Oilcraft

OILCRAFT

The Myths of Scarcity and Security
That Haunt U.S. Energy Policy

ROBERT VITALIS

STANFORD UNIVERSITY PRESS
Stanford, California

STANFORD UNIVERSITY PRESS
Stanford, California

©2020 by the Board of Trustees of the Leland Stanford Junior University. All rights reserved.

Printed in the United States of America on acid-free, archival-quality paper

Library of Congress Cataloging-in-Publication Data is available upon request.
ISBN 978-1-5036-0090-4 (cloth)
ISBN 978-1-5036-1234-1 (electronic)

Cover design: Kevin Barrett Kane
Cover photograph: Daniel Olah
Text design: Kevin Barrett Kane
Typeset by Newgen in 11/14 Granjon

For Marilyn Young (d. February 19, 2017) and
Ellis Goldberg (d. September 21, 2019)

CONTENTS

Oilcraft

1

OPENING

There is no reason we should end up going to war over resources, but that insight really becomes helpful only when the public, opinion leaders, and policymakers understand it.
—John P. Holdren, foreword to Ronnie Lipschutz,
When Nations Clash

IN THE RUN-UP to the 2003 U.S. invasion of Iraq, antiwar demonstrators marched under many different banners. "No War" and "Not in My Name" were prominent. But so were "No War for Oil" and its twin, "No Blood for Oil." The George W. Bush administration and its supporters in the major media, the academy, and think tanks tried hard to disabuse opponents of the idea that the United States was focused on Iraq's energy resources. "It has nothing to do with oil, literally nothing to do with oil," insisted Defense Secretary Donald Rumsfeld.[1] He and others emphasized that the war aimed to prevent Iraq's dictator from using (it turns out nonexistent) weapons of mass destruction, free Iraqis from tyranny, and permit democracy to bloom on the Euphrates.

Opponents weren't buying it. Hadn't the government lied or at least cooked the intelligence about Iraq's chemical weapons capability? Democracy promotion was just a facade, since Bush and his advisers appeared to care little about freedom a few hundred miles away in Saudi Arabia. The actual conduct of the war only increased the doubts. Why had the "liberators" ignored the wholesale looting of Baghdad's museums and ministries while defending the petroleum infrastructure (although looting had occurred there, too)? Future investigative reporting would reveal that, predictably, once ensconced in the Green Zone, some free market zealots in the Coalition Provisional Authority, the Defense Department's postinvasion government, had set their sights on selling off the publicly owned refineries, wells, and pipelines to private investors. Others dreamed of reopening an old pipeline to Haifa. Equally predictably, these plans never gained traction.[2]

Various journalists and bloggers could crow "we told you so" a few years later, when Alan Greenspan, the acolyte of Ayn Rand who headed the U.S. Federal Reserve between 1987 and 2006, came out with a memoir. Newspaper and television reports all led with the same one line from a book of more than five hundred pages: "I am saddened that it is politically inconvenient to acknowledge what everyone knows: the Iraq war is largely about oil."[3] Unfortunately, there is considerably less in that quotation than meets the eye, or so the country's most famous investigative reporter, Bob Woodward, would reveal in a follow-up interview. Greenspan said he wasn't explaining the president's thinking when Bush took the country to war in 2003 but merely his own belief: getting rid of Saddam Hussein would reduce the prospects for the disruption of oil supplies by someone who in Greenspan's mind was unconstrained by the market in which his country's and all other oil firms operate. Saddam in Baghdad ultimately meant higher prices for refiners in the future, although, with Saddam gone, the price of oil continued to rise, regardless, until the 2008 recession.[4]

The fact is that proof of the kind that Greenspan was thought to be providing—insight into the true but unstated objective of the president and his closest advisers—has never really mattered.

Certainly not to all those convinced beyond a doubt that somehow the world economy benefits or that the government enhances the security of its citizens or that a capitalist class preserves its domination over the globe through increasing projection of military might in the vicinity of the oil fields of the Persian Gulf. These beliefs, or in the case of the professors who espouse them, "theories," vary from the crude to the complex and at times arcane. For some, the United States seeks to keep oil "cheap."[5] For others, it is to restrict supply and so keep prices high.[6] Most commonly, it is presumed that the U.S. military assures the country's continued access to those energy flows, which otherwise would be in jeopardy. A subset of thinkers, though, purports to know better and insists that the military secures the flow of oil not to the refineries on U.S. soil, since imported oil has always come mainly from the Western Hemisphere, but to its allies. Most public intellectuals who think in these terms consider it the beneficent supply of a global public good, while a fringe see it as the armor of coercion that underpins the consent that Europe and Japan grant to American domination.[7] The point of this book is to demonstrate how such seemingly unshakeable beliefs are nonetheless false.

First, and simply, there is the idea that the Bush administration launched a war to get or steal Iraqi oil, but nothing remotely like that ever happened. On the day after his inauguration, at the headquarters of the Central Intelligence Agency, President Donald J. Trump declared that "we should have" taken the oil and that "maybe we'll have another chance."[8] Yet here are just a few reasons why this idea makes no sense.[9] It presumes that the United States needed to overthrow Saddam Hussein and install someone else in power to secure or maintain its access to oil from Basra or Kirkuk, but U.S. firms, through a little subterfuge, were already the single largest beneficiaries of the Iraqi oil that Hussein's government sold under United Nations auspices in the decade before the war.[10]

Assume that something different is meant by stealing the oil: that the output of Iraqi fields would come under direct ownership of the U.S. government, which would be unprecedented, to say the least. The U.S. government does not produce and refine oil on its own, and the last time such a plan was floated (and quickly defeated) was more than seventy-five years ago, during World War II. All civilian and military agencies purchase what they require on the market like any private business or trader. Then perhaps "steal the oil" is shorthand for the idea that the Bush administration wanted U.S. multinationals ("big oil") to enter the Iraqi oil business directly or was acting as the companies' surrogate. If so, then there was again no need to go to war. The government merely had to lift the sanctions that prevented U.S. companies from contracting with the Iraqi oil ministry, as is conventional in other oil-producing countries around the world, and as they do now in Iraq. Keep one more thing in mind, however. The putative *national* identity of the large integrated companies that sell their advanced technology expertise to and buy oil from Iraqi agencies—Exxon Mobil and its rivals—tells us little about where the oil is destined once it leaves the ground. That is, the U.S., Chinese, Indian, and European firms, whether privately held or government owned, all sell their refined products to many different buyers across the globe.

It's important to hold on to this last fact while turning to a more sophisticated contemporary geopolitics, from which vantage point the 2003 Iraq War appeared to confirm that the United States was locked in struggle with China and other powers for control of the dwindling world supply of natural resources, oil chief among them. The longtime *Nation* magazine defense correspondent Michael Klare wrote four books and produced one documentary between 2001 and 2011 on the topic—a windfall of sorts. Take *Blood and Oil* (2004). Klare argued there that America's dependency on—or to give it added moral muscle, addiction to—the stuff would lead to more and worse wars in the years to come.[11] Why? For three, to his mind, indisputable and covarying reasons: The United States was rapidly running out of oil, imports from the Middle East would have to grow, and prices would continue to skyrocket. The only sane alternative to "paying for our oil with blood," Klare warned, was an alternative energy policy that ended the country's dependency on fossil fuels.[12]

Well-known intellectual entrepreneurs shared the moral high ground with him, including the sustainable development champion Jeffrey Sachs, soft energy path pioneer Amory Lovins, and environmental activist Bill McKibben. Alongside them, one found a host of critics of the American empire, convinced that oil is the prize over which states have fought numerous wars in the past, with more likely to follow.[13] I also consider myself a critic of empire, and one who shares the environmental movement's alarm about climate change, with the caveat that, as Joshua Goldstein and Steven Pinker show, Western activists who seek to overthrow the fossil fuel regime would do so even if many billions of people in the global South would have to bear the costs—a variant of an old story.[14] But it is junk social science that Klare and others were selling. After the explosive rise in the production of oil from hydraulic fracturing that the high prices of the 2000s incentivized, the United States is today the world's largest producer and growing oil exporter. Imports from the Middle East hover around 18 percent, not 60 percent, as Klare feared. Prices also did not rise; they fell dramatically, as industry analysts had foreseen.[15] As is well known, however, there are no real costs when professors and other public intellectuals get their forecasts wrong.[16]

A veneer of references, footnotes, and quotations mask what is in essence an ideological construction, a set of deeply held, pervasive beliefs about the world, together with the actions these vivid truths license—op-eds and classified memorandums, documentaries, classroom lectures, naval patrols and calls at port, journal articles, podcasts, press conferences, and protests, to name a few. Call it "oilcraft," the close kin not of statecraft, or the art of diplomacy, but witchcraft, a modern-day form of magical realism on the part of many, diplomats included, about a commodity bought and sold on the New York Mercantile Exchange and elsewhere. The same as copper, coal, rubber, palm oil, tin, and so on, all of which were once imagined as vital, too. *Oilcraft* is about the reasoning that makes notions of oil-as-power unquestionably true, taken for granted, and my own claim suspect.[17] If you are unhappy with the witchcraft analogy, then think instead in terms of "doctrinal verities," to borrow a phrase from the linguist Noam Chomsky, who insists it is the United States' need to "control" Iraqi oil resources that led to war in 2003.[18]

A key feature of the mental terrain of oilcraft is what the environmental engineer turned historian Roger Stern calls "oil scarcity ideology."[19] Stern argues that moments of *perceived* decline in the world's known oil reserves—a false conclusion for which the only real evidence is that prices are rising—have repeatedly led to aggressive action. Some fear that rival powers are conspiring to gain exclusive control of foreign sources of supply, others that producing countries such as Iraq under Saddam Hussein or a less friendly Saudi monarchy will choose not to sell their oil. I am more cautious than he is in relying on the many histories that take for granted that states have repeatedly acted on these grounds. At times policy makers may have; at times not. The problem is that the historians, as believers themselves in the truth of the proposition that oil is power, often fail their discipline's norm of due diligence in judging evidence and questioning assumptions. Many examples are in the chapters to follow.

Alan Greenspan thinks in terms of scarcity, clearly. Thus, his advocating the removal of Saddam Hussein. I've met military officers and other intellectuals on the right who think like Greenspan. Michael Klare and many others on the left think in these terms, too, only they oppose these same, often imagined, aggressive policies to "secure continued access to" or "control" Iraqi and other Middle East sources of supply because they portend ecological catastrophe or because the costs are borne by Arab and other peoples of the region. But is it true? Do the oil resources of the Persian Gulf really "constitute a stupendous source of strategic power," as one State Department official put it in a 1945 memo that many treat as a kind of prime directive of U.S. foreign policy now, seventy-some years later?[20] Have successive U.S. administrations, from Woodrow Wilson to Donald Trump, acted (or are ready to act) on this belief, occupied countries, coddled dictators, threatened allies, overthrown governments, and even gone to war for oil?

For all the professors, investigative journalists, and best-selling historians turned entrepreneurs who have been telling versions of the oil-is-power story since the so-called energy crisis of the 1970s, the facts seem too obvious to question. Oil answers the need of those looking for the real or material objectives behind the government's rhetoric and what professors of international relations refer to as "strategic rationales." It is why documents unearthed from the archives are taken at face value rather than interrogated, treated as the equivalent of actual policy decisions or, worse, as previously stated, the prime directive followed by every post-1945 administration.[21] The common denominator among otherwise antagonistic perspectives—from right-wing grand strategists to left-wing critics of capitalist imperialism—is a belief that oil as lifeblood or weapon or prize is different or unique or exceptional in comparison to the myriad other raw materials that are mined or harvested and traded on the world market. But they're wrong.

Rethinking the Game of World Domination

Back in 1981, Douglas Feith was a twenty-eight-year-old National Security Council Middle East specialist who would go on to become undersecretary of defense in the George W. Bush administration. He counseled his then-boss, Richard V. Allen, who was Ronald Reagan's national security adviser, to stop worrying about the so-called oil weapon that many imagined the Saudis and the Organization of the Petroleum Exporting Countries (OPEC) wielding. As far as U.S. policy goes, "it is critical to recognize that oil is a commodity essentially similar to cocoa, tin, and pigs' bellies. It is subject to the laws of supply and demand, as are all commodities in trade, and one need not ingratiate oneself to any oil regime in order to buy oil."[22] The guy that General Tommy Franks, who led the Iraq invasion, called "the fucking stupidest guy on the face of the Earth," was nonetheless right about oil.[23] By the same token, the justification that then-president Ronald Reagan offered up in defense of a new military buildup in the Gulf, against "anyone that would shut off that oil" or in some other way threaten Western "access" wasn't credible, although many people think in these terms even now.[24]

Steve Coll, the Pulitzer Prize–winning staff writer for the *New Yorker* says that by 2003 Feith's view, once confined to wonkish pieces in the Heritage Foundation's *Policy Review*, had become the "quiet conventional wisdom" within the Bush administration.[25] Coll contrasts it with, to use Feith's evocative image, "the misguided Risk board model of the 1970s."[26] Its origins, though, go back much longer than the game itself, favored by the grand strategists of Harvard's Kennedy School, Georgetown's Center for Strategic and International Studies, Yale, and the Army War College on the one hand, and their radical antagonists on the other.[27] What has since been lost is the skepticism by imperialism's critics toward the "laws" that statesmen and other engineers of empire back then said compelled the pursuit of natural resources of all sorts, not just oil, else suffer the consequences. *Izvestia* editor (and author of *Imperialism and World Economy*) Nikolai Bukharin, for one, writing in *Foreign Affairs* in 1936, attacked the pseudosciences of race and *geopolitik* that provided the excuse for fascist expansionism and misled those in the West whose responses to the crisis drew on the same false ideas, for example, about the "need" for land or raw materials.[28]

Did the United States wage war in 2003 for the oil? I have no way of knowing what was in the hearts and minds of President Bush and his advisers. For what it is worth, though, I'd counsel against dismissing the reasons given by its architects as lies foisted on the public that are designed to keep the real and fundamental ones hidden. To do so would be to go down the same dead end that the critic John Hobson warned against more than a hundred years ago in *Imperialism: A Study*. It was wrong, Hobson said, to imagine that statesmen were "feigning blindness" or engaged in "deliberate conscious simulation of false motives" or had some kind of "consciousness of inconsistency."[29] That said, the evidence amassed so far by the believers in "it's the oil, stupid" thesis cannot bear even a moment's critical scrutiny. Not that the evidence really matters since, as has been stressed here, for the believers the answer is always already known, because of the hold oilcraft exerts over elites and citizens, professors in the service academies and the Ivy League, Democrats and Republicans, the provocateurs who lead Code Pink, op-ed columnists of the *New York Times*, and contributing editors of the *Nation*.

To be clear, the expansion of the U.S. military presence in the Middle East since the 1970s is no illusion. The Richard Nixon administration and the U.S. Army Corps of Engineers built a basing system in the Gulf as part of a mission to arm and train the Saudis and Iranians (the "twin pillars policy").[30] President Jimmy Carter organized the Rapid Deployment Force in response to the 1978

Iranian revolution, which evolved into today's Central Command, or Centcom. He then responded to the Soviet invasion of Afghanistan in 1979 in his last State of the Union address, declaring the Persian Gulf a vital interest to be protected by military force against efforts from outside power to gain control of its oil resources (the "Carter Doctrine"). The new Reagan administration, the one that employed Feith, faced almost immediate pressure from those who had backed him against Carter to reverse the policy of "appeasing" Saudi Arabia and to instead force the kingdom to accept U.S. troops on its soil.[31] Reagan rebuilt ties with Iraq, assisted Saddam Hussein in his war with Iran, and sent naval forces to protect shipping during the later years of the Iran-Iraq war. In the summer of 1990, the George H. W. Bush administration ordered U.S. troops to Saudi Arabia to protect the kingdom ("Desert Shield") and that winter the U.S.-led United Nations coalition of more than five hundred thousand troops launched a war ("Desert Storm") to reverse Iraq's occupation of Kuwait. The Clinton administration began a policy of dual containment of Iraq through a military-enforced continuing embargo that only ended with the war in 2003.

Among the many consequences, we witnessed the beginning of unprecedented violence against Americans in and outside the region, which has included kidnappings, assassinations, car bombings, and worse. As we would expect, each government provided multiple reasons motivating its policies, and the reasons differed, in part, in reflection of conditions confronting a particular administration regionally, globally, but also locally, in terms of the political coalitions arrayed for and against its preferences. Nonetheless, one specific rationale is common to practically all of them—namely, the defense of the region's oil resources and, in particular, securing or preserving access to them. This fact alone goes far in explaining how critics construct their own ideas about states and ruling classes and

the like and who imagine the wars in 1990 and 2003 as the fulfillment of "U.S. desires" dating back to 1973.[32]

The trillions spent are all the proof that believers in the idea of
U.S. control of Persian Gulf oil can muster, since there is certainly
no evidence that the actions of successive administrations have increased the supply or lowered the price refiners pay for oil in any
tangible or measurable way. That's more or less what Columbia
University political scientist Parker Moon thought back in the 1920s,
when trying to understand the "mid-Victorian mirage," "patriotic
haze," and the "mist . . . of national self-sufficiency" that had led the
governments of the United States, Great Britain, and other imperial
powers to spend enormous sums—although a drop in the bucket in
comparison to the costs of U.S. force projection today—to subsidize
the operations of private mining firms, rubber and sugar plantations,
and the like, which, through some kind of mysterious and unspecified alchemy, secured control of vital raw materials for the country
itself or its leaders allegedly on behalf of its people.[33]

> Such material treasures are something the public can visualize,
> something the statesmen can understand. Who can doubt . . .
> that a mandate [to wit, Iraq] permeated with petroleum, is a
> prize worth fighting for? It requires either sophistication or
> highmindedness to entertain such doubt.[34]

Moon's point has lost none of its force a century later. The geopolitical "mind" now, as then, presumes what needs demonstrating: What does control of oil mean and, more important, how does
this hidden (and in some versions not so hidden) power operate?
Those who have sought to do so—that is, subject their beliefs to
testing—have come up empty handed.[35] Worse still, others make
bold claims that cannot be falsified but must be taken on faith, like

the existence of God.[36] I've concluded that the idea of U.S. control is a mirage. And discovering in the archives that policy makers might have sought this objective doesn't resolve an analytical problem. Instead, it simply elevates one more "strategic rationale" above the others. It is no more meaningful than saying that policy makers were or are driven by concerns about credibility, power vacuums, civilizing missions, democracy promotion, and the like.

Policy makers persist in defending their actions in these terms—whether or not they believe them—given the high political costs in being second-guessed by domestic opponents and rivals. As the book shows, arguments about access are, like these other rationales, deeply engrained, and leaders find it too risky to do otherwise. As Peter Trubowitz persuasively demonstrates in *Politics and Strategy*, acting on such grounds may be costly in the long term. Presidents and their advisers, however, have high future discount rates and worry more about how failing to act decisively in the short term threatens to undermine their ability to win on other issues that matter, let alone their party's and coalition's political future.[37]

My presumption is that, in contrast to leaders, we can reliably take intellectuals at their word. That is, they believe it when they write that the Soviets posed a threat to Western oil supplies from the Gulf in the 1970s or that the United States controls the price of oil today through their "clients," the Al Saud ("House" of Saud), or controls its allies and rivals through its military presence or acts at the behest of Western oil firms or is locked in a geopolitical struggle to monopolize what remains of a dwindling strategic resource. They hold fast to their beliefs about oil the way others do about the biological existence of "race" and racial difference, while conjuring what they consider evidence in support in much the same way.

One objective of the book is the recovery of the early twentieth-century progressive era's original exposés of the strategic rationales behind the "new imperialism" and the ever-elusive security of the supply of raw materials of all kinds. Resource imperialism's bubbling cauldron of ideas—a mix of equal parts social Darwinism, neo-mercantilism, geographical determinism, and scientific racism—has lost little of its potency over the ensuing century. Oilcraft's debunkers today, no doubt unaware of the earlier refutations of scarcity ideology, are located primarily on the right, not the left, and promoted by the Cato Institute rather than the Open Society Foundations, Institute for Policy Studies, and the Type Media Center. The contemporary Anglo-American left appears wholly under its spell.

Three Propositions

In the sections that follow, I distill what economists and defense analysts have been telling us since the 1920s about peacetime world oil markets, about the kinds of threats most often imagined as challenges to market access, and about access during wartime. Collectively, they call into question much of what has been written about the prize by historians, self-styled energy security experts, and critics of U.S. foreign policy. They offer those new to the subject protection from scarcity ideology and the easy seduction of the Cold War's Risk-eyed view of the world.

In a market filled with buyers and sellers, everyone has access. The longtime Massachusetts Institute of Technology (MIT) professor Morris A. Adelman, an economist who studied monopoly and energy markets, among other subjects, was a controversial figure for most of his career. In one instance, Mobil Oil Company (now Exxon Mobil) used its regular *New York Times* op-ed page space to criticize his call for the United States to try to undermine OPEC, which he famously called "the clumsy cartel."[38] We forget now, under the incantatory accounts of the imagined 1973 "OPEC boycott," that pundits had already taken to describing the United States as being in

the midst of an "oil crisis" a year or more before the outbreak of the
1973 Arab-Israeli War. The crisis was a "fiction," Adelman argued,
following the mistaken belief—not for the last time—that there
was a looming scarcity of oil resources. He described the boycott,
correctly, as "meaningless," since others would step in and supply
U.S. refiners, which is indeed what happened.[39] But he was doing
no more than echoing what the secretary general of OPEC himself
had once said.

In a series of technical papers and books and articles for non-
specialists, Adelman exposed the factitious nature of much of what
passed for knowledge about oil and geopolitics in the 1970s and in
fact what passes now. He showed why the idea of an "oil weapon"
is a chimera. Administrations from Gerald Ford's on have been
obsessed by a false problem, that of access, and a misplaced solution,
energy independence, since, with price controls a thing of the past,
it is impossible to insulate the domestic market from price fluctua-
tions.[40] Adelman derided as sheer fantasy the belief (the "official
Washington gospel") that something called a special relationship
with Saudi Arabia somehow delivered oil to the United States at
lower prices or at higher volumes than would a less special relationship or less friendly oil-producing country. He called it "the pleasure
of self-delusion."[41]

> A trip to Arabia, to Africa, to a summit to discuss energy, or
> to the UN to lecture the producing nations on their duty to
> the world economy—these are all ego trips. The statesman
> believes he is gaining "access" to oil, or moderating the price
> rise and preventing long run shortage, or helping moderates
> against radicals, or improving North-South relations, or some-
> thing. . . . We all have a strong desire to believe we have some
> voice in determining the sauce with which we are to be eaten.[42]

He traced these "myths" back to the Ur myth, that the world is running out of oil (or any mineral for that matter), which he considered an impossibility. Why? Because estimates of recoverable reserves are not a matter of geology but of knowledge (or technology) and price at a given time. "The amount of mineral that is in the ground has no meaning apart from its cost of extraction and the demand for it."[43] These are determined "by a tug-of-war between diminishing returns and increasing knowledge. Historically knowledge has won . . . though this need not always be true."[44] The recent tremendous increase in oil and natural gas production in the United States, due to changes in technology, confirms the insight. It is a development that Adelman foresaw in the 1970s. In the decades since, his views have come to predominate among energy and natural resources economists, inside the industry, and, if Coll is right, then among some in the government. Feith himself credits Adelman for his view that the market rather than military might guarantees access during peacetime.[45]

The putative threats to oil price and supply that ostensibly motivate U.S. force projection are either not compelling or else cannot be dealt with efficiently by military power. Adelman's views on defense issues were scattered throughout his writings. In contrast to his economic analyses, however, they are unsystematic, if not off the cuff. He supported such measures as the creation of the Rapid Deployment Force in 1980, which was a means to promote security of supply in an "unstable" region. But he also dismissed as nonsense the idea that the USSR was planning to overrun the Persian Gulf to support its military command economy and coerce oil "dependent" Europe and Japan away from the United States.[46] And while he supported the use of force to reverse Iraq's invasion of Kuwait in 1990, he made clear that the problem was not that of access. After all, oil producers, friendly or radically opposed to U.S. policies alike, would continue to sell their oil to pay for all the goods, services, prisons, palaces, weapons, and so on that it buys. The oil rents themselves were the problem. More money in the hands of soon-to-be-dubbed "outlaw" or "rogue" states meant, Adelman presumed, a less peaceful world.

A second MIT professor and a specialist in defense issues, Barry Posen, though, takes up where Adelman left off in questioning the taken-for-granted assumptions of three generations of post-1973 energy security experts, foreign policy analysts, and reporters who parrot them. He published the results in *Restraint: A New Foundation for U.S. Grand Strategy*. It calls for a radical rethinking of the country's "unnecessary, counterproductive, costly, and wasteful" globe-spanning strategic posture and military force structure, in Europe, Asia, and, key for our purposes, the Persian Gulf. Posen goes as far as to reject any effort now or in the future to preserve the ruling Al Saud, or "House of Saud," in power under the assumption that Saudi rulers keep oil flowing to the United States or its allies at greater volumes or cheaper prices than other producers.[47]

After working through the set of routinely evoked claims that ostensibly justify the military presence—the presumed vulnerability of transit routes, the threat of a future Saddam Hussein–like figure who would raise prices or withhold supply—Posen dismisses most as either wild exaggerations, false, or not amenable to solution through use of force. Posen thinks that since the results of a cost-benefit analysis are both straightforward and inescapable, some other "factor x" must explain the enormity of the sums expended when the flow of oil itself has never seriously been at risk. "I suspect that global prestige and influence is this factor x," which is close to what some professors mean when they talk about U.S. hegemony, but, Posen adds, "even this argument is not self-evidently strong."[48]

Posen is no less dismissive of the idea that the military buildup in the Gulf is directed at and necessary in the highly unlikely event of hostilities with a rising power. There is no real danger of any great power conquering the Gulf, and, in the event of hostilities, "having the best submarines in the world and a large navy gives us a veto over who gets oil in wartime." When I asked him about those who believe hostilities with China are more rather than less likely in the medium term to arise, his response was, in the event of hostilities, "we don't need to be lords of the Gulf to intimidate every tanker captain into avoiding the route to China."[49] Wild exaggerations of the centrality of imported oil to its economy, and thus of the supposed existential nature of the threat to Beijing posed by U.S. dominance of the Gulf, is a mainstay of the we-are-at-the-dawn-of-a-new-great-power-conflict genre.[50]

Posen's skepticism about the need to secure the oil resources of the Persian Gulf in planning for or fighting a war with rival powers rehearses arguments made in the 1920s and again in the 1940s, based on the wars that had just been fought. For example, Bernard Brodie, the naval strategist who, as an employee of the Rand Corporation, went on to pioneer the theory of nuclear deterrence, argued that it was both unnecessary and quite likely futile to deploy U.S. force to protect the Persian Gulf in event of a war with the Soviet Union. The problem, he said, was that governments routinely confused or conflated strategic with economic interests, although he took pains to distance himself from those who detected in this fact "nefarious machinations of certain oil companies and of those governments which are presumed to be their lackies."[51] Presaging Adelman, he also dismissed fears of dwindling supplies, which had proved wrong in the past for reasons that Adelman would later develop at great length. Peacetime supply was assured by the market. And in the extraordinary event of a future war, the United States and its allies would once again rely on Western Hemispheric sources. U.S.

contingency plans in the early Cold War assumed the same. In the
event of conflict, one objective would be destruction of the region's
oil fields, not reliance on them, to keep them out of enemy hands.[52]

If there were public intellectuals in the 1970s and 1980s who
discounted the strategic value of physically occupying the Persian
Gulf in the event of war the way Brodie did—I don't know of any—
they stood little chance of gaining a hearing at the time.[53] Adelman's
experience confirms it, particularly once the Soviet Union invaded
Afghanistan in December 1979. As the book shows, political scientists inside the government portrayed the occupation as step one in
a campaign to seize the Gulf. Skeptics would have less of a chance
certainly than in 2003, when a large number of "mainstream" international security analysts came out in opposition to the Iraq invasion, Posen among them.[54] A plausible hypothesis is that what drives
the skeptics who have reexamined the logic of force projection is
how, after the collapse of the Soviet Union, military spending in
the Gulf theater nonetheless grew exponentially against lesser or,
to use the term of the art, "inflated" threats.[55] As one of the critics,
Roger Stern, emphasizes, U.S. Persian Gulf force projection has
cost about as much as the Cold War did and in virtually any year
exceeds the value of all oil exports from the region to the rest of the
world. In other words, what taxpayers pay for the impossible-to-
estimate good called energy security is roughly equal to what the
world pays each year for Middle East oil and ten times higher than
what U.S. refiners pay.[56]

Oil prices covary with the price of all other primary commodities. Roger
Stern is a one-time botanist who received a PhD in 2007 in environmental engineering from Johns Hopkins, where he began his
study of the history of Americans' powerful if misplaced fears about
threats to the energy supply. His work, like that of others who question the conventional wisdom, owes much to Adelman.[57] Stern,

though, has done something no one writing on oil and U.S. foreign policy has ever done, as far as I am aware. He compares the rise and fall of oil prices across the twentieth century with other commodities. The prices covary; meaning, they rise and fall in tandem.

Why is covariation significant? The simple answer is that it falsifies one of the most persistent beliefs about oil power: that particular agents—firms in some past accounts (the so-called Seven Sisters), and since the 1970s governments alone (Saudi Arabia) or in combination (OPEC)—have or had extraordinary abilities to control the price. Extraordinary in two senses. One is that it is a power unique to oil producers. Other raw material producers are price takers, as economists say, not price makers. Think about it. One rarely even sees news reports about the price movements of other commodities, save on the business pages, let alone about the strategies of copper or other mineral producers. More extraordinary still, the oil producers are imagined constantly to be deploying this unique power for political ends, evidence for which exists entirely in the mind of the writer or the geopolitical guru the journalist has talked to.[58]

What Stern shows is that, if Saudi Arabia at one moment is driving down the price, allegedly, to punish the Russians for their support of Syria or at another moment the Saudis, OPEC, and the Russians are ratcheting up the price, they are doing so with a remarkable degree of precision. Thus, these agents somehow get the movement, up or down, to align with the movement of all other traded goods.[59] Perhaps, though, there is another, simpler explanation. The effects of such efforts, even if real, are wildly exaggerated and, much more likely, imagined.

For Stern, it reveals the problem at the heart of oil scarcity ideology. It is the periodic spike in oil prices that allegedly demonstrated the correctness of each round of peak oil forecasts in the 1920s, 1940s, and 1970s, and thus the calls for aggressive policies to stave off economic decline (together with, in the 1970s, the countercalls either for the United States to pursue energy independence or to end its fossil fuel addiction). Yet, as he shows, prices of all other goods were rising at the same time, and presumably the world wasn't running out of cotton or bananas. What Stern and most other of today's historians of the international politics of oil miss is the fact that in the 1920s the statesmen and their varied ventriloquists fretted about access to or control of all sorts of raw materials. Oil was then just one and by no means the most important vital resource. So, in 1947, when historian and economist Herbert Feis, who served as the economic adviser for international affairs in the Hoover and Roosevelt administrations, looked back on supply problems during World War II, it was the shortage of rubber, not oil, that "presented the greatest threat to the safety of our nation and the success of the Allies cause."[60] Many, many materials mattered in the war. Scholars today, though, are barely aware of how radically they recast the past to tell their stories about the only one that seems to matter now.

Oil matters more today than other metals and minerals in one easily measurable way. The world pays some ten times more for the good annually than it does for gold, iron, and copper, the next three most valuable raw material exports.[61] But, to be clear, world trade in both electronic goods and machinery is larger, and growing, and the trade in oil declining relative to these other sectors.[62] If World War II is any guide, and it is open to question, then planners will be preoccupied with the supply of many materials rather than one. This is not the way the ranks of cultural critics, radical political economists, and environmental activists judge matters of course. Instead, oil is imagined as our "lifeblood," at the heart of "the American way of life," if not of capitalism itself ("petrocapitalism"). Not only are such cultural arguments contradicted by economic analyses that measure firms' reliance on oil across different industries.[63] They also faithfully echo the claims that analysts of other commodities make about cotton, the industrial revolution's "launching pad"; slaves, "the engine" that propelled Europe's rise; nitrates, which were fundamental to modern war making; bananas, the commodity that "changed the world"; sugar, ditto; and aluminum, which enabled "air power, the space age and moon landings."[64] Take your pick.

In what follows, I take up two foundational moments in the making of the doctrinal verities of oilcraft, the imperial rivalries of the 1920s, from the Caribbean to South Asia, and the 1970s, a moment of national trauma that effectively erased that past from memory. Along the way, I take apart some of the main myths of the energy crisis, for instance, the nonexistent "OPEC boycott," which continue to bedevil clear thinking, cogent analysis, and meaningful oppositional political action.

No one cherishes history for its own sake more than I do, but I have a second objective this time, which is to explicate what work these false beliefs about oil and geopolitics do today. We can either continue to remain fixed on the state's wholly unnecessary defense of access or on the left's unspecified, let alone empirically validated accounts of the project of hegemonic control—or we can extricate ourselves from the spell and concentrate instead on oilcraft's all too real effects. Consider the one first identified by progressives in the 1920s. In democracies, all favors, subsidies, and the like, whether to a single firm or entire industrial sector, must come dressed up as benefits to the public's "national security" interest. In other books I document how specific firms secured privileged access to the state in great detail for the case of the chemical, electrical equipment, and engineering industries competing in Egypt in the 1920s and after, and for oil giant Aramco in Saudi Arabia in the 1940s.[65] In the same way, we might compare the incalculable addition to "national energy security" provided by the just-lifted restrictions on U.S. crude oil exports, in place since the 1970s, with the much-easier-to-measure rents that accrued to the U.S. refining industry over the same period.[66]

The list of effects has grown significantly since the 1970s, in tandem with the expansion of the American military presence in the Persian Gulf and beyond. Let's start with the balance of payments and the global role of the dollar. In declassified records from the pre-1970s era, which is the era when private British and U.S. oil companies in the Middle East "controlled"—that is, made production decisions about—Saudi Arabian, Iraqi, Iranian, and Kuwaiti crude oil, we find a few instances where government officials sought to identify what this control signified for the power of the British state or how it added to the security of supply for British citizens, versus the case of a U.S. firm controlling that same source of crude oil. It didn't. The real benefit was to the Treasury, in terms of the balance of payments position, because refiners would pay the same price and the military would be supplied nonetheless. The U.S. ambassador to France had noted as much. The situation was identical for the United States in the years prior to the nationalization of firms' holdings throughout the region.[67]

Today, when oil producing countries (petroleum ministries or state-owned companies) rather than Western firms make production decisions, the balance-of-payment gains for the United States are even greater thanks to arrangements originally negotiated by the Nixon administration, in which Saudi Arabia, followed by other OPEC members, agreed to sell oil for dollars. The increased worldwide demand for dollars strengthened the U.S. foreign exchange position and underwrote deficits in the current accounts. In addition, oil producers invested billions of those dollars in U.S. securities. Private and not-so-private oil dollars flowed to real estate, capital goods, finance, engineering services, and, not least, the defense industry, to the benefit of the arms makers, sure, but also to the Pentagon itself, which gains from lower unit costs of major weapons systems.[68]

So what about the dramatic spread of U.S. military capabilities and bases into the Persian Gulf, Africa, and the Caspian basin since 1970s, as the instrument of what some call a deepening global hegemony, others the "new" turn to empire, and still others the latest phase of a continuous process of capitalist expansion? While many believe (and repeat like a mantra) that militarization is driven by the need to guarantee access or control of oil, nonetheless oil has been available regardless of the extent of U.S. force projection at any moment. More plausibly, the creation of a single integrated world market in oil has reduced the transaction costs of running the worldwide basing system (not to mention enriching the contractors who supply those forces and bases on cost-plus terms).[69]

Freeing ourselves from the "laws" of geopolitics and the spell of oilcraft entails costs. They may seem realer to many or at least easier to grasp, natural even, in comparison to the operation of oil markets. Utter the latter term and a critical theorist is apt to dismiss it with some judgment about the "neoliberal" fiction of "free" markets—a modifier not to be found anywhere in the pages to follow, needless to say. The value of course being that the critic never actually has to understand how a barrel of oil gets from a producing well in the Persian Gulf to a refinery on the U.S. Gulf Coast. For many, it means giving up what may seem like a winning oppositional stance. The gains, though, make it worthwhile, as I show, by reconsidering the question of the U.S.-Saudi special relationship, which confuses some and traps others unnecessarily into accepting what they imagine is a devil's bargain. The Al Saud does many things for U.S. investors, firms, regions, and government agencies, but guaranteeing the flow of oil or making it cheap or stabilizing the price isn't one of them. A post–Saudi Arabia may be a scary proposition for various reasons, but, some adjustment costs in the short term notwithstanding, markets will continue to operate more or less the same as now, and those routine operations, not the monarchy and not the U.S. Central Command, are what guarantee access to oil and all other commodities.

2

RAW MATERIALISM

AT LEAST SINCE PUBLICATION of Daniel Yergin's doorstop *The Prize* (1991), the interwar and World War II years have served to anchor beliefs about oil's outsized role in twentieth- and now twenty-first-century international relations: the ceaseless, intertwined struggle "for oil, wealth and power."[1] Those who believe that countries have fought and will continue to fight wars over oil point to Japan in the run-up to World War II. Environmental historian Brian Black argues that World War II was, in general, a "war for oil."[2] To put my objection to this radically reductionist view charitably, causes of war are complex, while historians like Black miss the fact that both world wars disrupted market access, and all combatants confronted massive supply problems.[3] This was true even of the United States in the period between 1939 and 1945—by far the most resource self-sufficient of the Allied powers.

Yergin doesn't make this basic mistake. He makes the other one, in imagining that Japan's oil dependency "*in particular*" and its efforts "to reduce its reliance on the United States, *especially for most of its oil*," best characterizes its leaders decision-making at a key juncture.[4] What else can he say given the book's premise? The only problem is that it isn't true. In fact, Japanese military and civilian planners identified dozens of strategic materials for which they depended on the West after launching a war with China in 1937 and while preparing for a wider war with powerful rivals. These included foodstuffs, machine tools, copper, aluminum, and above all, scrap metal. The latter was vital for making steel, and steel key to the ships and other weapons without which the Japanese forces stood not a chance against a rapidly rearming United States.[5]

There is no disputing that the late-nineteenth-century "new" mercantilist era of protectionism at home combined with aggressive government efforts in aid of the investors who sought to bring these resources to market had sunk deep roots. The Daniel Yergins and Brian Blacks of the first decades of the twentieth century argued that what best explained the "Great War and the unstable conditions which have characterized international politics since its close" was the unequal world distribution of a vast array of raw materials, including but hardly limited to "energy resources."[6] Back then a typically anodyne statement of the growing "raw materials problem" went: Would a renewed "struggle for colonies and raw materials" lead to another war between white people or would a theretofore unknown phenomenon, a "rising race consciousness of the East" and adoption of the white race's signature "imperialistic methods," lead instead to revolution and a race war against them?[7]

In the 1970s, a condensed but often no less racist conventional wisdom emerged. From the Soviet invasion of Afghanistan in 1979 and Saddam Hussein's failed effort at annexing Kuwait in 1990—the decade in which Yergin was hard at work on *The Prize*—to China's "going out" (going global) investment strategy in the 2000s, it is the threats to access to one scarce commodity alone—oil—that preoccupies the contemporary geopolitical mind. Yet, as Edward Mead Earle, one of the original and sharpest of oilcraft's debunkers, put it back in 1924, the "policy of the United States since the Armistice has been based upon two bogeys; the bogey of the rapid exhaustion of our domestic supplies of petroleum; the bogey of a

British monopoly of petroleum resources abroad."[8] Since then the list of bogeys or fears based on unreason has only gotten longer.

The views of Earle and a handful of other progressives in the 1920s who sought to expose the factitious nature of beliefs about raw materials and international insecurity deserve our attention. The Adelmans, Posens, Sterns, and like-minded critics of the strategic rationales that underpin U.S. primacy today are mostly unaware that Earle and others in what I call the Columbia School had done the same decades earlier when challenging the imperialist policies and aspirations of the United States and its great power competitors. For instance, they showed why colonies and spheres of influence had not and could not solve industrializers' raw materials problems. The pursuit of autarky, or self-sufficiency, via conquest, thus, was either irrational or else driven by other nonmaterial interests. Japanese civilian planners would tell their military counterparts the same thing and would be cashiered for doing so.[9] Meanwhile, citizens were being misled by governments that portrayed support for mining firms abroad on the grounds that it was the only means to guarantee domestic supplies of raw materials. They were right, and the argument stands the test of time. Consider the alarmism of the early 2000s about a zero-sum struggle with Chinese state-owned oil companies for a rapidly dwindling supply of a vital strategic good, although some 90 percent of the oil that those Chinese firms produced was purchased by customers outside China.[10]

In early 1920, the nearly identical imagined threat preoccupied politicians and statesmen (and they were all men back then) for the first but by no means last time. Warren G. Harding, then campaigning for president in Oklahoma, a Democratic Party stronghold, insisted that under President Wilson's watch, the country's security had been fatefully compromised. Great Britain had gained control of "90 percent of the world's known supplies," through its far-flung network of colonies and protectorates.[11] The only problem is that, as the *Wall Street Journal* reported, U.S. firms actually controlled 82 percent of the world's oil, the British Empire controlled 2.5 percent, and American-owned firms had been buying up new concessions throughout the Southern Hemisphere.[12]

A June 1920 *New York Times* headline screamed "Giant Struggle for Control of World's Oil Supply." Only the protagonists were two competing "industrial titans," not governments. One was Rockefeller-owned Standard Oil, which we now know as Exxon Mobil. The *Times* called it "the dominating power in the world's oil trade."[13] But Standard Oil's dominance had been built on monopoly power in the United States and through marketing its refined products around the world. It was late to seek oil supplies beyond U.S. borders. The rival, Royal Dutch Shell, directed by Henri Deterding, an Amsterdam-born naturalized British citizen—the better to secure backing of a second key state for his global venture—was attempting to best Standard through gaining exclusive access to new sources of crude, which had triggered the now-historic post–World War I competition for new foreign sources of supply. Mesopotamia was the latest site in this giant struggle, and the American oil interests eventually forced their way into the Anglo-French consortium through a deal with the rival firms. The spate of Senate resolutions calling on the government to block British private investments in U.S. oil bearing lands, State Department demarches, and appeals to "open door" principles that had accompanied the private bargaining were, once the deal was made, quickly forgotten—a pattern repeated frequently in the decades to come.[14] Great Britain's alleged control of "world rubber" would instead come to dominate the headlines.[15]

On what possible grounds would citizens of the United States, then the largest oil-producing country in the world, acquiesce to the idea that it was in their country's interest to confront the British

government in far-flung areas of the world? The argument was
that America was running out of oil. As one scientist with the U.S.
Geological Survey put it in 1920, "For the first time in her history the
United States is witnessing the day when one of her greatest stores
of mineral wealth—her most dazzling and spectacular endowment,
on which her prosperity, industries, and standards of living are so
largely dependent, and which imparts a characteristic and essential
quality to her civilization—is approaching exhaustion and so is no
longer able to meet her growing necessities."[16] Or consider what
seems the more soberly delivered but hardly less spectacular predic-
tion by the world's leading chemical engineering consulting firm,
Arthur D. Little (ADL), that the domestic oil production curve was
in permanent decline, with no new fields in the forty-eight states left
to be discovered. ADL issued that report just prior to what came to
be known as the Seminole Oklahoma boom and a few years before
the even more massive East Texas bonanza.[17] For the first but hardly
the last time, temporary shortages of supply were taken for proof
that domestic reserves were drying up.[18]

Then, and just as we saw in the 1990s, two groups in particular
picked up on the looming scarcity argument and ran with it: conser-
vationists and, for lack of a better term, grand strategists who advocated for the continued buildup of sea power after World War I.[19]
For the first group, oil was one of the vital "national resources"
that had to be preserved for future generations by the federal government, which meant restricting access to oil-bearing lands and
guiding or regulating the use of oil. For the strategists, "control" of
foreign oil fields had become a national imperative. Needless to say,
the biggest of the oil companies, the so-called instruments of U.S.
policy, opposed conservation but had few problems with the latter
idea that their rent-seeking efforts abroad were somehow vital to
the national security of the United States. It helped, too, that the Department of Interior had basically been captured by the industry.[20]

"Oil is power," some started to say, unselfconsciously deploying ideas going back centuries about how military prowess and state power depended on a monarch amassing stores of goods, such as timber, silver, and gold, in finite supply.[21] The best of many books to appear about the new "world struggle" among the great powers, *Oil Trusts and Anglo American Relations* (1923), sought to trace the origins of the oil-is-power idea, calling it a *great illusion*. "How and whence comes the evil in the possession of a commodity which, by its adaptability for human use and handling, is essentially one of the greatest servants of mankind?"[22]

The Progressives' Lost Account of the Roots of Resource Imperialism

Williams College President Harry Garfield, who had served as the federal fuel administrator in charge of coal and oil supply during World War I, brought the U.S. Tariff Commission chair, William S. Culbertson, to the college's Institute of Politics in 1923 to analyze the rising tensions over natural resources.[23] The institute's month of lecture courses and roundtables, launched with much fanfare in 1921 and dubbed the country's first summer school of world affairs, had received detailed coverage in the *New York Times, Christian Science Monitor, Philadelphia Inquirer, Los Angeles Times,* and *Washington Post.*[24] Culbertson ran the institute's first roundtable open to the public, "Problems of Raw Materials and Foodstuffs in the Commercial Policies of Nations," which became a two-year-long master class in the politics of international economic relations. A dozen experts gave papers at the first roundtable. The University of Pennsylvania–based American Academy of Political and Social Science would publish the transcript of the entire roundtable as a special issue of its journal the *Annals* the following year.[25] Culbertson then returned to Williamstown in 1924 to lead his second roundtable, "Public

and Private Finance in the Policies of Nations," and he brought
these materials together in his five hundred–plus page study of
the new mercantilism, *International Economic Policies.*[26] Culbertson himself is best described in those years as a Republican
internationalist in a party dominated by protectionists. He was on
the faculty of Georgetown University's School of Foreign Service.
In 1925, the Coolidge administration appointed him minister
to Romania and, in 1928, ambassador to Chile. The biographi-
cal details are important because the analysis he provides of the
capitalist roots of imperialism are today identified exclusively
with the 1960s New Left and its progeny.

"If we are to understand our modern world, we must recognize
that war follows in necessary sequence upon causes arising out of
the processes of production, trading, and financing." Competition
among firms "sooner or later reflects itself in rivalry between Governments and people." Culbertson noted how leaders and those
who parroted them dismissed the idea reflexively. They still do. "To
speak of the economic causes of war has been considered improper
and even disloyal."[27] This failure to recognize the economic dimen-
sion to modern conflict, however, leads the well-intentioned down
a dead end, to peace societies and naive calls to outlaw war, rather
than to promoting international institutions that would substitute
for imperialism as the means for the fair division of the raw materials and energy resources needed by Western civilization.

Culbertson underscored how the latter part of the nineteenth
century had seen a retreat from "liberal," or free trade, ideals and
reversion to policies that resembled mercantilism or "the use of the
power of the state to gain economic and political prestige."[28] What
was distinctive about the "new" mercantilist era was the primary
role played by industrial and financial capital in what he described
as "modern" or "economic imperialism," leading to a second,
more thorough and far reaching, "conquest of the non-European

world."[29] It is the turn to seeing industrialization as the linchpin of imperialism and, hence, of war that provoked the critics.[30]

At root, it was capitalism that was to blame. Mass production methods generated more goods and profits than could be sold and invested domestically. "The capitalistic class, therefore, which is in control of modern business, is constantly seeking new markets in which to dispose of goods and new opportunities for the investment of surplus capital."[31] For the political leaders of these new-styled "modern industrial states," power came to be seen as synonymous with "colonial possessions, the control by their own nationals of markets and resources of raw materials" through monopolistic concessions and similar kinds of direct and indirect investment "in economically backward countries."[32]

Culbertson was as forthright about imperialism and the "fear and suspicion" that drove it as he was about capitalism. "Little is gained by undiscriminating condemnation." At the same time, "we cannot understand our world by continually trying to explain away economic rivalry or by dressing up modern imperialistic policies in the robes of disinterested justice and liberty." This latter point is as relevant today as it was in 1924, when, as Culbertson pointed out, British officials insisted that the "principal object" of the agreement with France, to share in the exploitation of the Mesopotamian oil concession, was to benefit the yet-to-be-constituted state of Iraq. "Nations as such, as distinguished from self-sacrificing individuals and private humanitarian organizations do not engage in altruistic enterprises in parts of the world where they neither have nor seek material interest."[33] Ultimately, as he wrote the next year in the preface to *International Economic Policies*, in "practical world politics the difference between the South Manchurian Railway Company and the Japanese Government, between the Anglo-Persian Oil Company and the British Government, or before 1914, between the German Anatolian Railway Company and the German Government, amounts to the difference between Tweedledum and Tweedledee."[34]

Ed Earle pushed a little on this last point in an extended, very laudatory review essay, which uses the case of oil to illustrate "the new mercantilism" that Culbertson analyzes "in all its glory."[35] Specifically, Earle thought it odd that he names no "American corporation whose interests have been a special concern of American diplomacy." The *Oil Trusts* and other reporting of the time suggests he should have. Earle ends by suggesting that "a list of corporations dealing in bonds, oil, copper, fruit, sugar and rubber might lead to some interesting speculation concerning American policy in Mexico, the Caribbean area, Cuba, the Philippines and elsewhere."[36]

Earle's department at Columbia had emerged in the 1920s as the epicenter of the scholarly study of imperialism in (and by) the United States—what one critic called a distinct "American ... group of thought and propaganda."[37] Earle (1894–1954), Parker Thomas Moon (1892–1936), and Leland Hamilton Jenks (1892–1976) all wrote PhD dissertations in history. Earle and Moon then joined the history faculty. Jenks taught economic history and sociology for most of his career at Wellesley College.[38] To their detractors, the historians ought to have been questioning the validity of any "theory"—capitalism, underinvestment, overproduction, and so on—that by itself purported to explain such complex and varied phenomena as the European scramble for Africa, the outbreak of World War I, or U.S. intervention in the Caribbean.[39] Read carefully, these historians' works all appeared to me to do precisely that, while telling us something new and important about the thoroughly entangled business conflicts and great-power political concomitants that characterized the new mercantilism. The policies pursued by the great powers made no sense, they insisted. But that is an understatement. Countries that sought access to or control of raw materials for strategic reasons—to reduce dependency and attain "self-sufficiency"—through colonies, protectorates, concessions, spheres of influence, and the like operated on the basis of "illusions," or what Parker Moon called a "mid-Victorian mirage," haunted by "bogeys" and "phantoms."[40]

Imperialism may have increased the supply of raw materials and food on the world market, which the professors generally considered a "service to mankind," a point worth returning to, but it did nothing to reduce Europeans' growing dependence on imports from outside their own so-called spheres of influence and so increased security. *Statesman's Yearbook* data made that fact abundantly clear. Parker Moon used the example of France, with a large empire in North Africa and Southeast Asia. "After fifty years of active imperialism," its colonies supplied only 10 percent of the raw materials that its home industries consumed, and "three Great Powers," the United States, Germany, and Great Britain, ninety percent.[41] The course of the next war confirmed the quixotic element in such quests. England's very survival as a great power had allegedly required it to end its dependency on oil owned, refined, and transported by any other than firms owned and operated by British nationals. Nonetheless, U.S. producers would supply, according to one estimate, six billion barrels out of a total of seven billion barrels consumed by the Allies in World War II.[42] As the State Department's economic adviser, Herbert Feis, emphasized in his first-person account, "The geography and logistics of the war made it impossible" to access oil from many of the British-owned concessions.[43] And to my knowledge, no one has shown how precisely the empire's security had been enhanced by His Majesty's Government taking a majority ownership in British Petroleum (née the Anglo-Persian Oil Company) rather than leaving it to private firms to supply the military its fuel oil.

Both Jenks and Earle embraced the artful deconstruction of the oil-as-power idea in the *Oil Trusts*. The market guaranteed access in peacetime, and what mattered when peace broke down was not ownership of the wells but the ability to get the resource from the wells to the refiners via control of shipping routes, again, as World War I and, later, World War II would show. Yale's Bernard Brodie would make the same point in his early Cold War policy memorandum, as this book's opening demonstrates, and the contingency plans of the Joint Chiefs of Staff rested on the same assumption.[44]

Their explanation began with those who profited from "the growing alliance between business and diplomacy which confuses beyond hope of recognition the interests of individual Americans and the interests of the American people."[45] For example, Earle held that the U.S. oil companies together with such ventriloquists as Albert Fall, the secretary of interior who went to prison in the 1920s for accepting cash from his industry friends in the Teapot Dome Scandal, did much to conjure the "twin bogeys of dwindling resources at home and a boycott abroad."[46] Twenty years later, when Feis published his account of the diplomatic tangles in the emerging Middle Eastern oil and British- and Dutch-dominated Southeast Asian rubber-producing countries, the future giant of development economics, Bert Hoselitz, said the Columbia professors had been proved right. Feis's account was above all "an indictment of shortsightedness, stupidity, selfish interests, and greed, often on the part of private enterprise but not infrequently on the part of governments. If the book provides a moral, it confirms . . . rather than contradicts the theories of imperialism expounded by such men as Parker T. Moon and Harry Elmer Barnes."[47]

Such instrumental entanglements alone do not explain why publics believe in and support the politicians in such chimerical quests. Moon emphasized the role of "ideas" and "principles." Earle underscored how identification of the interests of firms with the "national welfare" had outlasted the war to become, as we say now, hegemonic. "Our philosophy is the discredited mercantilism of the eighteenth century combined with the pathological nationalism of the twentieth."[48] Moon stressed the force of economic nationalism and "national prestige" in these matters as well. "Many a Frenchman, for example, looks on the phosphate mines of French North Africa as an addition to the wealth of his nation. Such material treasures are something the public can visualize, something the statesman can understand."[49] And as he goes on to explain the fundamental error—"that raw materials, in general, are color-blind. . . . They follow the laws of supply and demand, and of distance and transportation costs. They obey economic rather than political control"—I can't help but think of my students who believe that the United States obtains its oil from the Persian Gulf, because why else occupy Iraq and continue to dominate the region militarily?

Moon went further, however, in emphasizing the role of "instinctive emotions" in "imperialist world politics," the most powerful and easily aroused of which was *fear*. Fear drove populations to back what we now call "preventive war": arms buildups; the takeover of the Philippines, Hawaii, and so on; and, not least, the impossible quest for control of raw material in time of war. Culbertson made much the same claim. "Fear and suspicion . . . are fundamental forces determining the psychology of imperialism."[50] Moon, however, appeared far readier than Culbertson was to dismiss any and all of them as ungrounded when judged against logic and evidence. "The unimpassioned student may perhaps inquire whether ownership of oil wells in some distant colony will be of value, in war . . . but to the 'man in the street,' such doubt rarely occurs."[51] The same holds true in our own time.

The Columbia professors presumed that political leaders knew roughly what they themselves knew and, thus, were acting "more or less unwillingly . . . at the instigation of business and other interest groups."[52] These same insiders were the source of "propaganda" or what, seventy years later, another Columbia professor called "myths of empire": false ideas consciously designed to play to the prejudices of the wider public to obtain their consent to bearing the costs.[53] But there are grounds for questioning this still-popular model of an elect inoculated against and encouraging the fear-driven misapprehension of events. Consider some other fear- and suspicion-driven efforts under way in the 1920s: immigrant exclusion legislation and the resurrection of the Ku Klux Klan in the northern and western United States, to stem the "rising tide of color" and preserve the white race from destruction.[54] There were Columbia University professors and others who challenged the science of "race" then, too, but it hardly mattered. Supreme Court justices joined the Klan, and presidents defended Jim Crow just the same. Racism was tenacious. So, also, were the delusions that Moon and others identified in the 1920s. Indeed, they are clung to tighter than ever today, almost a century later, by presidents, by professors, and by the public at large.

The policies that Moon and the others proposed on the basis of sober judgments about the working of raw material markets in peace and war were the ones that Adelman and other skeptics would advocate in the 1970s. The ones that actually made a difference. They urged more effective measures at conservation. Governments ought to stockpile raw materials as a short-term hedge against supply interruptions, including conflict. The powers should seek international agreements or other forms of cooperative arrangements. The nondiscrimination principle of the "open door" was important, although Ed Earle considered the Americans' advocacy of it hypocritical, given the many forms of protectionism that the United States employed domestically and in its own dependencies. He also endorsed the idea that Great Britain and the United States get out of the business of backing oil firms in their commercial battles. Culbertson considered it unnecessary and perhaps unwise. Later, Adelman would, too.[55]

The Heritage of Mankind

Parker Moon drew attention to one more principle that motivated the many "valiant feats of empire building" in the nineteenth and twentieth centuries. He labeled it, "for lack of a better term, aggressive altruism," which he defined as "using force, brutal force, to impose on unwilling native peoples the blessings of French, or German, or British, or American civilization."[56] Sure, the ideology of the "civilizing mission" or the "white man's burden" was central to how Europeans, including North Americans, South Africans, and other white settlers, thought and spoke about their conquests, with trade and its ancillary institutions themselves chief objectives and envisioned means of civilizing the "backward peoples."[57] What I want to draw attention to is a turn in argument in the 1920s and what brought it about.

Post–World War I defenders of the imperial order began to insist that the raw materials found in the tropics and semitropics were by right "the heritage of mankind." As the former governor of Nigeria, Frederick Lugard, framed the problem in his *Dual Mandate in British Tropical Africa* (1922), the races that inhabited these places possessed no "right to deny the bounties to those who need them." *It was a matter of life or death.* The cotton, groundnuts, rubber, and so forth had become "essential to the very existence of the races of the temperate climes."[58] Henceforth, these areas were to be governed in the interests of their inhabitants—the first mandate—but not by them. Commerce, which meant increasing exploitation of natural resources—the second mandate—required no less. Lugard's *Dual Mandate* would basically serve as a guide to legitimating colonial administration once the new League of Nations assumed oversight of the ex-German and ex-Turkish colonial possessions in Africa, the Middle East, and the South Pacific. However, the arguments about resource dependency and, thus, the necessity of controlling resources outlasted the league itself.[59] For instance, in 1949, Elspeth Huxley, the British-born settler in Kenya and author of *White Man's Country* and many other books, argued in *Foreign Affairs* that the "Black belt" was crucial to England's survival, and so there was no choice but to slow down the "pace of political advancement," or decolonization, as it came to be called.[60]

Therein lies the perceived threat to which the denial of resource sovereignty for "races" labeled "backward," "child," "dependent," and so on was a particular kind of magical thinking by the 1920s. Why? The fear for empire's future that many historians argue shaped Edwardian elites such as Lugard grew more, not less, palpable after World War I, with the prospect that "subject peoples are rising to throw off European domination."[61] "The revolt of Asia has become a popular topic," wrote Nicholas Spykman, a new assistant professor of international relations at Yale. Spykman traced the rise of "Asiatic nationalism" and creation of "movements for political independence" from India and Java to Indochina, the Philippines, and Egypt, where he had once resided, and found that they were the result of the increasingly capitalistic nature of imperialism.[62] It is what journalist and later professor of international relations Nathaniel Peffer called *The White Man's Dilemma* (1927). Whites needed the raw materials but they would not be able to continue to control them, given the growing militancy of nationalist movements across the world, without the use of force, and even then, "it might be a Pyrrhic victory."[63]

> We are caught in a dilemma and we shall have to seize either horn. . . . But since it is probable that we shall come to it in the end in any event, the preponderance of discernible evidence

seems to be in favor of seizing the one which will take us out entirely [i.e., renouncing imperialism]. The cost will be dire; there need be no self-deception on that score. But it is probably the smaller cost of the two. . . . Above all, our best hope lies in making the decision while it is still ours to make; either . . . to suppress the rebellious subject nationalities, now when the initiative is ours and there is more likelihood that we can; or at once to get about the business of liquidation and cut them loose, now when there is more likelihood that the surgery will not be fatal to ourselves.[64]

The arguments of Culbertson and the Columbia School theorists made little headway in the 1920s in the face of these apocalyptic accounts of looming scarcity, dangerous levels of dependency, colonial administrators conspiring against U.S. corporations, and an escalating, fanatical "fear and hatred of the West" on the part of "Asiatics," "Mohammedans," and the "brown race."[65] The U.S., French, and British elites all doubled down on their colonies, semicolonies (as China and Persia were sometimes referred to), and dependencies.

To Have and Have Not

With the collapse of global trade in the wake of the worldwide depression of the 1930s, elites in Japan, Italy, and Germany—by 1935 dubbed in the Anglo-American press the "have not powers"—began to demand a revision of the distribution of colonies as a life-and-death matter.[66] Japan invaded Manchuria in 1931, Italy seized Ethiopia (Abyssinia) in 1935, and German leaders advocated for the return of the Cameroons and its other territories for their raw materials and "expansion of her population."[67] The issue is what gained Soviet theoretician Nikolai Bukharin space in the otherwise staid monthly *Foreign Affairs* to attack the pseudosciences of race and geopolitics that the Nazis (and not only them) relied on, as we saw. What I found more generally is the adoption by elites in the United States and Great Britain of the arguments of Culbertson, Moon, and others. A spate of publications appeared in 1936 and 1937 in advance of the annual meeting at Geneva of the International Studies Conference, and in the published proceedings. Colonies "did not pay." They could not deliver the security of supply that the have-nots sought. The solution was, instead, a return to an open international trading system.[68] The have-nots had a ready answer, of course. "If the colonies are so bad, why do you keep them?"[69]

At the June 1937 Paris session of the International Studies Conference, a biannual forum created under the auspices of the League of Nations, the issue of the "colonial appeasement" of the have-not countries was front and center.[70] Many challenged the German claims that its position was exceptional ("all countries are, to a greater or lesser degree, 'have-not' countries") and that its economic problems could be resolved through return of its colonial possessions.[71] But one of the strongest refutations of the "it's the raw materials, stupid" position came from a most unlikely quarter, the unofficial German "observer" and newly appointed head of the German Institute for Foreign Policy Research, the jurist Friedrich Berber.[72]

To be clear, Berber had long championed the return of German possessions and served as adviser to the Nazi official most associated with the colonial appeasement issue, foreign minister Joachim von Ribbentrop. But after listening to the arguments about the economic needs of the so-called have-nots and whether return of the colonies was the solution, Berber scoffed. The idea of haves versus have-nots is a "classification which explains nothing, which is absolutely false, but which nevertheless is used in scientific research and discussion." Instead, return of the colonies was a question of "rights and justice," just as the French had long argued about the return of Alsace and

Lorraine.[73] Make of that what you will. One of the U.S. delegates, Eugene Staley, seized on it. "I have long thought that probably the main motive back of the German colonial claims was the kind of thing I understood Dr. Berber to emphasize. . . . This would imply that most of the talk about the need for raw materials and the possibility of getting them from the former German colonies is rationalization and not really the central issue."[74]

Savor the moment of maximum reach of the unsurpassed analyses that Culbertson and the progressives had pioneered in the 1920s because the mirages, bogeys, and phantoms that they warned of would soon return to haunt both the architects of the Cold War national security state and their critics on what came to be called the " New Left." The late 1940s and early 1950s saw a whole new cycle of fear, fomenting the belief that the United States was running out of the natural resources critical to industry and war while growing increasingly dependent on imports. University of Illinois economist John B. Parrish viewed the escalating cold war as turning on "steel power."[75] Contradictions abounded. Various departments and agencies promoted new U.S. foreign investment across the world's mineral frontiers (dependency fears notwithstanding), but the Eisenhower administration also protected the domestic industry from the crude oil that American and other firms produced in the Middle East, as if the faster depletion of U.S. stocks didn't matter.[76] Somehow, all such conflicting policies served national security. Roger Stern explains the moment as a consequence of "oil scarcity ideology," but oil was still just one of some seventy-two "strategic and critical materials" that loomed large in the minds of grand strategists.[77]

Three (or maybe four) enemies threatened to rob the United States of the gains from the recent victory: nature; fanatic nationalist and, thus, by definition highly irrational leaders of the emerging independent, "nonaligned," and as Americans imagined them "colored" countries; and the Soviet Union, allegedly driven by the objective of cutting off supply from Asia, Latin America, and the Middle East to the "free world," either through subversion or invasion. For the new Ford Foundation subsidiary, Resources for the Future, sponsors of a kickoff citizens' conference in December 1953, the real problem was the failure of the country's leaders and citizens to rationalize use of and so conserve what nature had provided.[78] It would take a few decades for the basic idea to catch on: "We have met the enemy and he is us."[79]

Tropical Raw Material Fever Dreams

The United States in 1956 was now a "Have-Not Nation," according to Peter Drucker, the management consultant who the *Economist* magazine would later call the "most enduring guru of them all."[80] The argument first made by president Truman's secretary of the interior, Harold Ickes (the guy who also tried to have the Roosevelt administration nationalize the American oil firms' concession in Saudi Arabia), emerged again with the publication of a massive five-volume study by the so-called Paley Commission, *Resources for Freedom* (1952). President Harry S. Truman had charged the radio and television executive William S. Paley with investigating the threat to the long-term raw materials supply as rising prices of raw materials during the Korean War prompted another round of scarcity fears.[81] Costs would continue to rise, it said, and the government would need to double down on support for private investment in Latin America and the European colonies and dependencies.[82] Later studies by the U.S. Senate and by Resources of the Future rejected the scarcity thesis, while future economists sought to explain why the Paley Commission's forecasts went so astoundingly awry.[83]

The American mining West and cotton-growing South put up stiff opposition to policies that encouraged U.S. investment in primary production abroad, let alone foreign aid for "far-off lands, many under the control of possible fickle allies or timid neutrals, some veritably under the guns of our potential enemies."[84] The western mining and Texas oil interests rejected the scarcity arguments as well, but even those who pushed for increased U.S. exploitation (giving a positive spin to that term) of resources in the so-called underdeveloped countries warned that "nationalistic" policies threatened "access on reasonable terms to the basic materials necessary to the continued growth of the American economy."[85]

The nationalistic policies were wrongheaded, according to the ex-diplomat, ex-Princeton professor, and president of the American Peace Society, Philip Marshall Brown. Imperialism no longer existed. Its "abuses" had "long since been eliminated." Colonial powers now acted solely in the interests of the various "dependent peoples" and of those in the West who needed the raw materials.[86] The viewpoint associated with the economists of the United Nations Economic Commission on Latin America, which posited that raw material–producing countries were structurally disadvantaged relative to the industrialized economies through worsening terms of trade (the ratio of export to import prices), was wrong. That is, if a young economist and assistant to the influential Soviet specialist George F. Kennan was to be believed. Rather "the terms of trade" was tending "to move against the industrialized countries" by dint of the failure of primary product producers to keep up with demand—a conclusion one could reach only by taking the Korean wartime conditions as normal. The alleged need for the production of raw materials in the colonial dependencies to catch up thus would require the "preservation of some colonial relationship" in the "interest of all metropolitan countries."[87] It gets better. As far as the United States goes, "the best possible situation is a series of "happy" colonial relationships, and so "the first political objective of the United States should be the discouragement of sentiment for independence rather than the promotion of it," while encouraging "reforms necessary for happy relationships."[88]

We can generalize the point. The gurus of (they hoped) a rehabilitated "geopolitics" in the early Cold War, Kennan chief among them, all opposed independence for the colonial dependencies on the grounds that it would inevitably starve the West of its needed raw materials. They reached for the heritage of mankind idea and deprecated the one about "sovereign rights."[89] As Kennan wrote about a trip to Caracas in 1950, where the new development minister and future founder of OPEC, Juan Pablo Perez Alfonso, forced Exxon's predecessor to share profits on a true 50-50 basis. "The local population had not moved a finger to create this wealth, would have been incapable of developing it, and did not require for its own needs the thousandth part of what was apparently there." Kennan dreamed of the "day when the morphine of oil company or steel company royalties and taxes would no longer enter the system of [the] Venezuelan economy . . . and when someone would have the unpleasant task of dealing with a terribly disoriented and intellectually debilitated population." Meanwhile, the West had "to find some better answer . . . between the needs of those economies which are capable of developing the natural resources of this earth and those other peoples who have been permitted to extend over those resources the delicate fiction of modern sovereignty."[90]

Robert Strausz-Hupé, the émigré attorney turned political scientist who founded the country's first right-wing international affairs think tank, the Foreign Policy Research Institute (FPRI), at the University of Pennsylvania in 1955, was an even more outspoken champion of a hard-headed approach to the preservation of colonial rule. The power position of the West depended on the raw materials, he insisted, and to promote or give into demands for (premature, unjustified, impossible to sustain) independence, would be to consign the European allies to decline and defeat. His *Balance of Tomorrow: Power and Foreign Policy in the United States*, the book that earned him a PhD, ranked iron and coal the most important of these resources. You need to build weapons, and only then does oil matter to the running of them. The list of strategic raw materials provided by the dependencies was long.[91] His 1950 textbook, *International Relations*, coauthored with another Austrian émigré and more militant right-wing thinker, Stefan Possony, is even bolder in its prescriptions for the preservation and upgrading of late-colonial rule or Western living standards were sure to plummet.[92]

U.S. officials seemingly failed to grasp just "how profound, how irrational and how erratic" the leading intellectuals and politicians were in what was coming to be called the "Third World." That's George Kennan's assessment, sent privately to the Truman administration's secretary of state, Dean Acheson, following the Iranian government's nationalization of British Petroleum's assets in 1951.[93] Iran was just a single example among many that decade, going back to the 1930s, of efforts by host countries to renegotiate concession terms, including subsoil and related property rights, with nationalization of the foreign firms' and landowners' assets, one increasingly likely outcome. And since such seemingly destructive choices were rooted in "the emotional and subconscious," the understanding of which would require delving into "the origins of various forms of neuroses," it was futile to hope that "the fanatical local chauvinisms of the Middle East represent a force that can be made friendly or dependable."[94] Rather—and you know what's coming, right?— "to retain these facilities and positions [the oil refinery complex at Abadan in Iran and the Suez Canal in Egypt] we can use only one thing: military strength. . . . There is nothing else that will avail us—least of all the attempts to incur the benevolent predisposition of these dreadful characters . . . on whose bizarre frames the trappings of statesmanship rest like an old dress suit on a wooden scarecrow."[95] Yet, at least in the eyes of hard liners Strausz-Hupé and Possony, postwar U.S. administrations took "childish delight" in undermining British and French efforts to hold on to their dependencies.[96]

The 1956 Suez "Crisis" confirmed it, no? Egyptian President Gamal Abdel Nasser nationalized the foreign-owned Suez Canal Company in July, driven, according to President Eisenhower's peculiar reading of motives, by a need to "to slap the white man down."[97] Three months later, Great Britain, France, and Israel invaded Egypt and seized control of the Canal Zone, until forced to withdraw under the threat of U.S. financial sanctions. Harvard government professor William Yandell Elliott, patron of future Secretary of State Henry Kissinger, among a legion of other defense intellectuals, argued that by sanctioning the nationalization,

> liberal circles [had] created the greatest possible threat to . . . resources vital to large and advanced populations. . . . If tribal chieftains, like the rulers of Kuwait, Bahrain, Trucial Oman, or the Yemen should claim absolute power over resources on which the whole of the western Europe depends for its industrial life-blood, it is evidently absurd to apply a concept as absolute as that of sovereign right without juridical or moral limit.[98]

Kennan went further. As the Eisenhower administration acceded to the Soviet invasion of Hungary and sold out its British and French allies (he cared little about Israel), while winning reelection in a landslide, Kennan said this "is now [vice president] Nixon's America, not mine," and later that month, "the Arabs are smiling at us." The American public "was content to believe that our posture had somehow shamed the imperialists and won us the gratitude of the helpless little people, who we could patronize and who we could show the paternalism which our own political system inhibits at home."[99]

Strausz-Hupé and confreres gathered at the Foreign Policy
Research Institute in 1957, still imagining it possible (and, needless
to say, preferable) to head off the "global anticolonial revolution"[100]
that they believed threatened to plunge the world "into economic
and political chaos."[101] How? The thinkers had little to offer to
match their hyperbolic accounts of the negative consequences of
"extreme economic nationalism," the predictions of the coming
"race wars" in Algeria and elsewhere, and of the minute hand of
the Communists' clock of world revolution moving that much closer
to midnight. Many proposed what we first saw proposed in the
1920s and every decade since, that colonial rule be recast in the real
interests of dependent peoples. Echoing Kennan's "happy colonialism," Harvard government professor William Y. Elliott called for
more "good colonialism" and for NATO countries to step in for the
United Nations as trustee powers, while selling "colonial peoples"
on the idea that the resources of the countries they inhabit are a
trust for the world."[102]

None of their apocalyptic visions—of Europe's collapse, new
brutal wars of conquest, and, not least, the irreplaceable loss of
"vital" raw materials—came true of course. Yet new visionar-
ies would emerge every decade from 1960, the year that the UN
General Assembly passed Resolution 1640, the Declaration on the
Granting of Independence to Colonial Countries and Peoples, who
spoke in the same apocalyptic, or if you prefer wildly "threat inflated," terms. And the norm established in that decade, of repre-
senting the leaders of anticolonial movements and newly independent countries—including Mossadegh (Iran), Sukarno (Indonesia),
Nasser (Egypt), Nehru (India), Ben Bella (Algeria), Qasim (Iraq),
Sihanouk (Cambodia), Nkrumah (Ghana), Jagan (Guyana), and
Lumumba (the Congo)—as irrational, mad, double-dealing, fanatical, hateful, and so forth—has lost none of its luster, either.[103]

What did the militants get wrong? A great deal in fact. But most basically, economic nationalism, including the expropriation and nationalization of Western holdings in mineral production, plantation agriculture, and the like, did not mean the end of export production.[104] Far from it. Industrializing countries needed the foreign exchange revenues from raw material exports to pay for the Western capital goods and technologies that would allow countries like Egypt, India, Brazil, Pakistan, and others to build domestic textile, steel, automobile, pharmaceutical, and weapons industries. Many in the West opposed these industrialization policies. Many western firms, however, happily continued to do business with the so-called socialist states and state-owned enterprises. The main examples of loss of raw material exports to Western markets occurred only when the United States imposed or went along with embargoes, for instance, on Iranian oil in the early 1950s or Cuban sugar after Castro's revolution. The United States is at it still. While a few nationalizations were reversed through covert intervention, in general, countries compensated private investors, and Western refineries and manufacturers had continued access to raw materials either through mercantile exchanges or through direct purchase from producing countries.[105] Culbertson and the Columbia School theorists were right in arguing that producing firms and states would not and could not afford to stop selling their cotton, copper, iron, or oil.

The anti-anticolonialists took for granted rather than thought hard about one more matter: that the U.S. or U.K. governments somehow gained strategic advantage by those plantations or concessions that were operated by private firms identified as "British" or "American." Plenty of policy makers believed this, too, of course. Yet on those occasions when government functionaries tried to unpack the idea of "control," they came up empty handed. Firms, not their government "partners," made production decisions. As one investigation concluded, the primary benefit to the United Kingdom from having British Petroleum rather than Exxon producing oil in Iran or Iraq accrued to the Treasury in terms of the balance of payments position.[106] In the 1960s, a few in the Lyndon Johnson administration began to mimic the argument that control by U.S. firms of Middle East oil concessions mattered above all to supporting the U.S. balance of payments position, but this particular strategic rationale never gained the traction it had enjoyed in London.[107] As the historian Stephen Randall says,

> American officials assumed that United States' strategic influence in the region depended on the strength of the private sector, *but American policy failed to provide the means to ensure control over the companies*; yet, it was assumed that the companies provided a vehicle for the attainment of larger strategic and diplomatic objectives.[108]

Unfortunately, the writings of Jenks, Earle, and their colleagues had been forgotten. Back in the 1920s, they had exposed the factitious nature of many of the beliefs about the need for controlling raw materials—let alone the ability to do so—or else face economic decline and conquest by rival powers. Instead, the emerging New Left accepted virtually all the arguments at face value. All the more so if it found a president or other official expressing these beliefs in a once-classified government document. The one difference is that the Right feared while the Left championed the Third World and capitalism's coming collapse.[109]

First Time as Tragedy

In 1959, the University of Wisconsin historian Williams Appleman Williams published *The Tragedy of American Diplomacy*, his landmark study of U.S. "open door imperialism," which he revised in 1962 and 1972. Highlighting its "free-swinging attack" on U.S. foreign policy, the *New York Times* selected it as a book of the year.[110] Williams argued that the commitment to overseas market expansion rather than territorial aggrandizement—the "Open Door"—in the age of empires resolved the debate between imperialists and anti-imperialists in the early twentieth century. Culbertson makes a brief appearance in the book, as one of the historic advocates of open-door principles. That concept had gained widespread acceptance in the years since. "As far as American leaders were concerned," Williams wrote, "the philosophy and practice of open-door expansion had become, in both its missionary and economic aspects, the view of the world. Those who did not recognize and accept that fact were considered not only wrong, but incapable of thinking correctly."[111]

The next decade witnessed a virtual point-by-point rehearsal of the 1920s to 1930s debate on U.S. imperialism, with Williams and his many students and acolytes roughly occupying the position of Columbia's "American school," committed to understanding the worldview that naturalized and legitimated U.S. economic expansion. Critics sometimes wrongly lumped them together with the new wave of Marxist thinkers who instead emphasized how the survival of U.S. capitalism itself depended on control of the raw materials and markets of the Third World, with the state being the agent of the "private autocracy." The many critics of these "revisionists" and "radicals" reproduced the arguments of the earlier generation of antagonists who challenged the idea that social structure determined U.S. foreign policy. Instead, they stressed either the selfless or else the strategic calculations of policy makers that they insisted better explained the course of post-1945 events from Berlin to Korea to Vietnam.[112]

Yet the 1960s New Left sociologists and revisionist historians differed in a fundamental way with the Columbia School thinkers of the 1920s. The former all took the arguments by policy makers and public intellectuals for the need to preserve or extend access or control of raw materials at face value. The United States or the advanced capitalist economies or the West depended on these resources, they wrote.[113] The evidence wasn't hard to find. There were the very public scarcity fears that seemingly animated the Truman and Eisenhower administrations' policies, such as the Point IV program; the declassified records of World War II planning in Southeast Asia; the stolen Pentagon Papers' references to U.S. control of nonferrous metals, tin, rubber, and so forth in the early years of the Vietnam War; let alone the campaigns by conservatives to do more to counter the imagined threats from "anti-western" Third World leaders and the "designs" of "hostile powers."[114] The moment is striking, not least for the convergence of the militant Right's and anticapitalist Left's versions of "realist" geopolitics. In one, the Soviets seek to take over resource-producing areas to force Europe and Japan to defect from the United States or else see those vital resources lost, I guess.[115] In the other, the U.S. government somehow controls the resources its allies need and so coercively secures their consent to its dominance, or, as is said now, hegemony.

In arguing that the U.S. capitalist order was imperialist by nature or necessity, the New Left theorists and historians were as vulnerable to getting the economic fundamentals wrong as those in the 1930s and 1940s were who argued that hanging on to the colonies was a matter of life or death. The international relations scholar Kenneth Waltz dismissed the idea that dependency on raw materials imports mattered or that it cost the United States anything.[116] Robert Tucker devoted the last part of what he called his "little book about the radical left in American foreign policy" to demonstrating, like those numerous 1930s cost-benefit analyses of imperialism, that the data on U.S. raw materials imports from, and foreign direct investment in, the Third World did not support the Left's claims about vulnerability and the significance for the gross national product. Tucker also dismissed as naive the view of geopolitics that thinkers like Harry Magdoff, coeditor of the Marxist *Monthly Review*, relied on when conjuring scenarios "of a sudden and complete denial of access to foreign sources of raw materials" that explained where and why the United States projected its power.[117]

This last is precious because just a few years later, Tucker reversed his own self-proclaimed "isolationist" commitments ("a more modest role for the United States") and in 1975 called for the United States to take over the Saudi oil fields because the Arabs were ready and somehow able "to deny us access."[118] Now he was sounding like Magdoff! Of course, as we saw in the first chapter, MIT's Morris Adelman also explained why the idea that the Arabs had done irreparable harm through a faux embargo was nonsense. We return to it in a few pages. But even earlier, in his first 1972 article for *Foreign Policy*, "Is the Oil Shortage Real?" Adelman undermined the Left's vision of the U.S. oil companies' dominance over developments in the Persian Gulf. Rather, they had been turned into OPEC's "tax collecting agency."[119]

Noam Chomsky, the brilliant linguist turned critic of the Vietnam War, lumped Tucker and his little book in with the many other political scientists he said were "experts in legitimation" of illegitimate U.S. power. Tucker did so, in part, by rejecting out of hand the importance that postwar administrations had seemingly attached to access to raw material resources in Indochina and elsewhere. For Chomsky, these were facts that reveal the extent to which "corporate interests influence foreign policy."[120] Specifically, the war in Vietnam followed from a professed need to preserve Southeast Asia as a source of raw materials for Japan, "linked by an essentially colonial relationship."[121] Tucker rejected the theory. Even if policy makers made such claims, citation "proves no more than conviction, and a mistaken conviction at that." Tucker then turned to International Monetary Fund records to show the insignificance of Southeast Asia for the Japanese economy.[122] Chomsky's answer? It is not a theory that Leftists have advanced but more simply a faithful rendering of "the expressed conviction of U.S. policymakers." He goes on: "Documentation of the conviction suffices to establish motive; *its accuracy is clearly irrelevant.*"[123]

The exchange underscores just how much analytical ground had been lost by the Left since the 1920s, when the Columbia School first exposed the beliefs about raw materials. Earle, Moon, and the others considered these fear-driven constructs to be dangers to world peace and sought to undermine them. Yet here was Chomsky arguing that their truth value didn't matter, which is a puzzle in at least two respects. For one, he, too, believes that the truth, in general, will set you free. His many books and articles, together with thousands of talks on U.S. foreign policy, seek to demonstrate that "the professed goals" of postwar U.S. administrations—from concerns about "credibility" and "containment of communism" to securing Asian peoples' "freedom"—are reliably false or incomplete or rationalizations for policies pursued for other ends. Thus, those ends must be "inferred from an evolving pattern of behavior."[124] For another, it is hard to understand what firms or sectors or corporate interests were promoting, let alone what they stood to gain from such a mistaken view of Japanese trade patterns. I think the answer is that Chomsky was really just scrambling to address an anomaly in what was basically a degenerative research paradigm. Puzzle solved.

There is a real puzzle going forward from 1975, just a year or two after Tucker, the academic New Left's most recognized antagonist and, not coincidentally, a skeptic of the idea that the Third

World mattered to U.S. strategic interests, was reborn as advocate for U.S. military occupation of the Persian Gulf.[125] Fifty years of hand-wringing about raw materials in peace and war had come to an end. Access to the seventy-some-odd minerals and other vital raw materials that allegedly drove wars in Asia from the 1920s on and were said to pose enormous threats to economic prosperity and national security disappeared as a "problem." Instead, a new "expressed conviction" seemed to take hold: that the United States and its free world allies had a vital national security interest in protecting the free flow of one commodity. Historians—none more richly rewarded for their efforts than Daniel Yergin—would go on to discover that oil (alone) turns out to have been the key to understanding a century of great power rivalry and conflict in Latin America, Asia, Europe, and the Middle East.

As we are about to see, the progressives of the 1970s were a pale imitation of their 1920s ancestors, using the so-called crisis to campaign for energy independence, or what used to be called autarky. The new dealers and those to the Left of them all portrayed the multinational oil companies as impossibly powerful forces that engineered the crisis and, later, U.S. military interventions in the Persian Gulf. Such views, though, failed to take into account the structural changes in the world economy and the game-changing importance of the nationalization of Western oil concessions. I'd argue that since 1979, the main "corporate interest" pushing policies of armed intervention in defense of energy security were the rapidly expanding ranks of energy security experts and other technicians and thought leaders who routinely exaggerated international dangers, overstated the benefits of intervention, and concealed the true costs. Doing so gave them all "plenty to do."[126] The critics of these overblown accounts of the energy crisis and the threats allegedly posed to national security were identified with the neoliberal and Libertarian Right, and, as far as I can tell, they went unread and certainly unreferenced by the most influential of the New Left thinkers, activists, and academics.

The puzzle for both the tenured radicals and the much more influential ranks of the American foreign policy elites is this: Since markets appear to have resolved an erstwhile fifty-year-old "raw materials problem," why is oil different?

3

1973: A TIME TO CONFUSE

ON OCTOBER 17, 1973, individual members of the Organization of Arab Petroleum Exporting Countries (OAPEC; the *A* matters), with Iraq the glaring and now-forgotten holdout, announced that they would reduce supplies of oil to some but not all buyers by 5 percent monthly, "until Israel withdraws from occupied Arab lands and 'restores the rights of the Palestinians.'"[1] The United States was singled out as a principle target. Why? Two of them, Egypt and Syria, non-OPEC members, had launched the fourth Arab-Israeli War eleven days earlier and were now in desperate straits, not least due to emergency U.S. arms shipments to the Israeli Defense Forces.[2] Three days later, some OAPEC members decided to stop all shipments to the United States and the Netherlands, a list of nations that grew to include Portugal, Rhodesia, and South Africa. The same embargo would be called off six months later, with Israel still occupying Arab lands and the Palestinians still under Israeli domination. During those same few months, imports to U.S. refiners may have fallen for a brief time by about 5 percent because supplies were being rerouted from non-Arab producers and Arab producers themselves failed to stay the course.[3] Keep in mind, too, that at the time, only about 7 percent of U.S. oil imports originated from the Middle East.

U.S.-based and all other refiners would ultimately pay a premium, however, as the price of imports skyrocketed. Taking advantage of the tight market, the governments of Saudi Arabia, Kuwait, Iraq, and Qatar did what they had unsuccessfully pressed the Western oil companies that produced the oil in their countries to do. They doubled the "posted price" of crude one day earlier, October 16, a move that the non-Arab members of OPEC supported. As a bidding war among buyers for future deliveries broke out, Iran, not an Arab country, a close U.S. ally, and a reliable oil supplier throughout the fall and winter, brokered the agreement among OPEC members to double the posted price once more to keep up with what frightened buyers were willing to pay for oil on the market.[4] The higher prices refiners paid were real enough, although the effects can't bear the weight that historians, who reproduce the rhetoric of the moment about "shocks," "turning points," and so forth, assign it.[5]

One year to the day of OAPEC's supply restriction announcement, on October 17, 1974, the Ford Foundation rolled out a five hundred–page study, *A Time to Choose: America's Energy Future*, the crown jewel in its $4 million, twenty-volume Energy Policy Project, begun in 1971. Its origins, thus, had nothing to do with a Middle East war that had not yet occurred, an embargo on the United States that had not yet been announced, or oil prices that had not yet quadrupled. Yes, Ford Foundation President McGeorge Bundy, who served as national security advisor to both presidents John F. Kennedy and Lyndon Johnson, launched the study in response to the country's "energy crisis," which by the summer of 1972 appeared to be escalating. Newspapers and television reported on fuel shortages, gasoline lines, and power brownouts in varied locales, proof for some that the country was rapidly running out of oil.[6]

President Nixon's "misguided oil import quota system" was really to blame, according to S. David Freeman, a lawyer, engineer, and modern-day progressive tapped by Bundy to head the project. Little wonder. Import quotas had created a sheltered market for domestic-produced crude and, not least, subsidized the Texas and Louisiana school systems.[7] In his speech before the Consumer Federation of America in January 1973, Freeman said the system should be abandoned and the market opened up to imports from the Persian Gulf and elsewhere. Three months later, they were. Ford was Freeman's springboard to becoming "Mr. Energy" once the Democrats took over the White House in 1976,[8] and for many decades since, he has tirelessly promoted renewable energy sources (great) and "our energy independence" (less so).[9] The latter wasn't yet a pressing concern of his in 1973, apparently.

Freeman had, however, already made up his mind about the U.S. oil industry, which he said could not be trusted to act in the public interest. Later, he claimed the speech had led the CEO of Mobil, an adviser to the Ford Foundation project, to try to have him fired.[10] Talk of a crisis, Freeman warned his audience of pro-consumer groups, "could well serve as a smoke-screen for a massive exercise in picking the pocket of the American consumer."[11]

Freeman would have many more opportunities that autumn and winter to share his views with congress and the public as he and the Ford Foundation scrambled to get out in front of the anguished debate about how to respond to the seeming existential threat suddenly posed by "foreign oil," "dependency," and "living at the mercy of the Arabs."[12] The problem was that Freeman and his staff were a year or more away from completing their work. As a stopgap, they released a preliminary report before consultants had completed many of the technical studies that had been contracted. The report nonetheless came out, in Freeman's words, for turning "our whole national policy around" via government programs to reduce energy consumption ("zero growth"), enhance conservation, shift away from energy intensive industries, protect the independence of U.S. foreign policy, and curb the power of oil companies and other industries whose interests conflicted with those of the public.[13]

When *A Time to Choose* finally appeared, with virtually identical conclusions and recommendations as the preliminary report, critics argued that Freeman had basically cooked the book. Many of the report's sixty-plus pages of dissenting commentaries by members of the advisory board said as much. Technical studies that did not support its claims were seemingly ignored. Bundy spun the fact in his introduction. Precisely "because it is a *Time to Choose* we shall not always be able to wait for 'all' the evidence before we act."[14] It didn't help that Freeman's own book published a few months later attacked "big oil" as the chief culprit behind the crisis and called for the government to go into the energy business itself.[15] Ultimately, foundation president McGeorge Bundy would be compelled to distance Ford from its own study while spending a great deal more of its money to commission work that would walk back some of its core claims.[16]

One more obstacle confronted the Ford Foundation upon the roll out of *A Time to Choose*. By late 1974, the gasoline lines were gone, luxury automobile sales were up, and oil supplies were plentiful. "The energy crisis seems to have vanished as suddenly as it appeared."[17] Adelman was correct in his judgment about the economic ineffectiveness of the embargo. The Nixon administration had encouraged the earlier OPEC price rises and had pretty quickly accommodated itself to the new round.[18] The economist and philosopher Kenneth Boulding, who served as an adviser to the Ford project, concluded that "the 1973 crisis was really a minor incident as far as the American economy was concerned; it did little more than ruffle it for a few months."[19] Subsequent studies showed that politicians (and others) exaggerated the economic costs of the supply disruptions, popularly framed as "crippling the American economy."[20] What underpinned all the more apocalyptic pronouncements was the old, old fear that the country was running out of a vital raw material, oil—all those other raw materials for decades in allegedly perilous short supply having been miraculously forgotten—and, thus, stood increasingly vulnerable to the whims of unreliable foreign sources. Weren't the gasoline lines proof?[21]

Adelman's debunking of these false beliefs was at the heart of the first report of the new conservative San Francisco-based Institute for Contemporary Studies, *No Time to Confuse* (1975), targeting the Ford Foundation study. "Everything said about oil and gas . . . was said about coal by W. S. Jevons in 1865," and many times since, as we have seen.[22] The neoliberal economist Armen Alchian, among other critics, did not pull his punches either, calling it arrogant, paternalist, politically naive, and demagogic. *A Time to Choose* belongs in "the Guinness Book of World Records for most errors of economic analysis and fact in one book." For these reasons, he said, the better title was *A Time to Confuse*.[23]

OPEC Blows Up the World

We are arguably more, not less, confused now, forty-five years later because the highly contested and suspect beliefs of a half-century ago are now seemingly unshakable truths—although *myths* is more like it—found in high school textbooks and passed on in the books that students turned historians write, the op-eds that are like oxygen to competitive thought leaders, and the article tie-ins that the publicity departments of publishing companies push in the hope of recouping a five- or six-figure advance.

You can try this experiment yourselves. Prior to writing this essay, I searched the phrase "OPEC embargo." The first link I found was to a website called the *Balance*, and a page titled "OPEC Oil Embargo, It's Causes, and the Effects of the Crisis." Kimberley Amadeo, president of something called WorldMoneyWatch.com, says that OPEC stopped selling oil to the United States. "The twelve members of the Organization of Petroleum Export Countries agreed to the embargo on October 19, 1973."[24] Only OPEC didn't embargo anyone, and no actions took place on October 19, 1973, that might be construed as an embargo by Arabs, OPEC, or anyone else.

You may think I am now stacking the deck by leading with a television and internet personality no one's ever heard of. If so, then consider Meghan O'Sullivan, the Jeane Kirkpatrick Professor of the Practice of International Affairs at Harvard, who directs its Belfer Center's Geopolitics of Energy Project. She wrote the same thing as Amadeo for Bloomberg on what she calls the fortieth anniversary of the OPEC embargo against the U.S. and "states that supported Israel," only she dates it October 17, 1973.[25] Wrong date. Wrong international organization. Not that other media outlets and acclaimed experts did much better, including the *Wall Street Journal* (Daniel Yergin), Reuters and the *Daily Star* (Warren Stroebel), *USA Today*, and the *Hill*.[26] If the A-listers and their editors can't distinguish OAPEC from OPEC or an embargo from a brief and minor production cutback, let alone keep the varied targets of these different discursive or symbolic acts straight, how do we expect lesser lights like science journalist Marc Lallanilla to get it right when he says OPEC launched an embargo that "eventually included western Europe and Japan"?[27] The most reliable short account I found, on the website of the *Oil and Gas Journal*, meanwhile, is embargoed behind a paywall.[28]

Many institutions, including academic ones, did not do any better. *National Geographic*'s web page "This Day in U.S. History," garbles the facts in remarkable fashion. The twelve-member OPEC cartel "decided to reduce the amount of oil available to the United States," and this "oil weapon" and "embargo" caused the price rise![29] The University of Georgia professor of public policy Andrew Whitford discusses the OPEC embargo in a technical paper.[30] National Public Radio's Alex Chadwick calls it the OPEC embargo.[31] James Madison University political scientist Glenn Hastedt confuses who is doing what throughout his account in *The Encyclopedia of American Foreign*

Policy.[32] The college textbook, *American Passages*, by a group of scholars led by Edward Ayers, the great Southern historian and onetime president of the University of Richmond, says OPEC ceased oil shipments to the United States, Europe, and Japan.[33] The website of the Smithsonian Institution's National Museum of American History calls it the OPEC embargo.[34] But so did *Diplomatic History*, the flagship journal of the Society for Historians of American Foreign Relations, which led one of its members, Georgetown University's David Painter, who knows better, to write a letter seeking a correction.[35]

To be clear, the problem ultimately is not with the mangled facts but with the truth, or, as we professors say, the "internal validity" of a story that casts in the starring role an ineffectual embargo by the "Arabs" or by a "cartel" of oil-producing countries that wasn't a cartel. That is, the majority of OPEC member states did not yet control how much oil was produced from its wells, let alone where it was or was not delivered, which is what economists take to be a cartel's defining feature.[36] This is in part why some observers back then—Freeman was by no means the only one—insisted that "big oil," the Nixon administration, or both had contrived the crisis.[37]

The embargo is best understood as political theater whose effects on its targeted audiences—Westerners and Arab citizens (or subjects)—were psychological. Let's see how far we get without the event itself for the moment in explaining two undeniably real phenomena of the time: the global price shock of 1973–1974 and the infamous U.S. gasoline lines of the fall and winter, photos of which serve as the clichéd symbol of a crisis that, back then, a majority of Americans blamed on the multinational oil companies—and that those confused retrospective accounts thus far cited now pin on OPEC. A basic convention of social scientific inquiry suggests we are on solid ground in doing so because OPEC raised posted prices again, five years later, without the benefit of another embargo. And it is now forty-five years and counting since any oil-exporting country has tried the boycott ploy again. Similarly, if you think it is what caused the shortages and gas lines in the United States, you have a puzzle to solve—namely, why residents of another embargoed country, the Netherlands, never waited in a single gasoline line before the embargo was called off in March 1974.

So why the price shock? What drove the rapidly escalating cost of oil on the spot market? It was this price spike that led OPEC members to force a change in the terms of the deal with Western oil companies—who unilaterally raised posted prices twice in an unprecedented fashion. This last statement is correct. OPEC did not cause oil prices to rise. It did, however, seek a fairer share of the windfall. Ultimately, the price shock of 1973–1974 is part of a bigger story about international economic change that the United States as a "superpower," or "hegemon," attempted to manage in the late 1960s and early 1970s. The problem, in other words, was a "structural" one, although to write this is to set an op-ed editor's head spinning, since thought leaders have only about five hundred words to get from the dramatic setup (OPEC embargo) to the supposed lessons the "history" teaches us today, a formula that became a cliché soon after the op-ed ("opposite the editorial") was invented in 1970.[38] Still, I try to be brief. There are a lot of new, good books to consult if you want to know more.[39]

Gulliver's Troubles

The years before the 1973 shock were tumultuous ones for the United States and the world economy, sometimes described as the unraveling of the post-1945 "Bretton Woods system."[40] For decades, the dollar, backed by gold, had served as the world's reserve currency. Confidence in the dollar declined as U.S. economic growth slowed, the country's trade deficit grew, and the cost-of-living rose. Holders of all those dollars abroad started cashing them in for gold, depleting U.S. reserves and leading ultimately to the Nixon administration's decision in August 1971 to end convertibility ("closing the gold window") and allow the dollar's value to fall. Nixon also announced wage and price controls for the first time since World War II, in the hope of controlling inflation and increasing the demand for U.S. goods. Why it mattered for oil exporters, and all other raw material producers, is, first, that the costs were increasing for the diverse Western manufactured goods and services critical to industry and state building, from turbines to radar, planes, and tanks, let alone the cars, air conditioners, televisions, and other luxury items that the newly enriched Saudi, Iraqi, Iranian, etcetera, ruling classes longed for. Raw material prices moved in the other direction. At the same time, the dollars that the various kings, colonels, and oil ministers earned in taxes and royalties were suddenly worth less. It is this double-squeeze that drove OPEC's efforts, successfully, in 1971, but not in 1973, to get oil companies to raise the posted price of their crude oil.

The key thing to understand is that by the 1960s the posted price, which as a result of OPEC's founding and near constant pressure on the concessionaires remained fixed throughout that decade, was a kind of accounting fiction used to establish the tax and royalty payments that the companies owed the sovereigns. We need to distinguish it from the much more variable "market" or "realized" prices that the companies actually obtained from contracts with their affiliates and third parties or that traders on the still relatively undeveloped spot markets of the era bought and sold at.[41] It is why Timothy Mitchell takes pains to emphasize in "The Crisis That Never Happened" that what OPEC did in October and again in December 1973 was to raise the *tax rate* that the companies had to pay on the oil then being sold by them on world markets at already record high prices.[42]

For most of the 1960s, the posted price exceeded the market price, which, as long as this was true, gained for the exporting countries of the Persian Gulf crucial advantages over exporters of other raw materials, such as copper and cotton. It meant that government revenues could be calculated in advance for planning purposes regardless of market conditions. It also protected them from the decline in revenue that virtually all other raw material exporters faced that decade.[43] The problem came when real oil prices started to rise toward the end of the decade, which drove the producers to demand an increase in their tax revenues. It was the only way to make sure that the companies did not pocket the whole of the windfall. The companies ultimately agreed in 1971 but stonewalled two years later, leading the Gulf producers to do so on their own, in October and again in December, this time following the Shah of Iran's lead. Keep in mind, though, that while this new, unprecedented posted price of $11.65 increased the tax rate to $7.00 a barrel, buyers on the world oil market were paying upwards of $17.00.[44]

Let's begin with the structural shift in oil supply and demand behind the price rise of the early 1970s, which, in conjunction with the spot shortages and gas lines, is what drove the talk of an energy crisis in the United States and led the Ford Foundation to launch the energy project. Most basically, demand from the advanced industrial economies had started to outpace supply, and getting additional quantities to market is a process that involves a time lag. One important source of the disequilibrium deserves highlighting. The U.S. government's efforts to "protect" domestic refiners from Middle Eastern oil, which sold on the world market at prices lower than crude produced in Texas, California, Louisiana, and Oklahoma, had contributed to the depletion of the country's reserves. The peak in production in both the United States and Venezuela (which was treated differently from other foreign producers) meant that supplies from the Persian Gulf would have to make up the shortfall, acknowledged not least by the decision of the Nixon administration to end the quota system and open the U.S. market, except that the price was no longer quite so cheap. Meanwhile, the 1971 wage and price controls would prevent domestic producers from selling their own oil at the price prevailing on the spot market. You don't need an advanced economics degree to understand that under such a system it is rational for firms to withhold supply.

Now factor in the consequences of uncertainty on price as war broke out in the Middle East on October 6, 1973. OPEC countries had convened a month earlier in Vienna to prepare for a meeting with company representatives on October 8. Both received more coverage than earlier rounds because of the heightened fears of oil scarcity the "crisis" that winter and spring was believed to portend. The producers demanded a doubling of the posted price. After consultations with their home governments, the companies quit the talks—ceding their role in the posted price regime, it turned out. The Persian Gulf producers then fixed the price OPEC had agreed on at Vienna on their own four days later. The rest of OPEC went along.

As I hope is obvious at this point, the price shock or, from the vantage point of the producers, the start of the oil revolution had nothing to do with the declaration of an embargo. Its announcement followed rather than preceded OPEC's successful effort to increase the tax rate the companies would have to pay, that is—to keep more of the revenues from the new, higher price of oil on the world market. The decision by the Arab-producing states to try to use their oil resources to force Israel and the United States to negotiate a settlement had nothing to do with OPEC's efforts to get more out of the companies. Historians err in imagining that the price increases reflected a sudden and dramatic cutback in production. Non-Arab members happily produced more not less oil and, soon enough, so did the so-called Arab radicals—Libya and Algeria—rather than lose market share. Saddam Hussein, meanwhile, increased exports of Iraqi oil to Europe.[45] All these developments occurred prior to the highly performative declaration of an end to the embargo that couldn't possibly succeed, as Adelman insisted at the time.

Professors like me like to think in terms of "counterfactuals." So instead of collapsing the two events into one, as was common at the time and as all those accounts cited still do, imagine that the Saudi and Kuwaiti rulers resisted the pressure or otherwise thought better than to threaten the United States over its support of Israel in the October 1973 War. OPEC would still have confronted the companies over the tax rate. Prices on the spot market and for future third party sales would still have increased. The accelerated turn to the nationalization of the oil companies' assets over the next years was overdetermined because it was taking place everywhere the oil companies had foreign concessions, not just in the Middle East.[46] And, finally, the regional shortages and gas lines in the United States were effects not of an embargo but of the price and allocation controls imposed in 1971, when these distribution problems first manifested themselves, and that were nonetheless kept in place for oil alone for the next ten years.[47] The phenomenon was unknown in the Netherlands, the other embargoed country. Gas lines reappeared in 1978–1979 in the United States, as markets were roiled by the revolution in Iran and the beginning of the Iran-Iraq War. And although supply disruptions, production cutbacks, and price rises have recurred many times since, no American has waited on a gas line again after the incoming Reagan administration dismantled price controls in 1981.[48]

The OPEC embargo, to paraphrase Adelman's debunking of scarcity, is a fiction, but belief in it is a fact, one that at the time added to the fears and panic buying that drove the price of oil to record highs.[49] Its effects were clearly psychological, although I may be understating it. Trauma inducing is more like it. The effects still manifest themselves today, in fact, in fears, for example, of an oil weapon that a succession of antagonists, from OPEC or the "Arabs" or Iranian "hardliners" to Saddam Hussein, Osama Bin Laden, and any and all future would-be hegemons possess and are ready to deploy (again).[50] These fears, in turn, animate the idea that something called "foreign oil" and the country's "dependency" on it threaten national security, although as Sebastian Herbstreuth details, only some and not all oil produced outside the country's borders, but refined inside them, constitutes a threat, apparently. Imports from Canada, Mexico, and Venezuela don't (yet). "Foreign oil" is, in fact, a euphemism.

A certain degree of overreaction or threat inflation is understandable among those who lived through the price rises, gas lines, and bluster of those first months. So economist C. Fred Bergsten, the former Kissinger aide and then senior fellow at the Brookings Institution, thought the basic principles taught in Economics 101, about the ineffectiveness of cartels, no longer applied. Instead, he warned Congress and readers of *Foreign Policy* that producers of bananas, rubber, tin, bauxite, copper, and so forth were likely to follow OPEC in holding up the world economy.[51] A half century later, and against all logic and evidence to the contrary, the conservative and self-styled global strategist Walter Russell Mead remains convinced that some Saddam Hussein–like figure could easily "blackmail the world" by cutting "the flow of oil from the Middle East to Europe, India, China, and/or Japan."[52]

Racism is, of course, the other entangled strand of the old raw materialism given new life in the oil crisis, intensifying fears that the world was running out of a now more-vital-than-all-other-commodities-combined product and confirming that access would require more vigilance and armed force than ever before. Some confined their dreams of righting the "holdup" of Western Europe and the United States by "Bedouin rulers" or ending the farce of "sovereignty" enjoyed by "various sheikhdoms" to their staff meetings or in their diaries.[53] William Simon, the businessman and treasury official appointed the country's first "energy czar," as the Shah of Iran successfully pushed through the second OPEC-posted price hike, was less circumspect. The key U.S. ally and buyer of all the weapons the Nixon administration would sell him was in the term of the art at the time a "price hawk." Simon, though, said this of the Iranian ruler: "The Shah is a nut."[54]

Others, distrustful of Nixon and Kissinger's appeasement policies (détente, shuttle diplomacy, and so forth) and outraged by OPEC's effrontery, pressed publicly for the U.S. takeover of the Gulf. Robert Tucker, as we recall, was just one of many. In 1975, *Harper's Magazine* published "Seizing Arab Oil," by unnamed Department of Defense analysts hiding behind the pseudonym Miles Ignotus, "Unknown Soldier." Edward Luttwak was one of them.[55] Berkeley political scientist Aaron Wildavsky, who made a career of cautioning against wild exaggerations that invariably yielded bad policy decisions, described OPEC as having set off a world-wide systemic "catastrophe" to which the United States had acquiesced, that had already led "to mass starvation in poor countries," was likely to destroy NATO, and allow the Soviet bloc to consolidate its power. Indeed, he insisted, the Soviets had orchestrated the crisis. He and his two coauthors, though, viewed the Israelis as allies who might help reverse Western decline by taking control of Libya while the U.S. seized Abu Dhabi and Kuwait.[56] Events seemed to have forced conservatives to shift the grounds of one of their venerable arguments about the economic losses that raw material–producing countries would invariably suffer at the hands of the Third World's overly emotional and neurotic nationalists.[57]

The absolute line of difference that the thought leaders and real leaders drew between the OPEC members and all the other actors central to the making of OPEC was a moral one. There was the Texas Railroad Commission, say, that fixed the price of U.S. oil for decades; the companies that had operated their separate and unequal compounds across the Caribbean, the Persian Gulf, and the Indonesian archipelago; and the successive U.S. administrations that embargoed Middle East oil, ended the Bretton Woods system, and eagerly armed the Shah of Iran. The producing-countries' actions, as a very early critic of this baseless double standard framed it, were routinely "condemned as a 'crime,' 'racket,' 'piracy,' and 'price hijack.'"[58] Even those who argued against seizing an oil field or two save as a last resort, such as Daniel Yergin, making his first tentative foray into the topic in the *New York Times Magazine* in 1975, condemned the price shock as unjust.[59]

The reality, however, is that the producers had seen the value of their only export and source of wealth decline with the end of Bretton Woods, the devaluation of the dollar, and the inflated costs of Western capital and consumer goods, as discussed. What the producers succeeded in doing by raising the posted price in dollars was to bring the price in terms of gold back within its decades-long historic range of ten to fifteen barrels per ounce of gold after oil had fallen by some 70 percent (or, put another way, after the oil price of gold had risen by almost 200 percent). "Rather than raising the relative price of oil, OPEC countries were only 'staying even'" for the rest of the decade.[60]

Certainly, the producers would have their work cut out for them in the years ahead.[61] The price shock of 1973 and the takeover of the foreign oil companies' assets were catalysts for upheaval in the industry, in part foreseen at the time. The obvious example is the development of new, non-OPEC areas of production, such as the North Sea, which began to be discussed almost immediately and became a reality just a few years later. Other changes emerged out of the disorder of the end of the concession regime—for one, new price concepts (marker or reference price, buy-back price, and so forth) in place of the old posted price system. Concentration in the industry declined with the growth of new entrants. The decade saw increased third party transactions and a new, unprecedented volume of trade on various spot markets. By the early 1980s, the first oil futures markets began operating in New York, Chicago, and London. Hard as it is for some to imagine, it is OPEC that deserves credit for bringing about "a proper world market for crude oil."[62]

The U.S. government played a role, although mainly a negative one, in this outcome. Policies focused more on increasing supply than on reducing demand. Thus, the mix of price and allocation controls in combination with the end of import restrictions contributed to the rapid rise in oil imports (by administrations ostensibly committed to "energy independence") and depressed investment in domestic production. Americans had started ordering gas-guzzling cars and turning up their thermostats again. The chickens came home to roost late in 1978, when the revolution in Iran temporarily shut down its oil industry. After four years of stable prices, the United States got to relive the trauma of 1973, with the reappearance of shortages and gasoline lines; runaway prices on the spot market; OPEC members' efforts to preserve their gains; a bruising, months-long battle in Washington by various interests over a proposed windfall profits tax on big oil; and not least, the generation of countless more "scary scenarios" of constantly rising prices, dwindling worldwide supply, and the nefarious designs on the Gulf by outside powers.[63]

Securing the Gulf

Leave it to an economist to produce one of the briefest yet devastating critiques of the unprecedented turn in 1979 to deploying U.S. military force for guaranteeing access—continuous, reliable, cheap, or other adjectives beloved by the growing ranks of self-styled energy security experts—to the oil resources of the Persian Gulf. Louisiana State University's Allan Pulsipher wanted to know what the intellectual sources of the dramatic pivot from Southeast to Southwest Asia were. What were the real objectives? As was obvious to him, Adelman, and other economists, even Iran's "fanatical" Ayatollah Khomeini would have to sell his country's oil to the Great Satan.[64] Pulsipher looked in vain for any mention of the need for U.S. force projection in the Harvard Business School and Ford Foundation studies charting America's post–price shock energy future. It just wasn't there, despite the presumption that, in the medium term at least, more not less of U.S. energy needs would have to be sourced from the "volatile" and "unstable" region. Yet an increasingly embattled President Carter set forth, in his January 1980 State of the Union address, a doctrine—that is, a pledge—to use force to prevent outside powers from seizing the Gulf, which soon begat a Rapid Deployment Force that morphed into what we now know as the U.S. Central Command.

Carter's successor, Ronald Reagan, and Reagan's successor, George H. W. Bush, each doubled down on the use of force, beginning with the 1982 intervention in the Lebanese civil war, a debacle that led to the blowing up of the U.S. embassy in April and a Marine barracks in October 1983 that was the largest single-day death toll of U.S. troops since the first day of the January 1968 Tet Offensive in Vietnam.[65] These were also among the first suicide bombings in the region. If Iran-backed militias carried out the attacks, which is likely, the U.S. government made no secret of its aiding Iraqi ruler Saddam Hussein in his brutal eight-year war with Iran.[66] By the time Pulsipher published "Watershed, Aberration, and Hallucination: The Past Twenty Years," the Reagan team had deployed the U.S. Navy in 1987 to protect oil tankers from Iranian missiles (the less said the better about the secret efforts by the same administration to sell arms to the Iranians with which to fund their wars in Central America).[67] In 1990, President Bush rushed troops and advanced weapons to "protect" Saudi Arabia's oil fields, wage a campaign known as "Desert Storm" to reverse Saddam Hussein's invasion of Kuwait, and enforce crippling economic sanctions on Iraq's population for the rest of the decade. For most of the rest of the decade, too, the Clinton administration pursued the "illogic," to quote a longtime specialist on U.S.–Persian Gulf relations, Gregory Gause, of the "dual containment" of both Iraq and Iran. It was illogical because the United States could at best contain one of those two adversaries but only with the help of the other.[68]

It is surely understandable why Pulsipher thought mainly in terms of the mistaken and what I have called racist beliefs about one or another dictator cutting off the West's oil supply (or seizing all the oil for himself and destroying the West by forcing up the price, a feat that OPEC itself had not remotely been able to accomplish in the ensuing decades). Thus, the imagined need for the United States to stop these nightmares from coming true. His resolution of the puzzle is also surely correct, as far as it goes. Since access was guaranteed by an enemy's seemingly insatiable need for revenue, he believed that U.S. coercive power was directed at *the oil rents* rather than the oil. As Pulsipher put it, the military would be used "if needed to keep the vast amounts of money to be made from the sale of oil out of the pockets of those who would use it to do us harm." As in most other realms, "it was money or something else, not oil, that was ultimately at issue."[69]

After all, as noted in the opening, the sanctions imposed on Iraq in the 1990s, or on Iran in 2018 for that matter, *reduce* the availability of oil for sale on the world market and, all else being equal, increase the price that buyers pay. And if, through slowly starving it, a population successfully rises up against Qaddafi, say, or the Baathists or the Ayatollahs, the gamble is that the successor, an equally oil rent–dependent dictatorship (no, we hope, democracy) will line up with, rather than against, the United States and its local "partners." Overthrowing an adversary directly may cost more in the short run, as we saw in Iraq in 2003, but the architects of that intervention swore that the ultimate payouts would be massively larger.

Pulsipher nonetheless had forgotten that the Carter Doctrine and the pivot to the Middle East was an answer not only to the downfall of America's imagined client in Tehran in January 1979 but to the Soviet intervention in Afghanistan eleven months later, which aimed to restore to power a not terribly reliable communist dictatorship. As

the archival record plainly shows, deliberations about the security
threat in the Gulf began in 1977 with the concern for the increasingly tenuous position of the Shah (and soon, the Saudis as well, not
for the last time), but it was the invasion of Afghanistan that was
"instrumental in paving the way" for the unprecedented change in
the U.S. strategic posture.[70] Some would call it a "strategic rationale."
Not least, it required wizardry of the highest order to turn the Soviet
Union—a major energy producer and exporter just starting to develop massive oil and gas fields in Siberia, financed by West Germany
and other European countries in the biggest "economic deal in the
history of East-West relations during the Cold War"—into a country
allegedly running dry and, thus, with designs for "control" over the
oil of the Persian Gulf.[71] Political scientists, including the ones that
the *Washington Post* called "rightist theoreticians," took to the op-ed
pages; they wrote position papers advocating intervention in the
Gulf for the presidential hopeful Ronald Reagan, policy briefs for
Rand, and secret studies for the "hawks" inside the Carter cabinet.[72]

We have already encountered the two most routinely cited advocates for military force projection, Robert Tucker and Edward
Luttwak ("an expert on everything"). Others included Amos Perlmutter, an Israeli teaching at the American University; Francis Fukuyama, who reworked his Harvard PhD dissertation on the topic
for the Rand Corporation; and Geoffrey Kemp, an arms control
specialist who worked for Paul Wolfowitz, in the Pentagon, on
a study of the Soviet threat to U.S. interests in the Gulf.[73] UCLA
graduate student Dennis Ross joined the team as well and would
write some of the most alarmist accounts of alleged Soviet designs
to gain control of or "leverage" over Gulf oil flows.[74] Ross clung to
the idea longer than most, in fact.[75]

The most important of the militant soothsayers by far was the
"hard-liner" and Harvard University political scientist Samuel A.
Huntington, Fukuyama's dissertation supervisor, as head of a team

writing not for the op-ed pages but for the Carter administration's eyes only. Presidential Review Memorandum 10 (PRM 10) is still classified forty-plus years later, although the turf battles involved were the subject of leaks even prior to its completion. Carter's national security adviser, Zbigniew Brzezinski, hired his old friend and coauthor as a consultant after Defense Secretary Harold Brown had turned him down for a Pentagon post. Huntington's job was to oversee the National Security Council's part of the largest review of national security strategy since the 1940s, a "comprehensive net assessment" of Soviet challenges to the United States across the globe. Brown grabbed the bigger part of the project, on military strategy and force posture, and got his own consultants to supervise the work.[76] Friends who Huntington had, in turn, begun to consult told the *Washington Post* that the hope was "to create a document that would scare the Carter administration into greater respect for the Soviet menace."[77]

What more we know about Huntington's study and its vision of the Soviet threat to the alleged inferior U.S. position in the Persian Gulf comes from the short history written by General William Eldridge Odom—another of the hawks who considered détente a disaster and who worked under Huntington—and from the research of a Norwegian historian.[78] Huntington portrayed the Soviet Union as poised to reap the gains from instability in Iran and Saudi Arabia as it had in Afghanistan. And what would follow would be (somehow) the denial of access to oil. The Soviet Union would then use its newfound control (somehow) of these resources to undermine the alliance with oil-dependent NATO and Japan. Brzezinski made strategic use of Huntington's study in the long and bruising bureaucratic battles that ultimately led to the buildup of naval forces there and the creation of a new Central Command.

These visions of a grand strategy of Soviet expansion toward the Gulf and of the chaos that a cut off of oil would produce reached a crescendo in the early 1980s.[79] First, the Democratic hawks had to compete with the assorted militarists and hard-liners advising Republican presidential candidate Ronald Reagan in advocating the use of force to protect "the lifelines of western civilization."[80] One of them, Edward Luttwak, more of an oracle really, claimed plans were afoot by the Russians to send Cuban troops to the Gulf.[81] No, Amos Perlmutter, another adviser, would argue one year later, the Soviets were gambling on an invitation from the Ayatollah Khomeini for arming his government in its war with Soviet-allied Iraq, so the United States would have to hold its nose and come to Iran's aid first.[82] Once elected, Reagan himself fought "some of America's most bruising foreign policy" battles inside the Beltway over plans to sell advanced arms and reconnaissance aircraft to Saudi Arabia as part of its defense of the Persian Gulf. As the *Washington Post*'s senior correspondent and columnist Jim Hoagland wrote, the coalition of "neoconservatives and Jews" that had helped bring him to power feared that Reagan was returning to President Jimmy Carter's game of placating untrustworthy clients, when he should have been pressuring them to accept U.S. bases on their soil as the only sure way to protect the oil against hostile takeover.[83]

Still, with the ascent of Mikhail Gorbachev to head the Communist Party Central Committee in 1985 and the beginning of reforms known as *perestroika*, the collapse of oil prices in 1986, and the withdrawal of Soviet forces from Afghanistan in 1988–1989, advocates for continued U.S. dominance of the Gulf would mostly turn to divining new threats in a world market awash in oil.[84] The consensus among a new generation of Soviet specialists was that Gorbachev sought to end the Cold War with the United States.[85] Brzezinski, though, remained implacable. In June 1987, he had called for yet "more muscle in the Gulf, less in NATO." Why? Because "the American-Soviet conflict is an historical rivalry that will endure for as long as we live." Moscow had not given up its design to "achieve predominance over Southwest Asia" to destroy the U.S.

alliance with Western Europe and Japan.[86] The Soviet Union collapsed five years later in 1991. Brzezinski died in 2017.

The Russian journalist and historian of modern Saudi Arabia, Alexei Vasiliev, is surely correct in his recent discussion of the "ideological predetermination" of the views of Brzezinski, his familiars, and the many others who imagined the Soviets driving from Afghanistan to the Gulf in fulfillment of the master plan for world conquest. It may be hard for readers now to believe that so many politicians and pundits back then believed such things about "the evil empire," in Ronald Reagan's phrase. Or maybe not. Vasiliev, though, is also right that those who began to think less in terms of invasion than subversion, with the Soviets somehow behind the instability in Yemen, Ethiopia, Iran, and so forth, still got it wrong. "The fragility of political structures that are mostly borrowed from the West but which have been painfully adapted to local conditions and traditions, and the growth of elites with their inevitable corruption and misrule quite naturally produced a form for internal instability." Most important, he argues, the "main fallacy" of the time was the idea that the Soviet Union was a "rising power," when, in fact, the country's "accelerating decline" made it more interested in the "status quo" than the United States itself.[87]

Lest one think a retrospective judgment somehow unsporting, the Irish radical, Fred Halliday, a brilliant student and intrepid researcher in the Gulf during those years, said it all at the time in his *Soviet Policy in the Arc of Crisis*, using the phrase Brzezinski popularized in support of the military buildup that the Reagan administration was recklessly escalating.[88] Halliday called the idea of a threat "illusory," for one, because analysts get the root causes of political change wrong. "The disproportionate focus by American commentators upon the role of Soviet policy, like that by Soviet commentators upon the activities of the United States, leads to tendentious analysis" and "simplistic policy" in response.[89] But Halliday also analyzed the "strategic alarmism," "anxiety," "psychology" of fear, and, not least, "new mood of raw material vulnerability" that contributed to the false picture of the Soviet threat.[90] In other words, Halliday had inadvertently returned to the pioneering arguments of Culbertson and the Columbia School theorists of the 1920s. Inadvertent because otherwise he would have realized that there was nothing "new" in the idea that whites fear potentially being denied access to raw materials, either by the producers themselves or by rivals seen as desperately seeking escape from the same imagined scarcity syndrome. Halliday insisted,

> But there are a number of problems with this scenario. First of all, even though voiced by right-wing analysts, it is a curiously economistic explanation, reminiscent in many ways of vulgar Marxist explanations of American foreign policy in terms of a quest for raw materials and markets. It is pertinent to make the same reply to the vulgar Marxists of the Right as to those of the Left: that foreign policy is rarely reducible to simple economic concerns, and that access to raw materials is not always best guaranteed by the pursuit of political domination in those areas where the minerals or markets are to be found. Despite the neat reductionism of so much writing on the subject, the Soviet policy in Afghanistan bears no serious relationship to its oil policy. Moreover, the Russians must have learned from their dealings with countries like Iraq, and from observing the fate of Western dealings with OPEC, that in the contemporary world raw materials producers, especially producers of oil, have a measure of independence unknown in previous decades.[91]

The Risk game view of the world let Brzezinski and all those other not-so-grand strategists act in willful ignorance of how oil actually gets to market, although as Halliday himself emphasized, even their understanding of geography, ostensibly their strong suit, was suspect.[92] So they repeated the mantra that the Soviets would somehow seize control of the production decisions of one or another sheikhdom, without considering how their own governments and those governments' imagined tools, the multinationals, had found themselves largely helpless to reverse OPEC's gains. Perhaps they believed along with many other ordinary Americans that Nixon and Exxon, and not the mercurial mad men of the Gulf, were behind the oil revolution. The Soviets themselves had a decades-long "patron client" relationship with Baathist Iraq, with zero consequences for Iraqi oil sales to the West.[93] As we have seen, Brzezinski himself feared above all that once in control of Arabs oil production, the Soviets would use the position to break up the NATO alliance because of Europe and Japan's dependence. This last is precious because, as has been noted, West Germany eagerly supported the development of Soviet gas production and pipeline facilities, becoming the biggest Western customer of these "strategic" energy resources, and NATO survived just fine (although the deal doubtless gave Brzezinski, not to mention competing companies, nightmares).

Vasiliev suggests why an even cursory knowledge of conditions as they actually existed at the time ought to have ended fantasies of Soviet designs in the long or short term for "seizing Middle East oil." Its leadership understood that the Gulf was a Western sphere of influence and any such action would've been seen as an act of war. Brezhnev said as much publicly and proposed initiatives to demilitarize the region, which the Reagan administration dismissed as propaganda. The Soviet Union simply could never substitute as an economic partner of the oil producers. It could neither absorb the amount of oil the region produced nor supply the goods and technology that oil rents paid for. Instead, the evil empire itself was growing more entangled in the world economy as an exporter of oil and gas, obviously, but also as an importer "of advanced technology, food and to some extent consumer goods." Its growing exports of arms and industrial machinery to the Middle East region meanwhile depended on the continued flow of oil rents to the producing countries. The "USSR was not interested in undermining the Western economy or in upsetting the region's economic ties with the West."[94] A historian, though, looks in vain through the thousands of pages of declassified documents from the time for evidence that principals like Brzezinski or their agents sought to reconcile their Risk game worldviews with the reality of the world economy.[95]

Ragaei El Mallakh, the Egyptian-born University of Colorado economist who pioneered the study of the effects of the oil wealth on the economic development of the Middle East, said that the United States in the late 1970s was suffering the "trauma of withdrawal" from cheap energy.[96] Agreed. Even as a traumatized 1973 generation came to see oil as "exceptional," it is uncanny how in other respects all the historic tropes of scarcity, insecurity, and existential threat from the 1920s and 1950s were evoked during the 1973 and 1979 "crises." A key one was the belief about the failure of stewardship on the part of the sheikhs, kings, and colonels over the resources that belonged not to those who lived there but to those who needed them. Racism undergirds all those calls for intervention by Tucker, Luttwak, and other militant raw materialists.

We have our work cut out for us, given all the myths that the blogs, textbooks, and even some professional histories keep alive in their accounts of 1973 as a "watershed" and "transformative" moment that somehow presaged and led inexorably to the wars of the late twentieth and early twenty-first century. Back in 2005, I raised a pointed question about the fabled fact-checking power of the *New Yorker* when it came to portraying the history of U.S. relations with Saudi Arabia. As we are about to see, the myths concerning the alleged "partnership" and "special relationship" continue to multi-ply.[97] Their staff writer, Lawrence Wright, award-winning author of the *Looming Tower*, about September 11, knows the subject, obviously. Consider this excerpt from the piece, though, that Wright published in January 2018, on the eve of his most recent big book, *God Save Texas*, with its seemingly authoritative account of how, for the true believers at least, the country has turned into Saudi America:[98]

> Michael Fowler, an oilman and a philanthropist in Houston, showed me a graph that depicted the U.S. production of crude oil over time. In 1970, American oil production reached nearly ten million barrels a day; that summit was followed by a slow slide, touching bottom, in 2008, at a little more than five million barrels a day. That decline was abetted by oil *embargoes*, price shocks, gas lines, shifting geopolitical alliances, and wars in the Middle East.[99]

It is hard to know where to begin. Wright, or, perhaps, Fowler abetted by Wright, imagines multiple embargoes after 1970, when there was only one, and pointedly one that didn't impact supply. As we noted in the opening, macroeconomic variables are what explain the largest part of the volatility in commodity prices over time. Wright and Fowler leave out the factor that mattered most in the decline—namely, the decades of "protecting" the domestic industry from cheap OPEC oil. And, finally, consider one implication of his idiosyncratic enumeration of events that he imagines led to the depletion of U.S. oil fields. Absent the OPEC oil price revolution that made investment in more marginal fields profitable, U.S. production of conventional oil would have fallen that much more rapidly, the "slow slide" replaced by precipitous decline.[100]

4

NO DEAL

THE SAUDI ARABIA of Americans' imaginations demonstrates like nothing else I know the hold that oilcraft has over us—its undiminished power to disarrange and misdirect thought. Fifteen years ago I began stripping away some old myths that served to obscure the underlying, not very complicated explanation of why and for whom in the United States the oil resources of Saudi Arabia first came to matter.[1] Two (later expanded to four) U.S. oil companies paid a significant sum for exclusive rights to explore for and produce petroleum there, eventually making a fortune for the principal owners, shareholders, executives, and favored engineering and construction firms of the Arabian American Oil Company (Aramco). The Al Saud, the family that had conquered the peninsula with the help of an army of religious zealots, did all right, too.

Back then, U.S. joint chiefs of staff, top economic policy makers, and even presidents had their doubts about subsidizing and protecting Aramco's operations on strategic or national security grounds. It is understandable. The firms certainly could afford the entire cost of developing the concession on their own. Populist sentiments against the old Rockefeller-owned Standard Oil (now Exxon Mobil) and the other partners ran extremely high. Even the minimal, mostly arms-length dealings with the Al Saud from the Roosevelt through the Kennedy and Johnson years generated enormous backlash among

Democrats, Jewish groups, labor, civil rights leaders, Western oil-bearing landowners, and those petroleum companies selling primarily on the domestic market (the "Independents").

These basic, indeed, mundane facts, though, were repeatedly forgotten in the ensuing blizzard of strategic rationales, many of which we are now intimately familiar with. The country was running out of the oil that would be needed to fight and win the next war. Great Britain was only the first of the rivals with improbable designs and, more incredibly, still intact capabilities to wrest the stupendous source of strategic power from—one would think—the concession owners. But no, from the United States itself, the rationale went.

Selling Americans on the Al Saud wasn't easy. The first king, Abd al-Aziz Al Saud, better known as Ibn Saud in the West, ruled a place that, as the cliché had it, was straight out of the Middle Ages.[2] Slavery was alive and well there. Democracy, not so much, although the oil company's PR portrayed him as a kind of "desert Democrat" and the George Washington of the Arabian Peninsula. They also tried to hide the fact that he and dozens of his sons were spending oil royalties even faster than they were "earning" them—on cars, palaces, payouts to the tribes, and so forth—with the firm and their bankers compelled to advance them more and more gold and dollars (not least why Aramco futilely sought postwar U.S. economic aid). The story went that all those advances were really for "development," led by the king's chosen successor, his son Saud, who was more of a "modernizer" even than Ibn Saud and dedicated to bringing the kingdom into the twentieth century. At the same time, they worried incessantly about the viability of this rickety family-based order going forward, as did the king, who, in failing to secure the weapons he wanted from the United States, blamed the Jews.

It's not surprising, therefore, that the firms' principals, their public relations divisions, their bankers, lawyers turned statesmen, and other company-subsidized institutions, from the Council on Foreign

Relations to Harvard and Princeton, embraced all these strategic and not-so-strategic rationales and two other more dangerous truths as they saw them. One was that Democratic administrations' support for Israel was itself a ticking time bomb. In private, company executives stole a page out of the Southern segregationists' playbook to argue that the early pro-Israel groups, like the civil rights movement, were fellow travelers in all but name, doing the bidding of the USSR.[3] The biggest threats of all, however, were the various "radical" nationalist, Pan-Arab, and, redundantly, anti-imperialist currents gaining ground among the workers, intellectuals, and, worst of all, military, all imagined as poised to overthrow the Al Saud and seize the oil fields. Doing so would cripple production (Arabs being unwilling or unable to meet market demand) and so deprive the west of a scarce resource that came to be viewed as the key to prosperity and to victory in war. Only, as we saw, nationalization did take place in the kingdom and elsewhere, and the oil continued to flow, with the old owners all adapting to the new order.

If those days are long gone, today's vastly expanded ranks of energy security experts, grand strategists, Saudi specialists, assorted crackpot realists, and an ever-widening circle of those on the Saudi payroll in one way or another have continued their hand-wringing about the threats to the Al Saud, which represent an existential danger to an ever-more oil-hungry world and to the idea—the reality being quite different—of a United States–Saudi Arabia "special relationship." As we are about to see, in the minds of many, the relationship is understood as a pact or agreement or alliance or, in the belittling words of the *New York Times* columnist Tom Friedman, a deal: "oil for security."[4] Here is President Donald boasting about upholding his end at an October 2018 Make America Great Again rally in Southaven, Mississippi: "We protect Saudi Arabia. Would you say they're rich? And I love the king, King Salman. But I said 'King—we're protecting you—you might not be there for two weeks without us—you have to pay for your military.'"[5] What about the oil, you might ask? Well, with prices down and incessant talk about U.S. energy independence at hand, there are, for the moment, more effective scary scenarios with which to energize the base.

Those long in the kingdom's corner have reached instinctively and repeatedly for the old clichés and myths at moments when Washington's ties to the Al Saud come under criticism, as in October 2018. Then, the new and power-aggrandizing crown prince, Mohammed bin Salman, lauded as a visionary and modernizer in the *New York Times*, as the paper has done for each of the kings and crown princes before him, ordered the murder of Jamal Khashoggi. His thugs strangled and dismembered the exiled Saudi journalist inside the Saudi consulate in Istanbul. David Ottaway, Khashoggi's friend and colleague at the *Washington Post*, who has been reporting on Saudi Arabia for decades, said that, as a result, relations with Congress and the public had plummeted to "their lowest point since 9/11."[6] To be clear, relations had sunk much, much lower in 2001, leading the kingdom's friends and not least its own public relations juggernaut to wield the story of President Franklin Roosevelt's one and only meeting with Salman's grandfather Ibn Saud in 1945 as a kind of charm against those who believed the Al Saud's agents had engineered September 11 or saw an opportunity to encourage the kingdom's downfall.[7] And so a new myth quickly came into being. What would be funny if it weren't so tragic is how a basically Saudi-inspired fiction is believed in and promoted by activists on the Left as exhibit one in an indictment of U.S. oil imperialism in the Gulf, a kind of original sin. These critics might selectively draw on declassified documents and read reference texts badly. Or they might not. Given the stakes, in their minds, they appear as willing as the spin doctors that the kingdom retains or relies on to just make shit up.

We begin with the myth of the deal since it affords a unique opportunity to see how oilcraft works in real time, before turning to a second, no less bizarre idea popularized in the United States by *New York Times* columnist Tom Friedman, about Mohammed bin Salman "returning" Saudi Arabia to the liberalizing path the kingdom was on in the 1960s and 1970s and to the "tolerant" version of Islam that was the norm under the Al Saud until the 1979 Iranian revolution forced bin Salman's uncle, the late King Fahd, to go rogue. All of them fantasies, needless to say.

Reading Roosevelt's Mind

The idea that the United States has a special relationship with Saudi Arabia based on the exchange of oil for security is only about twenty years old. Yet the deal itself is imagined to have been struck decades earlier, in February 1945, on board the destroyer U.S.S. *Quincy*, where President Roosevelt hosted warrior King Ibn Saud. William (Bill) Eddy, the intrepid Beirut-born, Arabic-speaking U.S. diplomat, oil company consultant, and spy, translated for the two ailing heads of state. Photos of the historic meeting are now ubiquitous in books, articles, and websites describing the deal.

The only problem is that no account of U.S.-Saudi relations for the next fifty years said any such thing. It is not in the first major postwar study of Saudi Arabia by Richard H. Sanger, the career diplomat, Eddy's relative, and head of Arabian Peninsula affairs.[8] The 1977 report commissioned by Henry (Scoop) Jackson, when he headed the Senate Committee on Energy and Natural Resources, *Access to Oil—the United State Relationship with Saudi Arabia and Iran*, doesn't discuss it.[9] You won't find it in *Saudi Arabia in the 1980s: Foreign Policy, Security, and Oil* (1981), by William Quandt, who was Zbigniew Brzezinski's Middle East specialist on the National Security Council before joining the Brookings Institution. There is no mention—either of the so-called deal or of Roosevelt's meeting, where it allegedly was sealed—in the five hundred–plus page, CIA-funded study by Harvard's Nadav Safran, *Saudi Arabia: The*

Ceaseless Quest for Security (1985). Historian Douglas Little's 2002 sweeping account of the United States in the Middle East says nothing about an oil-for-security arrangement, either.[10] There's good reason. We have only recently come to believe it, although no documentary evidence for it exists. It is a myth.

The idea of a relationship with the Al Saud based on trading oil for security itself appears in print for the first time in February 2002, when the *Washington Post* published a remarkable three-part, front-page series by staff writers Robert Kaiser and David Ottaway. They sought to explain the basis for the long entanglement with "an Islamic monarchy ruled secretly by one family, the huge Saud clan, in collaboration with Islamic fundamentalists."[11] Why? Five months earlier, fifteen Saudis and four other followers of one more Saudi-in-exile, Osama bin Laden, had killed thousands in New York and Washington, D.C. The place they came from had not been under such a bright spotlight since the 1973 oil crisis.

The series began by documenting the "shaky ties," in 2001, between the new president George W. Bush and Crown Prince Abdullah, the power behind the throne of King Fahd, who blustered about breaking relations with the administration. The cause was familiar. The U.S. supported Israel in its violent confrontation with Palestinians during the "second intifada," or uprising. Kaiser and Ottaway revealed the "extraordinary lengths" President Bush's team went to repair the breach. Knowing that the Saudis themselves made a big deal about Ibn Saud's meeting with FDR, an event that for Americans was "lost in the mists of time," the White House advisers sought to have the two leaders meet at the Franklin Roosevelt Library in Hyde Park New York.[12] Ten years earlier, King Fahd himself had talked about the summit on board the *Quincy* with Secretary of Defense Dick Cheney, as the two hashed out the agreement that led to the stationing of U.S. troops in the kingdom.[13] Abdullah remained unmoved.

Instead, the crown prince allegedly threatened to hit the United States where it mattered. Access to oil? Nah. Intelligence cooperation and the future of the close "Saudi-U.S. military relationship." The kingdom's ambassador, Prince Bandar bin Sultan, crowed that what the kingdom got out of the White House was a "groundbreaking" promise to support "the idea of a viable Palestinian state on the West Bank and Gaza Strip." Saudi and U.S. officials had allegedly even begun discussing next steps, before the flood of outrage over the destruction of the Twin Towers and the Pentagon, and over the monies that flowed from rich Saudis to support bin Laden and the jihad against Americans in Afghanistan.[14] The anger is understandable. After all, the Federal Bureau of Investigation assisted in the extraordinary evacuation of bin Laden's family and any stray Saudi royals in the United States when the planes struck. Once safely back in the kingdom, "some of them openly celebrated the attacks."[15]

The *Post* titled the second installment "Oil for Security Fueled Close Ties," though, as Kaiser and Ottaway detailed, the alliance had inherent tensions from the start.[16] Note carefully, however. They date the start of these close ties to the 1970s, not 1945, in the wake of the "Arab oil embargo" and the massive fortune amassed by the Al Saud following the price shock. "On the foundation of that wealth and the oil that produced it, the modern Saudi-American relationship was constructed." The article goes on to describe the growing entanglements, beginning with the story that journalists seem to rediscover every decade of the mission to the kingdom in 1974 by Nixon's energy czar turned Treasury Secretary William Simon to sell the Saudis on investing in treasury bonds.[17] More "recycled" Saudi petrodollars flowed to the treasury and on to U.S. corporations under the auspices of a U.S.-Saudi Joint Commission on Economic Cooperation, founded that same year, with an initial deposit of a billion dollars. Those sums paled beside the "over

$100 billion [spent] on American weapons, construction, spare parts and support."[18]

It's tempting to conclude, as one conservative critic of U.S. policy did, that an actual agreement was brokered in 1974, whereby the Saudis are imagined to have promised uninterrupted oil supply, constant prices, and all the petrodollars the financial market could absorb in return for guaranteeing "the dominance of the Al Saud dynasty."[19] Nothing like it happened, according to William Quandt, who served on the staff of the National Security Council at the time. Nor did the government later cut a deal with King Fahd in 1977 to raise production levels (which in any case did not happen) and turn millions of barrels over for the use of the U.S. government.[20]

Arms sales are, thus, the main measure of the "security" that Washington is imagined to have provided the Al Saud for fifteen years, until they reluctantly accepted the stationing of U.S. troops inside the kingdom as part of the massive Desert Storm campaign in occupied Kuwait, when "the oil-for-security bargain at the center of the Saudi-American relationship was fulfilled."[21] Only Kaiser and Ottaway have a hard time explicating the oil side of the equation—how, say, U.S. refiners obtained oil more cheaply or in greater quantities than all other sundry buyers in Europe and Asia or, as in the example just presented, how Saudi production decisions were different from what we would expect absent this so-called relationship. Really, the best the two reporters can do is leave the impression that the Saudis fulfilled their part of the bargain simply by selling their oil and forgoing further embargoes.

"Traditionally the United States' relationship with Saudi Arabia has been characterized as a basic bargain of 'oil for security,'" says Rachel Bronson, in her 2006 Council on Foreign Relations–subsidized book, *Thicker than Oil*, which argues, as her royal Saudi informants and their public relations firms did overtime after September 11, that the Saudis have delivered much more to Americans than just "the free flow of oil at reasonable prices." By my reckoning, the "tradition" or, more accurately, creation of the meme was then all of three years old. Bronson says that Roosevelt's meeting with Ibn Saud in 1945 had morphed into some "nostalgic, larger than life mythology" virtually "as soon as it ended," although her sole example dates from 2005.[22] As noted, one is hard-pressed to find the meeting referenced in the scholarship over the ensuing decades, let alone in accounts by those who were there, and no one in the United States besides Daniel Yergin followed King Fahd's lead in seeing the hosting of American forces inside his country in 1991 as somehow linked to his father's meeting with Roosevelt forty-five years earlier.[23] The Saudis, the PR firms, and their many friends in Washington, New York, Houston, and Los Angeles would milk the meeting with FDR for all it was worth after 2001. Descendants of the two tribes—the Roosevelts and Al Saud—met together on stage in 2005.[24] The wheeling and dealing Prince Bandar gave a framed copy of the iconic photo to CIA director Michael Hayden, which, Hayden says, "commemorated the unspoken contract . . . between the two countries: oil for security, security for oil. *Bandar was messaging*."[25] Now watch what happened.

Cable News Network's website, under the heading "Saudi Arabia Fast Facts," notes that since the end of World War II, "Saudi Arabia and the United States have maintained a relationship based on an exchange of oil for security."[26] Retired CIA agent and Brookings Institution expert Bruce Riedel writes that FDR had arrived in the Suez Canal to conclude a "bargain that would trade American security guarantees for access to oil."[27] The Public Broadcasting System's documentary arm, *Frontline*, insists that at the meeting, "the two leaders cemented *a secret oil-for-security pact*."[28] The self-styled muckraking site *Counterpunch* reports how FDR brokered "an oil-for-security agreement" and "vowed to defend the monarchy against all foes, internal or external."[29] Michael Klare calls FDR's decision in 1945 to "arm" the Saudis fateful.[30] Gawdat Bahgat, an Egyptian-born political scientist who teaches at the National Defense University says the two leaders forged an "unofficial alliance" that day on the *Quincy* "based on oil for security."[31] Marxist geographer Matt Huber says the deal was "about securing Saudi oil not for American consumers but rather for U.S. oil capital."[32] High school students can even access a downloadable essay on the topic, in case they need one. "The relationship between the United States and Saudi Arabia can usually be summarized by the term 'oil for security.' The theory behind it is that the United States needs oil and can get it from Saudi Arabia who, in return, ask[s] for security."[33]

The most egregious misrepresentations by far, though, are at the hands of self-identified "anti-Saudi activists." Phyllis Bennis, a DC-based critic and fellow of the Institute of Policy Studies, instructed a roomful of progressives in March 2016 that the two chiefs (misidentifying one of them "King Saud") "met on a warship . . . , where the great pledge is made, that amounts—it is technical how you word it—but the essence of it is a quid pro quo," access to oil, "although it wasn't only about access; it was more about control," in return for protection.[34] Medea Benjamin, a founder of Code Pink, the organization that sponsored the 2016 activist summit on Saudi Arabia, went on to write and tour behind her own book, *Kingdom of the Unjust: Behind the U.S.-Saudi Connection*. At one of those stops, at the Islamic Culture Center of Fresno, she described "the famous meeting" in 1945, in which, "basically, FDR said—not in these exact words—you, the king, can go about doing what you want inside your own country. We're not going to get involved and tell you how to rule internally, but we're going to make sure you don't get overthrown; as long as you . . . keep allowing Western oil companies to come in here and make a lot of money, and to export cheap Saudi oil, we're going to guarantee your security."[35]

Even with their disclaimers that "it is technical how you word it" and that it was "not in these exact words," how do they know what was said? It is tricky, since extant records of the meeting—the translator Bill Eddy's little book, *FDR Meets Ibn Saud*, published in 1954, and the later declassified State Department records—say nothing about oil, security, or alliances—tacit, explicit, secret, or otherwise.[36] Rather, until September 11, the 1945 meeting had served to anchor arguments about the evolution of U.S. policy toward Palestine, which was Roosevelt's main concern in visiting the king. The records are crystal clear on this. FDR famously asked Ibn Saud for help in "solving the problem of Zionism," and the king answered, "Give them and the descendants the choicest lands and homes of the Germans." They didn't see eye to eye, needless to say, and Eddy says the king began to lose patience when FDR complained that "the King had not helped him at all with the problem." Again, according to Eddy, using "very simple language, such as he must often have used in cementing alliances with tribal chiefs, Iban Saud then asked F.D.R. for friendship."[37] Eddy said the meeting ended with Roosevelt's famous promise. It was repeated in a letter to the king a week before his death and appeared in the *New York Times* a few months later—that he would do nothing "which might prove hostile to the Arabs," and "the U.S. government would make no change in its basic policy in Palestine without full and prior consultation with both Jews and Arabs."[38]

That's it. Far from promising to protect the kingdom, Roosevelt and his successor refused Ibn Saud's repeated requests for a treaty of alliance. No arms were supplied by FDR (he did, however, give the king a wheelchair). Ibn Saud sought in vain over the next few years to purchase arms and planes. He, ultimately, consented to the building of a U.S. base in Dhahran that the U.S. Air Force didn't need, the War Department refused to pay for, and that benefited, above oil, the private U.S. oil companies then busy expanding their fiefdom.[39] The successor Truman administration famously ignored the promises regarding Palestine made by FDR, at zero cost, because, as Nadav Safran underscored, the king's relationship with the United States was basically that of a "client."[40] The client would be rewarded for his acquiescence to U.S. recognition of Israel in 1948 with some token aid and military training, beginning in 1949, similar to what the king of Egypt and the shah of Iran received. Fateful? Probably more important in the end, American doctors helped to keep the king alive.

As for the "oil" in the factitious oil-for-security deal, nothing had to be arranged, negotiated, or secured. The king had awarded a sixty-year concession in the 1930s that gave the U.S. firms control of production and marketing of Saudi crude oil in return for tax and royalty payments. The oil was already flowing when FDR met Ibn Saud, and the firm was busy expanding its production capacity (paid for in part with the hard-earned dollars of U.S. taxpayers). Ibn Saud was desperate for revenue. That arrangement remained intact until 1972, when Aramco agreed that the Saudi government could have a partial-ownership stake in the firm.

Keep in mind, in light of the fantasies that have been concocted about oil for security pacts and the like, little of that oil reached U.S. refineries for a quarter century. Again, as we saw, Saudi officials tried but failed to get quotas lifted to up their earnings. Saudi imports grew, of course, in the 1970s and beyond, but the idea that as a result of a meeting in 1945 the kingdom "became the nation's most trusted supplier" is just another bizarre idea circulating after September 11.[41]

Old Ways Die Hard

What the American public knows about Saudi Arabia consists mainly of clichés. Many of them appear in the August 7, 1974, report filed from Taif by the then well-known *Los Angeles Times* syndicated columnist Nick Thimmesch. A "backward" kingdom ruled "by a fatherly king Faisal, benevolent and wise." Women cloaked "head to toe" in black. "Saudis like to wander, dream, and pray. There is much time to think. The Bedouin is the heroic ideal. Old ways die hard. A thief can get his hand cut off by law and murderers face execution by the sword. No nonsense about law and order." The trick was allegedly how to engineer the beginning of the modernization of the kingdom—educate the young, build roads, hospitals, and universities, and industrialize the kingdom while managing the "cultural dilemma."[42] It was also Thimmesch's first visit there. Those who returned to the kingdom after a period away, whether in the 1960s, 1970s, or after, instead would marvel at the dizzying pace of change "from camels to Cadillacs."[43]

The most overused cliché by far is the idea that every ruler, from Ibn Saud on, was a visionary dedicated to propelling Saudi Arabia out of the twelfth century into the present. Aramco executives never tired of making this claim about their "partner in progress," the king, where others spoke of him squandering the kingdom's new wealth and resisting necessary change. It is what U.S. officials routinely tell reporters (and perhaps themselves) in an attempt to rationalize support for the Al Saud's rule. When King Faisal ascended to the throne in 1964, a *Washington Post* editorial praised him for bringing the kingdom into the eighteenth century, which is what many first wrote about his brother, who Faisal dethroned. When Faisal died in 1975, the *New York Times* obituary added two centuries to the miraculous accomplishment, saying that he "led Saudis into [the] 20th century."[44] Lucky for us, the historian Abdullah Al-Arian has compiled seventy years' worth of such testimonials from the *New York Times*.[45] What Al-Arian missed, however, is how across those same seventy years, when the king or the crown prince, who rules in all but name, does something that troubles U.S. officials, the same politicians, reporters, pundits, and editorial boards are apt to discover a "dark side" or overzealous accumulation of power, blundered foreign policies, and squandered resources that threaten the stability of a key Western ally.[46]

The original and fact-challenged parable of a corrupt and profligate king versus a reforming crown prince that we will see commentators rely on in telling the royals' story dates to the decline and death of Ibn Saud in 1953. The United States heaped praise on crown prince Saud, who succeeded his father, as a farsighted modernizer who spent millions on weapons, infrastructure construction, the kingdom's first university, and the like, yes, along with palaces and Cadillacs, like all the royals before and after him, for which U.S. manufacturers and service firms were paid handsomely. New York banks loaned Saudi Arabia all the dollars it wanted as long as the U.S. oil company Aramco agreed.

These same stylized facts were then turned on their head when oil revenues decreased unexpectedly—the 1956 Arab-Israeli War cut off the main shipping route for Saudi exports—and, more crucially, when Saud acted independently of the Eisenhower administration's preferences and his government began to press Aramco on the issue of Saudization. Saud's brother and rival, Crown Prince Faisal, is celebrated until now, in fact, as the more savvy (yes) and fiscally prudent (no) modernizer who put the kingdom's finances in order (no) and implemented other far-reaching reforms at the urging of President John F. Kennedy (no again). These are imagined, incredulously, to have saved the kingdom from disaster. Disaster in this case comprised continuing elections begun by King Saud, the attempt to draft a constitution, growing labor militancy, the widest-ranging journalism that the kingdom has ever seen, and the worst of all possible developments, the threatened takeover of Aramco.[47]

After Faisal was shot dead by a nephew in April 1975, the editors of the *Washington Post* refrained from the kind of glowing tribute that they said too many others offered out of deference to his "immense oil reserves and bank balances." In their view, he "probably did more damage to the West than any single man since Adolph Hitler."[48] They were right about the first, although not about the second, and the easier answer to the puzzle is that, as we saw, the effects of the embargo and price shock have been exaggerated out of all proportion. Faisal's singular achievement was the centralization of power in his and his brothers' hands. That and the partnership with the United States Faisal committed to in the year or two before his death, as Ottaway and Kaiser reported in the *Washington Post*, the one that is obscured by the nonsense about a deal between his father Ibn Saud and FDR thirty years earlier.

The Benefits of Recycling

The west had high hopes, too, for Fahd following the short reign of his ailing brother Khaled, who died in 1982. The new king was lauded as "pro-American," a "progressive," and a "reformer," with a "strong sense of responsibility both toward the world" and Saudi Arabia, where, reporters told us, he would soon unveil a constitution. Who better to move "the country gently into the twentieth century?" He had even given up drinking.[49] Remarkable, given that seven years earlier Khaled was portrayed as the "moderate" and Fahd, appointed crown prince, a gambler and womanizer.[50] What really mattered more was that Khaled and Fahd would continue to spend billions on the purchase of U.S. goods and services for the modernization of the kingdom.[51]

The problem was that oil prices had tanked in the early 1980s, bursting the "Arabian bubble."[52] Though correlation does not prove causation, nonetheless what we witness in the kingdom after 1982, in addition to numerous bankruptcies, accounts in arrears, and dramatic slowdowns in new orders, is a rise in reporting of the religious police cracking down once more on Westerners—for example, Christians worshipping "too visibly or in too large numbers" and Fahd's "pursuit of policies likely to find favor with the conservative Wahhabi religious experts."[53] It is a turn that culminates with his adoption of the new title "Custodian of the Two Holy Mosques" in 1986. In place of the celebratory stories of new highways, airports, and weapons systems, we find an uptick in accounts of his unchecked personal spending, his luxurious foreign palaces in the Costa Del Sol and Geneva, and the building of a new one in Riyadh that "is a throwback to the time of King Saud."[54]

We know a lot more today about the emergence of radical Islamist currents (the "awakening," or *sahwa*) among Saudi university students in those years that some western reporters began to take note of, together with growing criticism inside the kingdom of the Al Saud's deepening relationship with the United States.[55] Recession, corruption, murmurs of dissent. Cue the hand-wringing about Fahd's grip on power and potential schisms among the princes. "It would be truly frightening if Saudi Arabia were to be taken over by someone like Libya's Moammar Kadafi [*sic*]."[56]

We need to consider one additional factor—the critical one, in fact—before we can adequately account for the print media and their go-to experts turning from one versus the other clichéd account of the Al Saud, and that is a king or crown prince who is not doing exactly what the White House wants him to. "Special Relationship Becoming Frayed" is how the *Washington Post*'s David Ottaway put it in his April 1986 analysis, deploying for the first time what has since become the third cliché in writing about the kingdom. "The cool Saudi treatment of [Vice President] Bush reflects a deeper malaise . . . between the kingdom and the United States, which is under attack from increasingly vocal anti-American elements in the kingdom and from pro-Israeli elements in Congress."[57]

Vice President George H. W. Bush had landed in Riyadh in April on a failed mission—a fantasy, really—to get the Saudis to save what was left of the Texas and Oklahoma tax base, retirement accounts, and real estate markets reeling from the collapse in oil prices then hovering at around ten dollars a barrel. Bush blamed the "free fall" on the Saudis and wanted them to stop selling so much of the stuff. But he was pretty incoherent about these matters, charging that the "Saudis wanted the highest price possible," which flew in the face of the fact that they were discounting their crude in order to preserve market share against other OPEC producers.[58] Squaring this mission with the Reagan administration's vaunted commitment to "the free market" would also prove tricky, but nowhere near as difficult as assuaging the Saudis about a visit that was supposed to signal the administration's continued support.

The Saudis had wanted new advanced weapons—air-to-air and ground-to-air missiles and dozens more F-15 fighter aircraft—but Democrats, who had just regained control of the Senate, opposed the sales, and the Reagan administration backed down rather than fight them and the Israelis, unlike in 1981. The Saudis bought British jets instead, in a deal rife with alleged kickbacks to Saudi Prince Bandar bin Sultan, and one that would come under investigation until the U.K. government closed the inquiry down on the grounds of national security. Bandar would go on to outrage his American friends even more by secretly negotiating a deal for Chinese missiles in 1986, which U.S. officials only discovered two years later.[59]

Before then, however, the Saudis had to cope with the fallout from the Reagan administration's Iran-Contra scandal, involving the U.S. secretly selling arms to Iran, with the hope of gaining the release of American hostages and using the profits to illegally aid counterrevolutionary forces in Nicaragua.[60] A series of investigative reports, culminating in the book, *Veil: The Secret Wars of the CIA*, by Bob Woodward, detailed Saudi funding for U.S. covert operations in return for the 1981 sale to the kingdom of the Airborne Warning and Control System (AWACS) mobile radar. These "favors" included the attempted assassination of the leader of Lebanon's Hezbollah, the arming of the mujahideen in Afghanistan, arms for the rebels in Nicaragua and Angola, and cash for the right-wing Christian Democrats in Italy.[61] These were sins to many liberal Democrats. The Saudis denied it all at the time, but after September 11, the intelligence chief in those years, Turki al-Faisal, and other members of the Al Saud would point to the various missions to show that the kingdom delivered especially good value to the United States.

For a brief moment, Fahd became the kind of king we could get behind once more. "Decisive in a crisis" is how the *Washington Post* put it in December 1990, four months after the king agreed to U.S. military protection following Saddam Hussein's invasion of Kuwait. Colin Powell promised "one hundred thousand troops for starters."[62] The Bush administration also agreed to sell the Saudis the F-15 fighters they were denied for the past half-dozen years—the very same model the Saudi air force would use to destroy Yemen between 2016 and 2019.[63] Of course, dependency on the United States for defense of the realm raised pointed questions about the "security" value of the many billions spent since the 1970s on weapons and training for the Saudi military.[64]

The Invasion of Arabia

Frayed relationship? No: a long, warm, and increasingly close one, built on "mutual trust and respect," or so Deputy Secretary of Defense Paul Wolfowitz said in a postmortem following Kuwait's liberation.[65] Of course, there were costs—that is, beyond the fifty-five billion dollars ultimately paid by Fahd for the war—including paying off the other Middle East coalition members. The tiny set of Saudi liberals of that era dreamed that the "crisis" would usher in a political opening. It wouldn't. King Fahd once again promised to establish a *majlis al-shura*, or consultative council, "soon."[66] More presciently, Yahya Sadowski, the smartest Middle East expert that the Brookings Institution ever employed, noted: "Already every Islamic movement in the Middle East is now depicting the Saudi Arabians as American puppets, rich sheiks sitting on barrels of oil while the poor suffer."[67] The real problem was that, as bills for the war came due, all that oil was still trading at far less than twenty dollars a barrel and would continue to do so for the next few years.

If, as one Saudi businessman complained, "King Fahd seems prone to bouts of amnesia when it comes to promises of political reform," the same would be true of the U.S. foreign policy establishment, or what we now call "The Blob."[68] By 1993, the experts were back to warning about the dangerous draw down of the kingdom's dollar reserves. Dangerous because religious dissidents, or what the embattled liberals in Riyadh called "Saddamist fundamentalists," were coalescing into an unprecedented aboveground protest movement that, according to Stéphane Lacroix, sought to lay the foundation for an "Islamic Democracy."[69] Saudi watchers in Washington viewed the problem in the now tried and not-so-true terms of a failure to reform—forty-seven women had driven in public for the first time in November 1990 to protest the curtailment of their rights—and a reduction in the social spending that they imagined had bought tranquility. "They have tilted the wrong way," according to another Brookings fellow William Quandt. "All the billions they've spent on arms haven't been very useful to them."[70]

Beyond the Beltway, there was a radically different explanation for the kingdom's political troubles: The massive U.S. troop

deployment that the Pentagon quickly expanded—quite openly—
into a long-term project of power projection in the Gulf and beyond.
It was a key piece of the strategy for "primacy" in a one superpower
world.[71] Bin Laden denounced it as an "invasion" and "occupation"
abetted by the Al Saud, and he would soon call for a jihad against
the Americans.[72] Even the *Wall Street Journal* recognized that, as the
editorial board put it, "Saudi Arabia has been more or less a U.S.
protectorate since the 1979 Iranian revolution," while urging the Al
Saud to stay the course.[73] These otherwise rival explanations for the
growing ferment converged on one point only: the corruption and
all-too-conspicuous consumption of the royal family during years
of dwindling reserves, reduced budgets, rising unemployment, and
other signs of economic distress.[74]

These woes were not serious enough, apparently, to stop the
incoming U.S. president, Bill Clinton—President Bush had lost the
election for a second term, largely because of the economic recession
at home—from squeezing the Al Saud some more. After Clinton appealed to him directly, Fahd agreed to buy additional tanks
and fighters to help keep "American arms makers afloat while the
American military shrinks."[75] The king also agreed to buy new commercial jets from Boeing and McDonald Douglas and pay AT&T
to overhaul its phone system, although their European competitors
had underbid them.[76] Perhaps Clinton had been inspired by the
Twenty-million-dollar check that Prince Bandar delivered to the
University of Arkansas for the creation of a new King Fahd Center
of Middle East studies just one month after his inauguration.[77]

The Saudis went on the offensive after the *New York Times*
ran back-to-back stories detailing their kingdom's financial woes,
borrowing the good offices of the Council on Foreign Relations
to help set the record straight.[78] The embassy sent smooth-talking
Adel al-Jubeir, who would become a council visiting fellow the next
year. He was joined by the vice chairman of the board of Morgan

Guaranty, the bank that loaned the kingdom the dollars to pay for Desert Storm, and Richard Murphy, a onetime assistant secretary of state who directed the council's Middle East program. All three pooh-poohed the report, and Jubeir gamely tried to defend the new weapons buying spree on national security grounds, but the price was a half hour or so of Saudi bashing. The king was as out of touch, much as the Shah of Iran was before his overthrow. The government was mismanaging the oil industry. The royal family was wasting the wealth of the country on themselves. Corruption continued unchecked. They better reform before it was too late.

King Fahd thought differently. While the Western press continued to focus on the country's deepening fiscal crisis, the increased opposition to the U.S. military presence, and the "chilly" state of relations with Washington, his security services began to crack down on the young Islamists, while the militant Osama bin Laden, who had fled to Sudan, was stripped of his citizenship.[79] Thomas Hegghammer dates a "final showdown" with the protest movement to mid-September 1994 following public demonstrations in Riyadh and the northern city of Burayda, which led to mass arrests, detention, and torture of clerics and their followers, and spurred the turn to violence on the part of jihadists.[80] Believe it or not, U.S. Secretary of Defense William J. Perry showed up in Riyadh on the heels of President Clinton's own first visit to request that the kingdom cover the cost of the new troop buildup under way on Saudi soil for containing Iraq and allow the Pentagon to preposition a brigade's worth of tanks and planes for future use. This time the king turned the Americans down.[81]

Jihad

On November 13, 1995, a car bomb ripped through the Saudi National Guard headquarters in the middle of Riyadh, where the Vinnell Corporation, a Virginia-based military contractor, trained Saudi personnel in the maintenance of U.S. weapons. Four Saudis carried out the attack, which killed five Americans, two East Indians, and injured dozens. Three of the militants had fought the Soviets together in Afghanistan. Their confessions would be broadcast live prior to their execution in May 1996.[82] The militants' objective was to end the U.S. military presence in Saudi Arabia. "If the Americans don't leave the kingdom as soon as possible, we will continue our actions."[83] American officials had trouble, at least in public, acknowledging this simple fact. It was impossible to say "whether the United States or Saudi Arabia was the principal target of the explosion."[84] Subsequent reporting settled on the Saudis, returning with a vengeance to the themes of corruption and mismanagement and the question first asked in 1953 and countless times since, would the Al Saud survive?[85]

So guess what the reporting looked like after King Fahd suffered a stroke (he died in 2005) a few weeks after the bombing and his half-brother Abdullah took over the day-to-day running of the kingdom for the next nineteen years, the last ten of them as king. Fahd was a "corpulent chain smoker," "one of the world's last absolute monarchs," a "playboy" who "frequented Mediterranean watering holes," who "looted the country" through the invention, allegedly, of "veiled ways of royal fortune making" that benefited his sons and cronies.[86] The crown prince, by contrast, was "an austere traditionalist with a reputation for piety," and who, thank God, "brings a markedly different style to the running of the world's largest oil exporter."[87] The reins of power were, again, in reliable hands. The relationship with the United States would be protected. Abdullah's reforms—belt-tightening, job creation, political change—would bring the kingdom into a fast-fading twentieth century.

Things didn't quite work out that way. In November 1996, nineteen American soldiers died and hundreds of Saudis and foreigners

were wounded in a second truck bombing, this time in Dhahran, at
the U.S. Air Force barracks (Khobar Towers). Abdullah's government hindered more than helped U.S. agencies in their investigation.[88] As noted earlier, the reporters began to insist that relations
with Saudi Arabia were at their worse since 1973, and that was
before the September 11 attack (that Abdullah's half-brother Nayef,
the "arch-reactionary" minister of the interior, insisted the Mossad,
and not his onetime client, bin Laden, had masterminded).[89] As
relations with the second Bush administration deteriorated even
more, journalists could be counted on to report on how a crown
prince was stumbling more than leading, a royal family was riven
by power struggles, and a kingdom just might lack "the political
resolve to undertake pressing domestic reforms judged critical to
Saudi Arabia's future stability."[90] Is it bad form here to point out
that the Al Saud has ruled since 1932 without ever undertaking any
of those vaunted reforms that two or, maybe, three generations of
Saudi hands have insisted are vital to securing its future?

For their part, Abdullah and his brothers were reportedly
stunned by the new Bush administration's decision to go to war
in Afghanistan and Iraq—using the kingdom to do so—and yet
were unwilling or unable to prevent it.[91] Throughout the region,
the "global war on terror" appeared as a war on Islam, a theme
hammered on in countless sermons, publications, and recordings
in and outside Saudi Arabia. As Thomas Hegghammer details, the
beginning of the Afghanistan war in October 2001 "brought anti-
Americanism in the kingdom to new heights." Worse, there were
some one thousand Saudis taking part in the jihad who would be
driven from Afghanistan and heading either home or to Iraq to
fight the crusaders who launched the war to overthrow Saddam
Hussein in March 2003.[92] While the Saudis sought to clamp down
on the most vociferous opponents of the coming war, those who
escaped the dragnet issued fatwa after fatwa, declaring cooperation

with the Americans as apostasy and calling for attacks on Western targets in and outside the kingdom.[93]

A nascent homegrown al-Qaeda franchise began operations in May 2003, with simultaneous car bombings of the Vinnell company complex and two other foreign residential compounds killing more than 30 foreigners and Saudis, and wounding 160. There were more attacks in the months that followed.[94] Hegghammer's painstaking research into the backgrounds and motivations of Saudi al-Qaeda recruits found that a majority fought first in Afghanistan, where they were radicalized, and returned "with a more global, anti-American, and intransigent ideological vision than Islamists who had never left the kingdom."[95] Saudi security services lent a hand, inadvertently, through the rough justice and torture meted out to suspects in the 1990s and early 2000s. "Virtually all" al-Qaeda "fighters were very anti-American," and were driven, above all, by the goal of ending "the perceived U.S. military occupation of Saudi Arabia" or the doctrinal variant of expelling "the polytheists from the Arabian Peninsula," rather than by "revolutionary" transformation or "hostility" toward the Saudi regime.[96] The Pentagon itself had recognized the potential destabilizing effect of its military presence a year or more earlier and came to a decision, together with the Saudis in April 2003, to withdraw its forces from the Kingdom to Al Udeid Air Base in Qatar.[97]

Crown Prince Abdullah swore he would be following the U.S. withdrawal with a series of far-reaching reforms. The Brookings Institution cheerleader for war with Iraq, Kenneth Pollack, an ex-CIA analyst, called it "Saudi Arabia's Big Leap" and advised the Bush administration to "hold the Saudis feet to the fire," since democratization was the only way to deal with the rise of terrorism inside the kingdom and the prospect of an Islamic revolution along the lines of Iran.[98] The *New York Times* chief correspondent Patrick Tyler referred to Crown Prince Abdullah as "the leader who will drag the kingdom into political modernity" (with just a little push from young Saudis "pressing relentlessly for change").[99] Thereafter, many column inches were dedicated to the progress, or not, of the imagined Saudi journey.

The *Christian Science Monitor* Beirut correspondent Nicholas Blanford reported on the "setback" to the kingdom's "reformist impulse" in June 2003. Jamal Khashoggi, then the editor of *Al Watan*, a leading Saudi newspaper, was fired after charging the Saudi religious establishment with abetting extremism.[100] The *Monitor* later complained that "Nation-Building in Saudi Arabia" wasn't happening fast enough, and by October 2004 had all but ground to a halt.[101] What about when the "reformer" Abdullah was crowned king in August 2005? True believers in Washington were growing less hopeful, although others said that Abdullah was being stymied by "hard-liners," and the Bush administration itself started fretting about the unintended consequences of pushing autocrats to democratize. Democracy promotion in Iraq resulted in an outsized influence for Iran, and elections in the Palestinian Authority resulted in Hamas, a victory for the Islamic resistance movement.[102] The editors of the *New York Times* were still counting on Abdullah in 2009 to "fulfill his promise to lead his country to greater tolerance and modernity." Two years later, popular uprisings in Egypt and Tunisia, known as the Arab Spring that brought down two Middle East "presidents for life," would scare all the other region's autocrats.[103] Abdullah sent the Saudi military to occupy Bahrain and crush an opposition movement there.[104] It is the last we heard of Abdullah-as-reformer among the Beltway's Saudi experts.

Perhaps they should have listened to Toby Craig Jones, the young analyst with the Brussels-based International Crisis Group, back in 2005, when Abdullah succeeded Fahd. He dismissed the idea of Abdullah as a liberal being hemmed in by "hard-liners." "Once people are in power, they have two missions: To manage the existing political system and to stay in power. So that's what they are going to focus on."[105] Jones said the best bet was that they would keep the autocracy intact. He was right. But what about the threat from the jihadists to which reform was the solution? The theory needed some tweaking. Crown prince and then King Abdullah devoted vast resources to overhaul the kingdom's security forces to defeat the jihadists, who, by 2005, saw new recruits slow to a trickle. Saudi propaganda, or, if you prefer, soft power, also helped turn the population, including other Islamists, against them. It was one thing to wage jihad against the U.S. occupation of Afghanistan and Iraq, where Hegghammer says a thousand or more Saudis joined the fight, and another thing entirely to terrorize the population of Riyadh and Medina.[106]

Now recall the world of difference that the experts stressed between the profligacy of Fahd and the austerity of Abdullah, who, nonetheless, entertained visitors at home in a hall "the size of six basketball courts, next to . . . an Olympic-size indoor swimming pool," and with a floor-to-ceiling aquarium that stretched the length of the room.[107] The *Washington Post*'s longtime Saudi watcher used *Fortune* magazine's list of the world's richest to bolster the case against Fahd's ill-gotten wealth. He was ranked sixth in 1993 with assets estimated at ten billion dollars.[108] *Forbes* ranked Abdullah third in 2011 with eighteen billion dollars. It is an ambiguous measure to be sure, and Abdullah and the rest of Al Saud benefited handsomely from the skyrocketing price of oil between 2000 and 20008, and again in 2011, following the end of the global recession. The rising prices in that decade were what drove all those predictions of the world running out of oil and warring over what was left.

In November 2017, as part of the newest "reformist" efforts by Crown Prince Mohammed bin Salman to, yes, "bring Saudi Arabia into the modern world," he had two hundred leading Saudis arrested.[109] The *New Yorker*'s Dexter Filkins called these Saudis the kingdom's "leading plutocrats." True, they were confined not to prison but to the Ritz Carlton Hotel, but they were, nonetheless, brutally interrogated. The cost of release was a coerced transfer of unspecified billions. MBS, as the crown prince is known—we now refer to royals the way the CIA have done internally for decades— likes to crow that he recovered "over a hundred billion for the state" this way. Princeton's Bernard Haykel, who markets his friendship with the crown prince to Western businessmen, lauded the move: "He was sending a message that the old era was over, that corruption would no longer be tolerated."[110] None of Fahd's sons were arrested on corruption charges. The story was different for Abdullah's sons, suggesting that maybe the journalists treated him a little too easy on this score. Miteb bin Abdullah, the ousted head of the National Guard (Abdullah's longtime power base) turned over a billion dollars or so to settle accusations of malfeasance.[111] Mishaal and Faisal were released, but no Saudi official would say how much it cost them.[112] Turki, the ex-fighter pilot and governor of Riyadh was still under detention a year later, in prison rather than a five-star hotel, where his chief of staff was killed while in custody.[113]

Tom Friedman's 115th Dream

No one in the United States championed Mohammed bin Salman in traditional fashion more than Tom Friedman, the Pulitzer prize–winning author and foreign affairs columnist for the *New York Times*. One reason may be that MBS and his entourage played him, most obviously by feeding his own fantasies about the kingdom back to him. While he has long experience in the Middle East, beginning in Beirut as a United Press International correspondent in 1979, his first byline from Saudi Arabia appeared only in September 1990, when he was chief diplomatic correspondent for the *Times*, accompanying Secretary of State James Baker to the kingdom.[114] Six years later, following the

Khobar Towers bombing, Friedman called the Al Saud "a loyal and important ally" that should not be abandoned—which would simply play into the hands of the "fringe groups" that wanted "to drive the U.S. out"—but the United States needed to do more on the energy conservation front to "make ourselves less vulnerable to changes in *that desert kingdom, which is far, far away, and about which we understand very, very little.*"[115]

The idea that those "fringe groups" were politically motivated was buried in the rubble of downtown Manhattan. Just days after September 11, Friedman denounced the perpetrators as nihilists, driven by hatred, who targeted the United States for its "way of life"—what it stands for rather than its policies.[116] He held Saudi Arabia and its "Wahhabi brand of Islam" responsible because it defines "infidels as enemies" and inculcates these values throughout society via the schools, "sermons, TV shows and the Internet."[117] Saudi Arabia had permitted the hijacking of Islam by "anti-modernists," or what he called "bin Ladenism," as a kind of survival strategy.[118] Meanwhile, America's need for oil prevented the president from telling the Saudis the truth. ("Addicts never tell the truth to their pushers.") Their "antimodern and antipluralist brand of Islam—known as Wahhabism—combined with their oil wealth has become a destabilizing force in the world."[119]

We might give him the benefit of the doubt. We all needed to know more than we did about Islamist movements and political activism in Saudi Arabia, although in the years since we have learned a great deal from the scholars who gained unprecedented access to the kingdom in the wake of September 11. There is nothing to be explained by a nonexistent, monolithic, or essential Wahhabism. The religious field in Saudi Arabia is a dynamic one. It has been shaped by waves of Muslim Brothers from Egypt who were welcomed by the "reformer" Faisal. He built an elaborate religious educational system staffed by Brothers and their protégés that were Faisal's weapon of choice to combat communism and Arab nationalism at home and abroad in the 1960s. The religious field is also a fractured one, as we saw, with the rise of the religious dissidents in the 1980s and 1990s, when al-Qaeda failed to gain much traction among the country's "extremists." A close look also reveals the continuous existence of non-Wahhabi and non-Salafist traditions within the kingdom, including Sufism, Shiism, and various orthodox Sunni legal schools.[120]

The problem is that Friedman appears unaware of these realities, while continuing to trumpet the views of whatever "friend" he talked to with the deadline for his next column looming. In 2005, Raymond Stock, an itinerant Arabic instructor who has never been to Saudi Arabia, told him that one needed to go back to the seventh and ninth centuries to understand the "jihadist fanatics."[121] Five years later, Friedman's essentialist views of Wahhabism took an abrupt turn because another friend told him that the Saudis only began promoting fundamentalism in 1979—a kind of big bang theory. They allegedly cut a deal with the clerics at home ("let us stay in power and we will give you a free hand in setting social norms"), while turning to "export" their brand of fundamentalism abroad, allegedly to counter the Islamic revolution in Iran. "Islam lost its brakes in 1979, said Mamoun Fandy."[122] Only, these stylized facts won't stand up to scrutiny.[123]

Friedman judged Abdullah "a decent man," personally, who was being prevented from carrying out essential reforms. "The problem with Saudi Arabia in 2003 is not that it has too little democracy. It's that it has too much. The ruling family is so insecure, it feels it has to consult every faction, tribe and senior cleric before it makes a decision." He urged Abdullah instead "to break heads at home" and "force some sustained reforms on his religious establishment."[124] As we have seen, Crown Prince Abdullah did the former and ignored the latter. In Friedman's early September

2015 column, "Our Radical Islamic BFF," he said the generals and admirals were getting it wrong (the United States was then in the midst of arguing over the Iran nuclear agreement). It was the rulers in Riyadh, not Tehran, who were the "greatest purveyors of radical Islam throughout the region and throughout the world." The kingdom was actively promoting terrorism through exporting its "Wahhabist ideology, which basically destroyed the pluralism that emerged in Islam since the 14th century."[125]

There is no way, though, one could have anticipated the about-face and autocritique Friedman executed just three short months later, in November 2015. "Saudi Arabia is a country that's easier to write about from afar, where you can just tee off on the place as a source of the most austere, antipluralistic version of Islam." But after traveling to Riyadh to look "for clues about ISIS," he discovered that it "is not your grandfather's Saudi Arabia" or, quoting his friend Adel al-Jubeir, who we have encountered before, "Actually, it's not even my father's Saudi Arabia anymore—it is not even my generation's Saudi Arabia anymore."[126]

The Saudi "Arab Spring at Last"?

On Sunday December 3, 2017, Friedman was hosted by Bruce Riedel at the Brookings Institution to discuss the future of Saudi Arabia. He had come under fire two weeks earlier for his long love letter to Crown Prince Mohammed bin Salman in the *Times*, "Saudi Arabia's Arab Spring, at Last." According to Friedman, Salman was leading a "top down" reform program that might well "change the character of Saudi Arabia" as well as "the tone and tenor of Islam across the globe." He repeated what Fandy told him about the sudden 1979 puritanical turn and praised the crown prince's plan to "bring Saudi Islam back to its more open and modern orientation." He also bought—hook, line, and sinker—a fantasy that MBS and his loyal Twitter followers be-

lieve about the 1970s as a moment of liberalization in the kingdom that got shut down. It's true. Friedman was even shown a
YouTube video proving that Saudi Arabia had movie theaters
before they were outlawed after 1979.[127] He didn't take criticism
of this fact-challenged, clichéd reporting well.[128] "I just want[ed]
to stick my head up and say, god, I hope you succeed. And when
you do that the holy hell comes down on you. Okay, well, fuck
that is my view okay."[129] His audience laughed and applauded.

Here is the problem. The two big books written about the kingdom in that era, one by a longtime resident and the other by one of
the best investigative reporters ever to cover the region, say nothing
about a liberalizing moment short-circuited by events in 1979.[130] The
idea should raise the eyebrows of anyone who knows anything about
the era. As we have seen, the rise in riches led to massive spending on
U.S. goods and services, with Westerners arriving in the kingdom
in numbers never seen before or since. A place that had drawn very
little attention previously was also now under the microscope. So,
what did the *New York Times*, the *Washington Post*, the paper that
last employed Jamal Khashoggi, and other major papers uncover
about the years before 1979?

Neil Ulman, the career *Wall Street Journal* reporter and editor
writing from Abqaiq, site of one of the original Aramco oil camps,
as they were once referred to, in the midst of expansion in February
1975. There were more than ten thousand U.S. citizens employed
in senior positions in banking; the national airlines; education; oil
production, of course; running airports; training the military; over-
seeing construction of roads, buildings, hospitals; and "installing
sophisticated weapons systems." The expatriates had spread out
beyond the confines of the oil compound, and Ulman described how
Westerners either "endured or circumvented" Saudi religious pro-
hibitions against alcohol, motion pictures, and the like. It is a story
that could have been written in the 1930s. Aramco showed films

then and thereafter in the confines of the company's compounds, and other Western firms began to do so "semi-clandestinely for their employees with Saudi officials often invited."[131] By "employees," Ulman meant expatriates.

Author Phyllis Kepler ventured into the kingdom with her family for a short time in 1975, as well, and later marketed the experience in guide books for U.S. families working and living abroad. She described their efforts to accommodate the strictures on dress enforced by the Saudi religious police and the hardships Westerners faced outside work hours. "There are no movie theaters, cocktail lounges, night clubs or legitimate theaters."[132] The next year, Jonathan Randal, on a break from covering war zones for the *Washington Post*, reported on the "Sly Sin in Stern Kingdom." Randal contrasted the streets in which the religious police enforced the rules "of Islam's strictest sect, the puritanical Wahhabites, who rule according to the Shariah," and "what goes on between the four walls of one's home." The goings-on in Western and rich Saudi homes alike might've included the manufacture and consumption of the "local moonshine called Sidiki,"—the drink of choice before and every decade since—the use of videocassette machines, and, for the very affluent Saudis, "a hundred specialized shops" that "rent home movie equipment." Why? The "ban on public commingling of the sexes, which has meant no movie theaters."[133]

Judith Miller plowed some of the same ground in 1977, when she worked for Wisconsin's great *Progressive* magazine. The *Washington Post* published her feature on the rising tensions in Saudi Arabia stemming from the influx of two distinct classes of foreigners: the million-plus "miserably poor" Yemenis, Pakistanis, and others who "do the work Saudis refuse to," and the "highly paid American and West European technocrats who do the jobs the Saudis cannot yet perform." They lived, separated by "high walls" (the Westerners) and "barbed wire" (Muslims from the "Third World"), from

Saudi society. But she noted that the rich Saudis she met also lived in homes surrounded by walls, in which "the black veils women wear are discarded ... and families watch the latest American and European TV programs and movies on their television sets." The point was to underscore the stark difference "with the evident austerity of Saudi public life."[134]

The *Los Angeles Times* reported the same year how "Saudi Arabia's renewed Islamic evangelical fervor" at home resulted in pressure being put on Ras al-Khaimah, one of the seven United Arab Emirates, to close down the casinos (where "local citizens are not allowed") and bars. Elsewhere in the Gulf, the same "conservative wave" was leading to extending the reach of religious (Sharia) courts and dissolving "fledgling parliaments."[135] Note that we are quickly running out of years for that liberalizing moment to reveal itself.

Thomas Ferris, who lived in the kingdom and edited the English-language *Saudi Gazette*, did a big story for the *New York Times* in March 1979, two months after the fall of the Shah, on the underside of the Saudi boom. Ferris focused on Jiddah, the old sea port where all foreign embassies had been located—far away from the Al Saud's heartland and Riyadh—until the mid-1970s. "To the foreigner's eye, the oil boom had been cruel to Jidda.... Three years of flat-out, haphazard building have made the city a vast construction site." It was also "a jarring contradiction to the Saudis' stated goal of preserving Islam and maintaining their ancient society." There "the tidal wave" of foreign workers "seeking their fortunes" had led to rising crime rates, slums, prostitution rings, and drug markets, together with a few illicit cinemas "in a string of roofless abandoned buildings." Saudis seeking cheap thrills more typically bought "X-rated television cassette films in what has become an international center for pirate recordings."[136]

This is the only contemporary account I've found of motion pictures ever being screened outside the company compounds, embassy buildings, and princes' palaces. If pursuit of illicit pleasures by young Saudi males is what constitutes the "liberalizing track" Friedman believes Saudis once were on before "fun was outlawed," then it never really ended. One need only pick up Pascal Menoret's eye-opening ethnography of young hard-drinking, drug-taking Saudi "joyriders" or "drifters," who steal, race, and smash cars along the miles of highway that crisscross Riyadh. That city's massive expansion is what proved that every crown prince from Saud on was a farsighted reformer. The fortunes that royal family members and their protégés realized from sales of every about-to-be-developed tract of land across the kingdom over the past fifty years are what proved that corruption had stymied meaningful reform—until now. And those roads the drifters ply are the ones leading from "the Middle Ages to the 21st century."[137]

The Not-So-Special Relationship

President Nixon and his successors cheered Faisal and each so-called reformer as they set off on a never-ending journey and, crucially, as they financed the federal government's budget deficit; spent billions on U.S.-designed development projects; bankrolled U.S.-allied counterrevolutionaries; paid for the CIA's covert wars; kept General Dynamics' assembly lines humming; contributed cash to foundations, centers, charities, universities, K Street, and the paid-to-think tanks; and aided the Pentagon's bottom line. Although I'm sure I've left something out, oil isn't one of them. The gamble for the Al Saud was that, in turn, the United States would keep it in power, although Faisal and his brothers could never be sure. Why? First, as Gregory Gause, the leading scholar of U.S.-Saudi relations, holds, no such explicit commitment has ever been made.[138] "Territorial integrity" is one thing. Who rules in Riyadh is another. There is no deal, however many times the idea gets repeated on the op-ed pages and at Code Pink confabs.

More crucially, as the Al Saud surely knows, many other equally "special relationships," with the likes of the Duvaliers in Haiti, Manuel Noriega in Panama, Anastasio Somoza Debayle in Nicaragua, the Shah of Iran, Fernando Marcos in the Philippines, and Hosni Mubarak in Egypt, crashed and burned. Immense oil reserves and bank balances may only go so far.

Many Americans, of course, opposed the backing of these right-wing dictatorships as well as the counterrevolutionary forces ("freedom fighters") that sought restoration of the old order in those cases in which the dictators had been overthrown. So, it was the successful effort by the U.S. Congress in 1982 to cut off aid to right-wing rebel groups in Nicaragua that led to the Saudis' involvement there. It was true about Saudi Arabia, from the days when the oil company Aramco mattered much more than the U.S. government did to the Al Saud's rule.[139] Recall that through the 1970s it was conventionally believed that the big oil companies rather than the OPEC countries were the real engineers of the energy crisis. When Aramco organized tours and meetings with the president for King Saud and Crown Prince Faisal these were opposed by, among many others, New York's leaders. Mayor Rudolph Giuliani returned the ten million dollars donated by Prince Al-Waleed bin Talal, following September 11, after he opined that it was the failure of the United States to support peace with the Palestinians that led to the attack.[140] Aramco executives gave a reductive account of the source of this opposition: "The Left-Wing and Zionist-American Press." The Saudis did Aramco one better. As Faisal told Kissinger (and countless others), Khalid told Reagan, and Fahd told Clinton, the problem was "the Jews."[141]

Criticism of the U.S. embrace of the Al Saud grew more powerful in the ensuing decades, through the bruising battles to sell the Saudis arms, the attacks on U.S. installations in the 1990s, and the destruction wrought by bin Laden and al-Qaeda in 2001. Afterward, we saw the first calls in twenty years to seize the Saudi oil fields, or possibly topple the royal family ("there is an "Arabia," but it need not be "Saudi.""), threats that the Al Saud took seriously.[142] The 1990 war to defend the kingdom and Kuwait was an anomaly in which, for a brief moment, a majority of Americans held a favorable view of the kingdom. Gallup polls taken regularly since the attacks on New York and Washington show a strong and consistent lack of support for the kingdom among the public through 2018.[143] Gause argues that it is both remarkable and a testament to the efforts by U.S. and Saudi officials that relations survived more or less unscathed in the aftermath of the September 11 attacks.[144] It is a relationship that he seeks to preserve against the ill-advised calls—given the destructive effects of American elsewhere in the region—in 2018, to replace MBS, whose foreign policy decisions were some of the kingdom's most erratic since the mid-1950s, when King Saud first sought an alliance with Egypt's Gamal Abdel Nasser and then tried to have him killed.[145]

Some deeply held beliefs about oil-as-power are at work here, obviously, among many otherwise outraged men and women who fear that access to Saudi oil would be threatened by pressing princes too far or sanctioning Saudis who supported al-Qaeda or even providing the public with a full and unredacted version of the *9/11 Commission Report*. The refrain goes, "We're stuck with Saudi Arabia.[146] Maybe not, according to others. For the first time since 1973, the United States is producing more oil than Saudi Arabia and all other producing countries. There are those who believe that the so-called "fracking revolution" can free the country from its putative devil's bargain. Two University of Pennsylvania colleagues told an audience in 2014 that fracking would end our dependence on the kingdom and gain us new leverage over the Saudis, for instance, in countering their support for jihadists in Syria and Iraq.[147]

But is it even necessary? Aren't other interests to blame for whatever tensions exist that threaten access? That's what the undercover air force intelligence officer who was a member of my study tour to Saudi Arabia told me back in 1996. It was just after the Khobar Tower bombings, and she knew some of the victims. The problem, she said, was that U.S. policy had been hijacked by the Israel lobby. Saudi Arabia's oil mattered more to the national interest than Israel, she said, and it is mainly our backing of the latter that drove the jihadists. A prince told me more or less the same thing on that same trip. And I told him the argument is an old one, made by every king and crown prince, in fact, to every U.S. president since the 1940s. MBS has turned it on its head. His evolving rapprochement with Israel has gotten conservative American Jewish organizations on Saudi Arabia's side for the first time since 1948.

No, the problem is of our own making. Ramping up production of fossil fuels domestically won't solve the problem on its own. "America is addicted to oil," insisted Tom Friedman, just one of many who stole the line from President George W. Bush's 2006 State of the Union address and ran with it.[148] Addiction became his meme of choice for bringing together two strands of his musing in his *New York Times* foreign affairs column: about U.S. energy policy, going back to 1996, although, as a reporter in the 1970s, one of his beats had been OPEC affairs, which he still thinks is a cartel, and about "religious fanaticism" in Saudi Arabia, which he first took up after September 11. He wrote a dozen columns on these, he believed, entangled issues, culminating in the documentary *Addicted to Oil* in June 2006, a *New York Times*–Discovery Channel joint venture that Friedman coproduced.

Friedman calls for "living green" as a "geostrategic, tough-minded, and patriotic" solution to dependency on foreign oil.[149] By living green, he means relying on "renewable resources, domestic

production and energy efficiency."[150] Doing so would mean the
United States would no longer be "funding both sides of the war on
Terrorism"—that is, "the U.S. military with our tax dollars and supporters of Islamic militants through our gasoline purchases."[151] His
vision, though, suffers all the blind spots and unresolvable tensions
discussed in the introduction. It presumes Centcom is necessary to
guarantee access and, I guess, that access will be a problem for some
other power—China, India, Russia, Japan, or Germany—to solve
in the future. He has no answer to the fact that in a world market—
and Friedman was globalization's indefatigable cheerleader in the
1990s—there is no way to insulate the United States from the effects of "price spikes," save by erecting a massive new regulatory
regime. And if the rest of the world is buying Middle East oil, how
precisely does that end funding for "Islamic militants"? He doesn't
say. Oilcraft's illusions can't help him out of this jam; nor can they
help those of us who are serious about challenging the militarization
of U.S. foreign policy and Washington's decades-long infatuation
with the House of Saud.

5

BREAKING THE SPELL

IN 2012, KAREN AND BARBARA FIELDS published *Racecraft: The Soul of Inequality in American Life*. The puzzle the two authors and sisters raise is why a scientifically discredited idea of "race" persists. The belief that humans are naturally divided into distinct groups identifiable by certain physical and other traits is a kind of magical thinking or imagining that people find impossible to let go of. The belief itself exists and can be analyzed, both on its own merits but, more important, in terms of the work it does, that is—on the basis of its effects. The main and insidious one is the continuing legitimation of inequality.[1]

"Racecraft" is their term for the rational "processes of reasoning" that makes "race" appear "to the mind and imagination as a vivid truth," in the same way that witchcraft once appeared real to very smart people. Readers of the books we write and students in the classes we teach don't believe in people riding broomsticks. "Americans acquire in childhood all it takes to doubt stories of witchcraft." Yet, as the Fields analogize, "Little in our childhood leads us to doubt racecraft." Rather, "daily life produces an immense accumulation of supporting evidence for the belief." They then drive home the analogy to devastating effect. Believers in witchcraft had "authoritative sources in the science and law of the day." For the ancestors but, no less for us, "it often is (or seems) impossible for so much evidence to accumulate around a conception which has no basis in fact."[2]

The Fields helped me resolve a problem that I had been wrestling with for a while. Popular and scholarly beliefs about oil-as-power also have no basis in fact. Evidence for the belief, such as it is, continues to accumulate in the form of U.S. officials, past and present, proclaiming the need once to control and now secure access, stabilize prices, or prevent hostile powers from holding the world economy hostage. As we have seen, plenty of mandarins, public intellectuals, and energy security experts urge them on, in their briefs, memorandums, hearings, and op-eds. Only, nothing the policy makers armed with these incantations have done can be shown to have made the price of petroleum more stable than other commodities traded on the world market or to have secured for refiners greater quantities at lower prices than had the same policy makers refrained from, say, subsidizing Aramco's expansion in the 1940s, feting kings in the 1950s, selling advanced weapons to the Iranians and Saudis in the 1960s and 1970s, intervening in the Persian Gulf in the 1980s, deploying tens of thousands troops to Kuwait and Saudi Arabia in the 1990s, and launching wars without end in 2001.

Militarizing the Gulf has not insulated and cannot protect the world economy from regular if unpredictable supply disruptions due to accidents, natural disasters, and political upheaval. Far from it. U.S. sanctions policies are themselves a continuing source of supply instability, a fact that has led some thinkers on the Left to argue that the objective of the United States must be securing the profitability of oil and arms firms ("the weapondollar-petrodollar coalition") and managing the petroleum sector's structural problem of oversupply.[3] Keep in mind, too, that instability in the supply of oil has not yet set the U.S. or world economy into a tailspin.

For all those who, nonetheless, believe in an objective national security interest in protecting the global oil supply from strategic threats, the best they can argue is that absent the military buildup in the Persian Gulf, more and worse disruptions would have resulted, an argument that is impossible to falsify. To give it more oomph, they conjure not the run-of-the- mill refinery fire or civil unrest but extraordinary "severe and profound" supply failures at the hands of "hostile powers" that "would be economically devastating and potentially catastrophic" for the United States.[4] As we have seen, defenders of the mystical U.S.-Saudi special relationship do something similar each time they underscore how the kingdom has fulfilled its part of the imagined oil-for-security bargain by doing what all oil exporters do and refraining from use of the oil weapon. Only, as we have also seen, in 1973, the weapon—that is, the boycott—didn't matter, as the economist M. A. Adelman predicted and as subsequent reports confirm. The Saudis themselves quietly continued to supply oil to the largest consumer, the U.S. military. Rather than lose market share to its competitors, the Arab producers called the boycott off without having achieved any of their demands.[5] In any event, consuming countries have long since worked out an effective response to all the real, rather than hypothetical, supply disruptions by hedging, diversifying, and stockpiling, similar to firms and regions dependent on other globally traded natural resources.

The costs of this chimerical exercise in securing the free flow of oil are notoriously difficult to assess—somewhere between seventy and one hundred billon dollars per year, according to one recent report, although these estimates exclude the costs of the Afghanistan and Iraq wars.[6] And to be clear, as the economist Allan Pulsipher guessed at the time of the 1990 Gulf War and as subsequent government reporting suggests, exposing the strategic rationale as false would not lead to a reduction in defense spending.[7] It might not even lead to a different defense posture—retrenchment or "restraint," in Barry Posen's words—in the Gulf.[8] Why? Centcom pursues multiple missions at one and the same time—shows of force, enforcement of no-fly zones, and humanitarian operations.⁹ In addition, as we have seen, a forbidding "mental terrain" of "pervasive belief, action, and imagining" has to be confronted and overcome before we can even hope to tackle the formidable bureaucratic and institutional impediments to demilitarization.¹⁰

I started by examining the 1920s, when critics began to question the emergent belief that growing demand for scarce natural resources threatened violence, war, and, worst of all, imperial ruin. Markets or, as they said then, commerce could not be counted on to supply an importing country's needs for the raw materials necessary for modern life. The Columbia School thinkers were at their best when exposing the many problematical assumptions and factitious beliefs of the "new mercantilism." We have gone around and around now for about one hundred years over the sufficiency or not of the alternative "social" or "interest" driven explanations they and other progressive era thinkers provided for the new burst of imperialism in the Caribbean, the Middle East, and Asia after World War I. What I have gained a new appreciation for is their emphasis on the psychology of fear and suspicion that gripped citizens and leaders alike in the need, as it was imagined, to control the tropics and their resources.

They had their blind spots, too, of course. The progressives believed as wholeheartedly as the new imperialists in the superiority of their "race" and the inability or unwillingness of the "backward," "overly-emotional," and "irrational" darker peoples, nationalists, *caudillos*, chiefs, and kings to make sufficient quantities of cotton, copper, gold, rubber, diamonds, and dozens of other vital materials available to those who depended on them. As we saw, many held that whites (the West, civilized peoples, and so on) actually possessed more moral and legal right to those resources than the people incapable of exploiting them on their own, whose ownership claims were due to an accident of geography.¹¹ According to the progressives, the problem was that the mining syndicates, rubber producers, and oil companies put profits ahead of the protection and promotion of the welfare of the natives, thereby playing into the hands of the resource nationalists. The progressives advocated for international institutions to play a greater role in mediating among stakeholders to avoid supply disruptions and other threats to access.

One would be even more hard-pressed to find progressives in the 1920s questioning the meaningfulness of the idea of absolute limits to the stock of the world's mineral resources. It was simple. The remaining quantities were calculable. Growing demand meant declining reserves. Prices were bound to climb. Powerful states might risk war (or unintentionally bring war about) in an effort to guarantee the security of supply. As we saw, the progressives focused on the rival business interests whose competition for market dominance sometimes conjured or exaggerated scarcity or threats to access. But the laws of geology were seemingly no more circumventable than those laws of biology that determined racial hierarchy and the degenerative offspring resulting from miscegenation. Defenders of the Anglo-Saxon world order held up both entangled truths, as we saw, for instance, when scarcity fears in the 1950s drove the militant raw materialists' call to reverse decolonization lest the Third World leaders with a visceral hatred of whites starve the West of what was legitimately the common heritage of mankind.

The point is to take heart from this long-forgotten moment. None of the dire predictions came true. The fears of the raw materialists proved unfounded. It is also true, by the way, of the racists' fears in the inevitability of "race war" in all those raw material–producing countries if the national movements there were ever to gain power.[12] C. Fred Bergsten's forecast that other primary commodity producers would piggyback on OPEC, notwithstanding, most professors, politicians, and the public seemed to forget about all those other far more important raw materials that the market could not be counted on to deliver uninterruptedly in sufficient quantities and at prices that would keep machinery and weapons-manufacturing lines humming.[13] In the article and footnote wars between different tribes of diplomatic historians, raw materialism came to be associated exclusively with the 1960s New Left thinkers, as we saw. In any event, no one explains the U.S. wars in Southeast Asia any longer by the putative needs of the "aerospace industry" for bauxite, tungsten, tin, rubber, and so forth from Indochina, Indonesia, and Thailand.[14]

Only, there never was any real sustained professional or technical debate about these matters. There is no record of international relations scholars, say, carefully correcting for their discipline's errors and concluding that the neomercantilists, converts to the seeming truths of geopolitics, scarcity ideology, and racism of the first half of the twentieth century, mostly got it wrong. Had there been, we might have more easily prevented or inoculated ourselves against the mutation in which oil went from one among many and more vital resources to *the* commodity over which rival powers are imagined to had been locked in combat since the end of World War I. Diplomatic historians might have identified the "presentism" in post-1970s studies of oil-as-power among other effects of the national trauma induced by the price shock and of what Ronnie Lipschutz called "hysteria about events in the Persian Gulf and potential Soviet threats to Western supplies of oil."[15] Why believe the case of oil in light of all the other failed cases of copper, bauxite, gold, iron, aluminum, or rubber? Those who do believe it have their work cut out for them, and, thus, it may, indeed, be rational in terms of protecting the value of their brand for our specialists in the geopolitics of energy to continue writing specious accounts of the OPEC embargo and of the need for the United States to maintain the flow of oil by military means. After all, many actual historians of that moment haven't done much better.[16]

The high prices of the early 2000s that drove all those predictions that the world was running out of oil, that we needed the Gulf's production more than ever, and that we'd soon confront challengers eager to take "what was left" for their own seems a world away in 2019. Today, some imagine the United States a stone's throw from energy independence. The rise and fall of scarcity fears confirms the insight of Ronnie Lipschutz, the University of California, Santa Cruz, professor of environmental politics. "This cycle of increasing and decreasing visibility suggests that strategic material dependence is not a 'problem' in the usual sense of the word; rather, it is an issue that is used for other purposes."[17]

Recall MIT's Barry Posen's invocation of a "Factor X," or "global prestige and influence," necessary to resolve the puzzle of the buildup of U.S. armed forces in the Persian Gulf since 1979 against threats to access that are either "not compelling" or "that cannot be dealt with efficiently by military power."[18] Lipschutz reached the same conclusion fifteen years earlier—that is, before the U.S. wars in Kuwait and Iraq. He called the Carter Doctrine an "empty threat," one that "disregards" what military strategists had long understood as "the difficulties of maintaining the flow of oil" from the Gulf in the event of internal stability, let alone in a war against a major adversary." The dilemma is in successive U.S. administrations, "declaring vital an interest that might be gotten along without and is almost impossible to protect."[19] John Holdren, the future science adviser to President Barack Obama and director of the White House Office of Science and Technology Policy, distilled the essence of Lipschutz's text for those not ready to wrestle with the overdense manuscript: "We are in the Middle East more to protect our status as a superpower than to protect access to oil for oil's sake."[20]

So why is the strategic rationale of access to oil so pervasive? In part because some "policymakers and military leaders" believe it and in part because of its "ready acceptance by the public."[21] The Left is a component of that public, of course, and what distinguishes many of their analyses is their unshaken faith that big oil is the driver and that a better world awaits the overthrow of the fossil-capital-led order. Consider the analysis of the 2003 Iraq War by Jim Paul who, in the 1970s, helped transform the Middle East Research and Information Project (MERIP) publication, *MERIP Reports*, from an irregularly issued newsletter to a critical resource for scholars and the public, and, in the 1990s, founded the Global Policy Forum to monitor UN policy making. "The war was primarily a 'war for oil,' in which large multinational oil companies and their host government acted in secret concert to gain control of Iraq's fabulous oil reserves and to gain leverage over other national producers."[22]

Nothing reveals the continuing power of oilcraft today "to hijack the minds of the scientifically literate" than the widespread belief that in February 1945 Franklin D. Roosevelt and Ibn Saud secretly agreed to cut a deal, conclude a bargain, forge an alliance, sign a secret pact or fast-track a special relationship for oil in exchange for security.[23] The Cold War historian turned energy consultant Daniel Yergin first tried selling the idea beloved by the Al Saud and the old timers among the Americans then still in Saudi Aramco's employ to the commentariat and the public-at-large in 1990. It was his modest contribution to the massive deployment of U.S. troops and the war that President George W. Bush and his secretary of defense, Dick Cheney, launched to protect the Saudis, "the prize," and "the balance of power."[24] Many ordinary folks didn't see it that way, of course, and started to raise the old objections to U.S. arms sales and other entanglements with Fahd and family once more. "Why are U.S. troops in the Middle East? Surely there are plenty of robust, patriotic Saudi Arabians eager to defend their country's oil."[25]

It should be obvious, now, that following the 2001 terrorist attacks on the Twin Towers and the Pentagon, the it-all-begain-in-1945 story was a talisman to protect "the special relationship" from harm and the banner under which the believers rallied in a holy war. These were the days when the outrage of U.S. citizens fueled sales of such books as *Sleeping with the Devil*, *Hatred's Kingdom*, and *House of Bush, House of Saud*, and earned millions for the provocateur Michael Moore, who made *Fahrenheit 9/11*, the highest-grossing documentary of all time.

In response, the London-based Saudi anthropologist and critic Madawi al-Rasheed writes:

> From the high towers of academia to research centers and think tanks, money was invested in projects, annual lectures, conferences, seminars and publications whose main objective is to promote Saudi interests, absolve the country from any wrongdoing and polish its image among increasingly sceptical American and European audiences.[26]

It worked. That is, it came to be believed, repeated, enhanced—to become whatever the writer, content provider, or mobilizer chose to make of it. David Ottaway, who cowrote the 2002 *Washington Post* series about the post-1973 origins of the U.S.-Saudi alliance, now begins the story with the two leaders aboard the U.S.S. *Quincy*.[27] As we saw, so do the activists who would reverse the fateful course they believe was set in motion by a wholly factitious bargain of oil for security.

The story told here, although brief, provides ample grounds for opposing the continued embrace of Salman and the reckless despot in line in 2019 to succeed him, or any future autocrat-in-waiting. Why should activists oppose him? The latest Freedom House review backs them up on the nature of Saudi rule.

> Saudi Arabia's absolute monarchy restricts almost all political rights and civil liberties. No officials at the national level are

elected. The regime relies on extensive surveillance, the criminalization of dissent, appeals to sectarianism and ethnicity, and public spending supported by oil revenues to maintain power. Women and religious minorities face extensive discrimination in law and in practice. Working conditions for the large expatriate labor force are often exploitative.[28]

The noise about reform and taking Saudi Arabia back to a mythical era of religious moderation and pluralism, the easy mixing of men and women, movie theaters, and so forth—what shortly before his death Jamal Khashoggi called "peddling revisionist history" by paid propagandists and those like Friedman pleased to hear his own crazy ideas echoed—distracts from Mohammed bin Salman's efforts to crush his opponents and ease the job of those in the United States who back his war in Yemen and side with the kingdom against Iran.[29] There is nothing new here.

The ritual incantations of the kingdom's powerful oil weapon, a bin Laden–like figure seizing power who might hold the world supply hostage, the Saudis' role as a "reliable supplier," "swing producer," the leading OPEC "moderate," and the like may be an even more important source of distraction because, as we have seen, the transactional nature of relations with the kingdom predates the Donald J. Trump administration by decades.[30] Buying treasury bonds outside normal channels and in secret, selling Saudis arms, buying U.S. commercial airliners, selling them more arms, paying Washington lobbyists and consultants, doing "dirty work" in the Cold War, reducing the impact of Pentagon budget cuts, calming financial markets, obliging the rest of the world to pay in dollars for their oil, channeling funds to presidential libraries, Nancy Reagan's "Just Say No" campaign, the University of Arkansas, Harvard, Princeton, Georgetown, the Middle East Institute, the Council on Foreign Relations, and other blue chip organizations—all of it produces a lot of good will, testimonies to the vital nature of the special relationship, and working overtime "to make our Gulf friends happy."[31]

Saudi rents return political dividends everywhere, it seems, but the United States, to judge from insider accounts of the U.S.-Saudi relationship.[32] Investigative journalists tell a different story, at least in those moments in the early 1980s over the AWACS battles, after September 11, and in the fallout over the 2018 murder of Jamal Khashoggi. That is, when the "curious and close liaison" comes under heightened scrutiny and the elites on both sides do what they can to shore up the relationship against its critics.[33] The first line of defense is always American difference. The government's relationship to firms and whole industries in no way resembles what goes on elsewhere around the world where investors pay to play.[34] It would be extraordinary if some U.S. administration were to make a "strategic gesture" for "commercial reasons."[35] The paid-to-think-tanks, congress, and parties raise cash confident that they perform their functions disinterestedly. Noam Chomsky once explained to a BBC interviewer how ideological conformity works: "I'm sure you believe everything you're saying. But what I am saying is that if you believe something different, you wouldn't be sitting where you are sitting."[36] So it goes without question, save at the Cato Institute, that access to Saudi Arabia's oil is a problem of transcendent economic and strategic proportions.

Since that is the case, the critics and their motives are what represent the real problem. "The Jews" as Faisal used to say, or the Israel lobby, the many unwitting dupes of the Soviets back in the day and of the Muslim Brothers now, along with the professors like me, driven, we are told, by the conviction that the United States and its leading corporations are "evil."[37] The professors who, instead, believe that oil is power and that the grand strategy of successive U.S. administrations correctly prioritizes protecting the prize and securing the uninterrupted supply of oil for the West at reasonable prices will—indeed, are hardwired to—dismiss the idea out of hand that Saudi money matters to the elites, Boeing, MIT, Wall Street, and K Street.[38] They'll, instead, tar it with the label "conspiracy theory." It is no such thing.

Start with economist Allan Pulsipher's point about the 1990 Iraq war, that it was the rents that counted, not the oil, which would flow regardless of who governed in Baghdad. Now imagine Riyadh ruled not by the Al Saud but by radicals in a renamed Islamic Emirate of Arabia choosing to use their oil wealth to end the country's and region's subservience to the United States. While totaling up the costs, both Democrats and Republicans together with the commentariat will commence to blaming the rival party for the newest Middle East foreign policy debacle. Even those in the universities who believe that the national interest is truly calculable and carried out without regard for profits or campaign contributions will identify the setback to Israel's security, counterterror efforts, and other key interests as one more oil-producing country transits from the category ally to adversary, similar to Iraq in 1958, Iran in 1979, and Venezuela in 2002. The consolation, meager as it is, is that the U.S. administration might finally begin to oppose, in the words of former Human Rights Watch staffer Sarah Leah Whitson, Riyadh's "thuggish and lawless leadership, hellbent on exacting sadistic vengeance against any citizen who dares to think freely."[39]

Is it really a mystery why Washington and its expert auxiliaries, ex-CIA analysts, retired diplomats, and the like, prefer the status quo? Why they work assiduously to protect the relationship from political fallout and trip all over themselves in the rush to prove the monarchy is dedicated to reform? And why, when a crown prince is overzealous in imprisoning rivals or murdering a journalist (no, a secret Muslim Brother), the chief worry is that inept interference in the kingdom's domestic affairs might result in destabilizing the country? Intervention to force political changes on the kingdom is itself highly unlikely if the past is any guide— and I am not advocating it. What should worry us is any effort in the future to preserve the Al Saud in power. Why fear an "Arabia without Sultans"?[40]

What economists have long realized and defense intellectuals such as Posen have come to recognize is that a post–Saudi Arabia can be counted on to sell its oil on the world market. Iraq's Saddam Hussein did after the nationalization of foreign concessions. Iran did so after the 1979 Islamic revolution. Venezuela, too, remained a reliable supplier of oil to U.S. refineries, some of which were owned by the Venezuelan oil company through its Houston-based subsidiary, Citgo, even as official U.S. enemies Hugo Chávez and Nicolás Maduro ruled there. The Trump administration imposed economic sanctions on Maduro's government in 2019. In a post–Saudi Arabia, the main obstacle to continued access in the long term will be a choice by a future administration to impose crippling sanctions in the case of a not-so-special relationship with those who rule Riyadh and Dammam.

The opponents of U.S. imperialism or primacy or hegemony on the Left lag far behind the critics, for lack of a better term, on the Right in recovering from the national trauma of the factitious OPEC boycott and belief in the supernatural power of big oil. Like the foreign policy and national security experts, the activists and their oracles remain entranced by oilcraft's illusory, yet seemingly vivid, truths about our world. Their journal articles, books, think pieces, blog posts, protest signs, and appearances on the C-SPAN network, *Democracy Now!* public TV news hour, RT (Russian TV), Al Jazeera English news channel, and the like conjure a world in which the interests of Western oil companies explain the endless wars in the Middle East, and in which successive U.S. administrations through their agent the Al Saud control world oil prices and supply in fulfillment of a wholly imaginary bargain struck in 1945. Those who activists and intellectuals hope to enlist in efforts to rethink and reverse the militarization of U.S. foreign policy deserve better.[41]

ACKNOWLEDGMENTS

I first started to question my own deeply held beliefs about the role of oil in U.S. foreign policy more than two decades ago. Identifying all the people I have discussed and argued these matters with, texted, and learned from and who hosted talks and workshops, commissioned essays, and made me rethink things is daunting. The folks I remember and owe a debt of thanks are Osman Balkan, Duccio Basosi, Alex Beasley, Joel Beinin, Arthur van Benthem, Dan Bessner, Elisabetta Bini, Rosie Bsheer, Nate Citino, Juan Cole, Jeff Colgan, Pat Conge, Zach Cuyler, Joel Darmstadter, Chris Dietrich, Tim Di Muzio, Gaetano Di Tommaso, Manuel Dorion-Soulié, Kaveh Ehsani, Rusti Eisenberg, Noura Erakat, Anusar Farooqui, Tom Ferguson, Ted Fertik, Irene Gendzier, Avery Goldstein, Joel Gordon, Vicky de Grazia, Guy Grossman, Bassam Haddad, Deborah Harrold, Waleed Hazbun, Jim Henson, Mike Horowitz, Aida Hozic, Meg Jacobs, Toby Jones, Lola Jusidman, Arang Keshavarzian, Assaf Kfoury, Laleh Khalili, Zuhair Khan, Philip Khoury, Michael Klare, Atul Kohli, Bruce Kuklick, Mazen Labban, Mark LeVine, Zach Lockman, Roger Louis, Shana Marshall, Melani McAlister, Victor McFarland, Tom Meaney, Emily Meierding, Yoram Meital, Pascal Menoret, Fareed Mohamedi, Marta Musso, Greg Nowell, Gwenn Okruhlik, Ido Oren, Roger Owen, Patrick Porter, Barry Posen, Daryl Press, Haggai Ram, Sayres Rudy, Madawi al-Rasheed, Peter

Rutland, Andrew Schlossberg, Adam Shatz, Cyrus Schayegh, Relli Shechter, Nate Shills, Ahmad Shokr, Ben Smith, Roger Stern, Ted Swedenburg, Dawn Teele, Peter Trubowitz, Alex Weisiger, Stephen Wertheim, Brandon Wolfe-Hunnicutt, and Marilyn Young.

I won't ever forget the ten friends and colleagues who took time from their own work late in the spring and summer of 2019 to write detailed comments on and criticisms of the entire manuscript. Their generosity reminds me of what I love about the academy even in these dismal times. I thank Samer Abboud, Jason Brownlee, Giuliano Garavini, Greg Gause, Ellis Goldberg, Clem Henry, Ian Lustick, Mike Lynch, Tim Mitchell, and David Painter.

I have had the singular honor to work with Kate Wahl and her colleagues at Stanford University Press, not once but twice. She is the best editor I know, and the press is a vital national resource.

I wrote the book on the third floor of our house in Mount Airy, at McMenamin's Tavern, at Uncle Bobbie's in Germantown, at Starbucks in Chestnut Hill, and for a few mornings at the Flourtown Swim Club. It is the first one I've written without decamping for weeks at a stretch to work in various archives. So I didn't need anybody's money this time. I couldn't have done it, though, without JSTOR and ProQuest. But I took a sabbatical and borrowed on a future one (who knew?), so my thanks go to Anne Norton and Rogers Smith for arranging it.

Streaming music has messed things up for me, because the choices are now limitless, but while writing I kept returning to Phoebe Bridgers, Ferron, I Think Like Midnight, Lianne La Havas, Kendrick Lamar, Lee Morgan, Kacey Musgraves, Oliver Nelson, Horace Silver, the Stylistics, Taylor Swift, Thundercat, and Neil Young's archive releases.

I managed the meals and my share of the pickups and drop-offs and had the thrill of watching Phoebe's play, swim meets, and circus performances. Chloe gave me the space and inspiration to do the work. I love the two of them so much.

I dedicate the book to Marilyn, who kept pushing me to write it, and to Ellis, who for three decades encouraged me and modeled for me how to work against the grain. We lost them both too soon.

NOTES

CHAPTER 1

1. John Esterbrook, "Rumsfeld: It Would Be a Short War," *CBS News*, November 15, 2002, http://www.cbsnews.com/news/rumsfeld-it-would-be-a-short -war.

2. Greg Palast filed a number of valuable stories in the London *Guardian* and elsewhere, which are reworked in his *Armed Madhouse* (New York: Penguin, 2006). The radical activist Greg Muttitt dissected and dissented from what most believed about the oil business in *Fuel on the Fire: Oil and Politics in Occupied Iraq* (New York: New Press, 2012). And *New Yorker* writer Steve Coll followed up on some of these issues in *Private Empire: ExxonMobil and American Power* (New York: Penguin, 2012). On the dream of getting Iraqi oil to Israel, see Gary Vogler, *Iraq and the Politics of Oil: An Insider's Perspective* (Lawrence: University Press of Kansas), 2017.

3. Alan Greenspan, *The Age of Turbulence: Adventures in a New World* (New York: Penguin, 2007), 463.

4. Bob Woodward, "Ouster of Hussein Crucial for Oil Security," *Washington Post*, September 17, 2007, http://www.washingtonpost.com/wp-dyn/content/article/2007/09/16/AR2007091601287.html.

5. Rashid Khalidi, *Sowing Crisis: The Cold War and American Dominance in the Middle East* (Boston: Beacon Press, 2009), 15.

6. Matthew Huber, *Lifeblood: Oil, Freedom, and the Forces of Capital* (Minneapolis: University of Minnesota Press, 2013), 150.

7. Stephen Brooks and William Wohlforth, *America Abroad: The United States' Global Role in the 21st Century* (New York: Oxford University Press, 2017); G. John Ikenberry, *Liberal Leviathan: The Origins, Crisis, and Transformation of the American World Order* (Princeton, NJ: Princeton University Press, 2011); David Harvey, *The New Imperialism* (Oxford: Oxford University Press, 2003); Doug Stokes and

Sam Raphael, *Global Energy Security and American Hegemony* (Baltimore: Johns Hopkins University Press, 2010).

8. Robin Wright, "Donald Trump, Pirate-in-Chief," *New Yorker*, January 30, 2017, http://www.newyorker.com/news/news-desk/donald-trump-pirate-in-chief.

9. Patrick Porter makes a similar claim in his critical account of the Blair government's decision-making in *Blunder: Britain's War in Iraq* (Oxford: Oxford University Press, 2018), 5–18.

10. See Paul A. Volcker, Richard J. Goldstone, and Mark Pieth, "Manipulation of the Oil-For-Food Programme by the Iraqi Regime," October 27, 2005, https://www.foxnews.com/projects/pdf/final_off_report.pdf.

11. Michael Klare, *Blood and Oil: The Dangers and Consequences of America's Growing Dependency on Imported Petroleum* (New York: Henry Holt, 2004), 10, 193.

12. American Empire Project, "Blood and Oil," http://americanempireproject .com/blood-and-oil (accessed October 19, 2019).

13. Even higher up the ladder of geopolitical thought we find formulations such as "fossil capital," "petrocapitalism," or the "military-petroleum complex," but the underlying idea is the same. For statistical and archival analyses that demonstrate why this commonly held view is wrong, see Jeff Colgan, *Petro-Aggression: When Oil Causes War* (Cambridge: Cambridge University Press, 2013), 3n4.

14. See Joshua S. Goldstein and Steven Pinker, "Inconvenient Truths for the Environmental Movement," *Boston Globe*, November 23, 2015, https://www .bostonglobe.com/opinion/2015/11/23/inconvenient-truths-for-environmental -movement/esDloe97894keW16Ywa9MP/story.html.

15. See for one Michael Lynch, *The "Peak Oil" Scare and the Coming Oil Flood* (Santa Barbara: Praeger, 2016). The book collects Lynch's technical papers and popular commentaries on the topic.

16. Richard Posner, *Public Intellectuals* (Cambridge, MA: Harvard University Press, 2003).

17. The title pays homage to Karen E. Fields and Barbara J. Fields, *Racecraft: The Soul of Inequality in American Life* (London: Verso, 2012).

18. Noam Chomsky, letter to the editor, *London Review of Books*, August 17, 2017, p. 4.

19. Roger Stern, "Oil Scarcity Ideology in U.S. Foreign Policy, 1908–97," *Security Studies* 25, no. 2 (2016): 214–257.

20. Gordon Merriam, "Draft Memorandum to President Truman," enclosed with "Memorandum by the Under Secretary of State (Acheson) to the Secretary of State," October 9, 1945, https://history.state.gov/historicaldocuments/frus1945v08/ d20. Klare's documentary leads with the quotation. Noam Chomsky has used it in interviews and writings since the 1970s.

21. See Robert Vitalis, *America's Kingdom: Mythmaking on the Saudi Oil Frontier* (Stanford, CA: Stanford University Press, 2005), for many examples of diplomats and oil executives engaging in what professors call "threat inflation" as a means to move policies in ways favorable to their interests.

22. Letter from Douglas Feith to Richard Allen, June 4, 1981, Box 81, National Security Council Files, Ronald Reagan National Library, cited in Meg Jacobs, *Panic at the Pump: The Energy Crisis and the Transformation of American Politics in the 1970s* (New York: Hill and Wang, 2016), 282. *New York Times* op-ed columnist William Safire had just called for the U.S. to "smash" the cartel. William Safire, "Glut to the Gluttons," *New York Times*, June 3, 1981, p. A23.

23. The irony here is that "Franks . . . was widely regarded as a dim bulb, even by fellow officers." His cluelessness drove Secretary of Defense Rumsfeld crazy and, according to Fred Kaplan, colored the latter's views toward the army generally. See Fred Kaplan, *Daydream Believers: How a Few Grand Ideas Wrecked American Power* (New York: Wiley, 2008), 40–41.

24. Ronald Reagan, "The President's News Conference," October 1, 1981, https://www.reaganlibrary.gov/research/speeches/100181b. To be clear, Feith, a protégé of hawkish Soviet expert Richard Pipes, supported the military buildup against the Soviets while criticizing the deference showed to Saudis and other Arab oil producers, which he called a surcharge on the price Americans paid. Douglas Feith, "Radical Sheiks," *American Spectator*, April 1980, pp. 11–15; Douglas Feith, "Love and Oil," *New Republic*, November 22, 1980, pp. 20–23.

25. Coll, *Private Empire*, 239–240.

26. Ibid., 239.

27. The board game first appeared in the United States in 1959 as Risk: The Continental Game. It was originally created in France in 1957 and called La Conquête du Monde (World Domination). American toy manufacturer Parker Brothers bought the game, releasing it in under the title Risk: The Game of Global Domination. See Alan Axelrod, *Adversaries and Allies: Mastering Strategic Relationships* (New York: Sterling, 2009), x. Risk is now owned by Hasbro and continues to sell.

28. Nikolai Bukharin, "Imperialism and Communism," *Foreign Affairs* 14 (1936): 563–577.

29. John A. Hobson, *Imperialism: A Study* (London: James Nisbet, 1902), 207, 218, 223. For a counterview, see Ahsan I. Butt, "Why Did the United States Invade Iraq in 2003?" *Security Studies* 28, no. 2 (2019): 250–285.

30. The Nixon administration began developing the regional proxy strategy prior to the 1973 "crisis" and not as a response to it. See F. Gregory Gause III, "British and American Policies in the Persian Gulf, 1968–1973, *Review of International Studies* 11, no. 4 (1985): 247–273, and the extremely detailed account based

on declassified records by Tore T. Petersen, *Richard Nixon, Great Britain and the Anglo-American Alignment in the Persian Gulf and Arabian Peninsula: Making Allies Out of Clients* (Brighton: Sussex Academic Press, 2009).

31. See Robert Tucker, "The Middle East: Carterism without Carter," *Commentary* 72, no. 3 (1981): 27–36, and the account by the *Washington Post*'s Jim Hoagland, "How Strong Are the Saudis?" *New York Review of Books*, April 1, 1982, https://www.nybooks.com/articles/1982/04/01/how-strong-are-the-saudis.

32. See, for example, Edward Said, "Thoughts on a War: Ignorant Armies Clash by Night," in *Beyond the Storm: A Gulf Crisis Reader*, ed. Phyllis Bennis and Michel Moushabeck (New York: Olive Branch Press, 1991), 1.

33. Parker Thomas Moon, "Raw Materials and Imperialism," *Proceedings of the Academy of Political Science in the City of New York* 1 (July 1926): 180–187.

34. Parker T. Moon, *Imperialism and World Politics* (New York: Macmillan, 1927), 545.

35. See, for example, Simon Bromley, "The United States and the Control of World Oil," *Government and Opposition* 40, no. 2 (2005): 225–255.

36. For example, see the recent claim by independent reporter Tom Stevenson that the "US's inherited mastery of the Gulf has given it a degree of leverage over both rivals and allies probably unparalleled in the history of empire," lest it, "if it wished, cut them off from their main source of energy." Tom Stevenson, "What Are We There For," *London Review of Books*, May 9, 2019, pp. 11–12. He offers no evidence of the effectiveness of this "leverage" (he cannot), while, as the book shows, those who specialize in military strategy for a living have demonstrated that U.S. force projection provides no advantage of the kind that Stevenson and many other enchanted amateurs imagine.

37. Certainly, firms, sectors, and regions may benefit as a result of the increased defense outlays, contracts to let, and so forth, but these gains by themselves can't explain why governments choose to intervene in the Gulf or other regions. As Trubowitz puts it, these kinds of societal or domestic-interest-focused explanations are "underdetermining." Peter Trubowitz, *Politics and Strategy: Partisan Ambition and American Statecraft* (Princeton, NJ: Princeton University Press, 2011), 132. I prefer to think of them as effects.

38. Douglas Martin, "Morris A. Adelman Dies at 96; Saw Oil as Inexhaustible," *New York Times*, June 9, 2014, p. B8. For his view on OPEC, see M. A. Adelman, "The Clumsy Cartel," *Energy Journal* 1, no. 1 (1980): 43–53.

39. M. A. Adelman, "Is the Oil Shortage Real? Oil Companies as OPEC Tax Collectors," *Foreign Policy* 9 (Winter 1972–1973): 69–107.

40. M. A. Adelman, *The Economics of Petroleum Supply: Papers by M. A. Adelman, 1962–1993* (Cambridge, MA: MIT Press, 1993), 351.

41. Ibid., 534.

42. Ibid.

43. Morris A. Adelman, "The Real Oil Problem," *Regulation* 27, no. 1 (2004): 16.

44. Adelman, *Economics of Petroleum Supply*," 538.

45. Douglas Feith, interview by the author, September 26, 2017.

46. According to Adelman, "Unfortunately, there is a powerful legend or stereotype of the energy-famished bear stretching his greedy paw toward the Persian Gulf because he cannot 'satisfy his needs' with domestic supply. But 'needs' should be spelled 'nonsense.' All the USSR can get out of occupying the Persian Gulf is cheaper energy. This is not worth the cost, still less the risk of war. It is deplorable to see our Secretary of Defense [then Casper Weinberger] repeat the legend that the Soviet Union is about to become an oil importer, particularly when his own Defense Intelligence Agency has concluded . . . that the Soviet Union will continue as a net hydrocarbon exporter throughout the 1980s." Adelman, *Economics of Petroleum Supply*, 515–516. For the role that this factitious idea played in the shift of the U.S. military from Southeast Asia to the Middle East, see William E. Odom, "The Cold War Origins of the U.S. Central Command," *Cold War Studies* 8, no. 2 (2006): 52–82, 61–62.

47. Barry Posen, *Restraint: A New Foundation for U.S. Grand Strategy* (Ithaca, NY: Cornell University Press, 2014), book jacket.

48. Ibid., 112.

49. Barry Posen, email to the author, February 28, 2019.

50. Aaron Friedberg, for one, sees the consequences of the United States restricting China's access to imported oil as "far reaching and potentially devastating" to its "economy, social stability and war-making capacity." Aaron Friedberg, *Beyond Air-Sea Battle: The Debate over US Military Strategy in Asia* (London: Routledge, 2014), 106. Accounts of this type sidestep the fact that coal, not oil, provides the largest share of China's energy needs, and that its vaunted Belt and Road initiative is a policy to diversify trade routes for goods, in general, rather than for oil and gas resources, in particular.

51. See Bernard Brodie, "Foreign Oil and American Security," Yale Institute of International Studies Memorandum no. 23, September 15, 1947, p. 1, http:// www.fdrlibrary.marist.edu/_resources/images/ergen/ergen1937.pdf. For an unsurpassed discussion on Brodie, see Fred Kaplan, *The Wizards of Armageddon* (New York: Simon and Schuster, 1983), 9–50. The Rand (Research and Development) Corporation was what we now call a think tank. It began in 1945 as a project of the Douglas Aircraft Company under contract to the U.S. Air Force, spinning off as an independent nonprofit organization in 1948 with funding from the Ford Foundation. Rand focused originally on weapons planning.

52. Vitalis, *America's Kingdom*; Percy Bidwell, *Raw Materials: A Study of American Policy* (New York: Harper Brothers, 1959), 332–333; Shibley Telhami and Fiona Hill, "America's Vital Stakes in Saudi Arabia," *Foreign Affairs* 81, no. 6 (2002): 167–173, 170; Ronnie Lipschutz, *When Nations Clash: Raw Materials, Ideology and Foreign Policy* (New York: Harper and Row, 1989), 106–120. Charles Glaser claims something quite different—that military planning counted on the Gulf supplying European forces in event of a war—but offers no evidence in support. See Charles Glaser and Rosemary Kelanic, eds., *Crude Strategy: Rethinking the US Military Commitment to Defend Persian Gulf Oil* (Washington, DC: Georgetown University Press, 2016), Kindle ed., loc.407.

53. Patrick Porter explains why the beliefs that primacy's defenders consider self-evidently true are so hard to change in "Why America's Grand Strategy Has Not Changed: Power, Habit, and the U.S. Foreign Policy Establishment," *International Security* 42, no. 4 (2018): 9–46.

54. "War with Iraq Is *Not* in America's National Interest," *New York Times*, September 26, 2002, http://www.bear-left.com/archive/2002/0926oped.html.

55. John Mueller, *Overblown: How Politicians and the Terrorism Industry Inflate National Security Threats, and Why We Believe Them* (New York: Free Press, 2006). For the best discussion I know of the militants who led the disastrous campaign to remake the Middle East, see Jacob Heilbrunn, *They Knew They Were Right: The Rise of the Neocons* (New York: Doubleday, 2008), 228–278.

56. Roger Stern, "United States Cost of Military Force Projection, 1976–2007," *Energy Policy* 38, no. 6 (2010): 2816–2825. For more conservative estimates, see Securing America's Future Energy, "The Military Cost of Defending the Global Oil Supply," *Issue Brief*, September 21, 2018, p. 4, http://secureenergy.org/wp-content/uploads/2018/09/Military-Cost-of-Defending-the-Global-Oil-Supply.-Sep.-18.-2018.pdf.

57. Jon Gilbert Fox, "Powerful Ideas About Oil," *JHU Engineering*, Summer 2007, https://engineering.jhu.edu/magazine/2007/07/powerful-ideas-oil/#.We9f3oZrz-Z; Stern, "Oil Scarcity Ideology"; Roger Stern, "The Lie That Changed History: Peak Oil, Science, and America's Path to the Middle East," unpublished manuscript, 2017, in author's possession.

58. See, for instance, Vijay Prashad, "Saudi Arabia's Oversupply of Oil Has Little to Do with Economics and Everything to Do with Politics," *AlterNet*, March 3, 2016, https://www.alternet.org/world/saudi-arabias-oversupply-oil-has-little-do-economics-and-everything-do-politics.

59. Robert S. Pinkyck and Julio Rotemberg, "The Excess Co-movement of Commodity Prices," *Economic Journal* 100, no. 403 (1990): 1173–1189; Eric Blankmeyer, "Do Commodity Prices Still Show Excess Co-movement?" *Southwestern*

Economic Review 33, no. 1 (2006): 149–160; Norges Handelshøyskole, "Price Co-movement in Energy and Commodity Markets" (master's thesis, Norwegian School of Economics, Bergen, Norway, 2011); David S. Jacks, "From Boom to Bust: A Typology of Real Commodity Prices in the Long Run," NBER Working Paper no. 18874, March 2013, https://www.nber.org/papers/w18874.pdf.

60. Herbert Feis, *Seen from E. A.* [Economic Affairs] (New York: Knopf, 1947), 4.

61. Jeff Desjardins, "The Oil Market Is Bigger than All Metal Markets Combined," *Visual Capitalist*, October 14, 2016, https://www.visualcapitalist.com/size-oil-market/. I owe the argument to the University of Florida's Ben Smith, one of the great debunkers of (I kid you not) the so-called oil curse. Similarly, Guliano Garavini pointed me to the work of Bernard Mommer on why prices remain higher than we'd expect on the basis of production costs alone. See Bernard Mommer, "The Shocking History of Oil," in *Oil Shock: The 1973 Crisis and Its Economic Legacy*, ed. Elisabetta Bini, Giuliano Garavini, and Federico Romero (London: I. B. Tauris, 2016), Kindle ed., loc.310–672.

62. Esteban Ortiz-Ospina, Diana Beltekian, and Max Roser, "Trade and Globalization," *Our World and Data*, 2014, https://ourworldindata.org/international-trade.

63. See the discussion in Christiane Baumeister and Lutz Kilian, "Lower Oil Prices and the U.S. Economy: Is This Time Different?" *Brookings Papers on Economic Activity*, Fall 2016, p. 293. Their models show oil prices matter to firms that "directly or indirectly rely on oil (or oil-based products) as a major factor of production." It would include transportation, of course, "some chemical companies, and rubber and plastic producers." It simply doesn't matter to most other industries as opposed to final consumers. Ibid.

64. Adam Hochschild, review of *Empire of Cotton*, by Sven Beckert, *New York Times*, December 31, 2014, https://www.nytimes.com/2015/01/04/books/review/empire-of-cotton-by-sven-beckert.html; Devin Leigh, review of *Capitalism and Slavery*, by Eric Williams, *Lakefront Historian*, July 8, 2014, https://lakefronthistorian.com/2014/07/08/review-of-capitalism-and-slavery-by-eric-williams/; Dan Koeppel, *Banana: The Fate of a Fruit That Changed the World* (New York: Hudson Street Press, 2008); April Merleaux, *Sugar and Civilization: American Empire and the Cultural Politics of Sweetness* (Chapel Hill: University of North Carolina Press, 2015); Mimi Sheller, *Aluminum Dreams: The Making of Light Mobility* (Cambridge, MA: MIT Press, 2014), https://mitpress.mit.edu/books/aluminum-dreams.

65. Robert Vitalis, *When Capitalists Collide: Business Conflict and the End of Empire in Egypt* (Berkeley: University of California Press, 1995); Vitalis, *America's Kingdom*. Also see Ken Silverstein, *The Secret World of Oil* (London: Verso, 2014).

66. "When Congress in the 1970s made it illegal to export domestically produced crude oil without a license, the goal of the legislation was to conserve domestic oil reserves and discourage foreign imports. In reality, the export ban did not help accomplish either of these objectives." Blake Clayton, "The Case for Allowing U.S. Crude Oil Exports," Council on Foreign Relations *Policy Memorandum* 34 (July 2013).

67. Steven Galpern, *Money, Oil, and Empire in the Middle East: Sterling and Postwar Imperialism, 1944–1971* (New York: Cambridge University Press, 2009); Robert Vitalis, review of *Money, Oil, and Empire in the Middle East: Sterling and Postwar Imperialism, 1944–1971*, by Steven Galpern, *Business History Review* 84, no. 2 (2010): 371–373; Lipschutz, *When Nations Clash*, 58; Ezra Davidson, "Visions of Political Islam and the American Military Presence in the Middle East—from Carter to Reagan" (PhD diss., New York University, 2011).

68. Robert Vitalis, "The Closing of the Arabian Oil Frontier and the Future of Saudi-American Relations," *Middle East Report* 204 (July–September 1997): 15–21, 25.

69. According to Georgetown University historian David Painter, the U.S. military consumes more oil than two-thirds of the world's nations. See David Painter, "Oil and U.S. Foreign Policy," *Oxford Energy Forum* 53 (May 2003): 9.

CHAPTER 2

1. Daniel Yergin, *The Prize: The Epic Quest for Oil, Money, and Power* (New York: Simon and Schuster, 1991).

2. Brian Black, *Crude Reality: Petroleum in World History* (Lanham, MD: Rowman and Littlefield, 2012), 136–137.

3. For works that bring conceptual and statistical evidence to bear on the widespread, false belief that needs for oil and denial of access leads to conflict, see Lipschutz, *When Nations Clash*, and Colgan, *Petro-Aggression*.

4. Yergin, *The Prize*, 309 (emphasis added).

5. See the extraordinarily researched Michael Barnhart, *Japan Prepares for Total War: The Search for Economic Security, 1919–1941* (Ithaca, NY: Cornell University Press, 2013).

6. Brooks Emeny, *The Strategy of Raw Materials: A Study of America in Peace and War* (New York: Macmillan, 1938), 1; Lipschutz, *When Nations Clash*.

7. "Caucasian Solidarity Urged to Insure Safety of World," *Christian Science Monitor*, August 27, 1923, p. 3; William S. Culbertson, "Raw Materials Breed Animosities," *New York Times*, December 17, 1924, p. X17.

8. Edward Mead Earle, "Oil and American Foreign Policy," *New Republic*, August 20, 1924, pp. 355–356.

9. Barnhart, *Japan Prepares for Total War*.

10. See David G. Victor, "What Resource Wars?" *National Interest* 92 (November–December 2007): 49.

11. "Harding Sees Oil in British Control," *New York Times*, October 10, 1920, p. 2.

12. "American Position in Oil Industry Supreme," *Wall Street Journal*, June 5, 1920, p. 8. "Most of the current talk as to the future control of oil is widely astray from fact. It bears all the earmarks of propaganda either to facilitate promotion of British oil companies or to conceal activity by leading American oil interests." Ibid.

13. A. Percival, "Giant Struggle for Control of World's Oil Supply; Standard and Royal Dutch Shell Engaged in Battle of Billions for Mastery of Fuel Vital to Merchant Marine—Vest Stakes Awaiting the Victor," *New York Times*, June 27, 1920, https://www.nytimes.com/1920/06/27/archives/giant-struggle-for-control-of-worlds-oil-supply-standard-and-royal.html.

14. "Eventually . . . the problem goes away, and its political salience declines. This cycle of increasing and decreasing visibility suggests that strategic material dependence is not a "problem" in the usual sense of the word; rather it is an issue that is used for other purposes." Lipschutz, *When Nations Clash*, 147.

15. See Silvano Wueschner, "Herbert Hoover, Great Britain, and the Rubber Crisis, 1923–1926," *Essays in Economic and Business History* 18 (2000): 211–221.

16. David White, "Petroleum Resources of the World," *Annals of the American Academy of Political and Social Science* 89 (May 1920): 111–134.

17. "Declares Oil Industry Can't Fulfill Contracts," *Los Angeles Times*, November 14, 1920, p. V6. For the dark side of the Oklahoma boom, see David Grann, *Killers of the Flower Moon: The Osage Murders and the Birth of the FBI* (New York: Random House, 2017).

18. "World's Oil Resources Practically Unlimited," *Wall Street Journal*, July 27, 1920, p. 7. Stern, "Oil Scarcity Ideology."

19. For the best account I know of the relationship of these two currents to oil scarcity ideology, see Gaetano Di Tommaso, "America's Energy Transition, the Evolution of the National Interest, and the Middle Eastern Connection at the Dawn of the Twentieth Century" (PhD diss., University of Bologna, 2017).

20. Ibid., 260.

21. Hamid Mowlana, "Roots of War: The Long Road of Intervention," in *Triumph of the Image: The Media's War in the Persian Gulf—a Global Perspective*, ed. Hamid Mowlana, George Gerbner, and Herbert Schiller (Boulder, CO: Westview Press, 1992), 36–37. The discussion reengages the oft-cited view of Lord Curzon that the allies had floated to victory on a sea of oil.

22. E. H. Davenport and Sidney Russell Cooke, *Oil Trusts and Anglo-American Relations* (London: Macmillan, 1923), vi. Davenport was an Australian journalist; Cooke, a stockbroker, secret agent, and one of John Maynard Keynes's lovers. For the book's significance at the time, see Earle, "Oil and American Foreign Policy," and Leland Jenks, review of *Oil Trusts and Anglo-American Relations*, by E. H. Davenport and Sidney Russell Cooke, *Social Forces* 2, no. 5 (1924): 761–763.

23. Garfield was the son of the assassinated U.S. President James A. Garfield. His elder brother, James, served as President Theodore Roosevelt's secretary of the interior and played a leading role in the conservation policies for which the administration is known. For Harry Garfield's role in World War I, see Di Tommaso, "America's Energy Transition," 237–238.

24. Chief Justice of the Supreme Court Howard Taft presided at the highly successful inaugural 1921 session, and subsequent years saw growing numbers of college presidents, military officers, attorneys, diplomats, and others with interests in foreign affairs enrolling. See Robert Vitalis, *White World Order, Black Power Politics: The Birth of American International Relations* (Ithaca, NY: Cornell University Press, 2015), 73–75.

25. William S. Culbertson, "Problems of Raw Materials and Foodstuffs in the Commercial Policies of Nations," special issue, *Annals of the American Academy of Political and Social Science* 12 (March 1924).

26. William S. Culbertson, *International Economic Policies: A Survey of the Economics of Diplomacy* (New York: Appleton, 1925).

27. William S. Culbertson "Economic Control Urged to End War," *New York Times*, July 31, 1923, p. 4.

28. Culbertson, "Raw Materials," 4.

29. Ibid. 5–6.

30. My discussion does not constitute an endorsement of Culbertson's ideas, but the extent to which journalist John Hobson, from whom Vladimir Lenin borrowed a great deal, came to influence liberals in the United States by World War I is remarkable. See the earliest criticisms by Tufts College economist E. M. Winslow, "Marxian, Liberal, and Sociological Theories of Imperialism," *Journal of Political Economy* 39, no. 6 (1931): 713–758, and the German-Jewish émigré who taught at the Hebrew University of Jerusalem, Richard Koebner, "The Concept of Economic Imperialism," *Economic History Review*, New Series 2, no. 1 (1949): 1–29. Many more critiques and countercritiques (the so-called economic versus political explanations for imperialism) would follow in the 1960s and beyond, with Culbertson and the other influential writers I discuss eventually disappearing from "the canon."

31. Culbertson, "Raw Materials," 4.

32. Ibid., 6.

33. Culbertson, "Raw Materials," 125.

34. Culbertson, *International Economic Policies*, vii.

35. Edward Mead Earle, "The New Mercantilism," *Political Science Quarterly* 40, no. 4 (1925): 594–600. Earle's is a combined review of *International Economic Policies*, Davenport and Cooke's *Oil Trusts*, and Pierre l'Espagnol de la Tramerye's *The World Struggle for Oil* (New York: Knopf, 1924). L'Espagnol de la Tramerye, a true believer in the "oil is power" idea, criticized French authorities for failing to reverse the country's dependence on the United States and Great Britain.

36. Earle, "New Mercantilism," 600.

37. Koebner, "Concept of Economic Imperialism," 4.

38. Earle wrote one major work, the unsurpassed *Turkey, the Great Powers, and the Baghdad Railway* (New York: Macmillan, 1923), before suffering a debilitating disease. His return to prominence as an early appointee of the Institute for Advanced Study at Princeton in the 1930s coincided with his reinvention as a grand strategist. Moon produced more, including *Imperialism and World Politics*; *Modern History* (New York: Macmillan, 1928), coauthored with his ex-adviser Carlton Hayes; and *The United States and the Caribbean* (Chicago: University of Chicago Press, 1929), coauthored with Chester Lloyd Jones and Henry Kittredge Norton at the behest of the Chicago Council on Foreign Relations, which wanted a book dealing with "the subject of our so-called 'imperialism.'" Jones, Norton, and Moon, *The United States and the Caribbean*, vii. Moon, who moved to Columbia's Department of Public Law as an assistant professor of international relations in 1925, also died young. Jenks wrote the highly influential *Migration of British Capital to 1875* (New York: Knopf, 1927) and *Our Cuban Colony: Sugar* (New York: Vanguard, 1928), one of a number of imperialism studies commissioned by Harry Elmer Barnes, another Columbia PhD who taught there in the 1920s.

39. Winslow, "Theories," 737–746. See Moon, *Imperialism and World Politics*, 25–28, where he makes clear his rejection of monocausal explanations on the grounds that they are "unhistorical," and 67–76, where he discusses animating fears and related "ideas."

40. Moon, "Raw Materials and Imperialism," 180, 187. University of Chicago economist Eugene Staley would soon write of "the pathological sense of insecurity which has come to dominate the thought of many nations on the subject of raw materials" in his Strategy of *Raw Materials* (1937), quoted in David Popper, "Arms and the World," review of *The Strategy of Raw Materials: A Study of America in Peace and War*, by Eugene Staley, *Saturday Review*, August 28, 1937, p. 16.

41. Moon, *Imperialism and World Politics*, 555.

42. Keith Miller, "How Important Was Oil in World War II," *History News Network*, October 11, 2001, http://hnn.us/articles/339.html.

43. Herbert Feis, "The Anglo-American Oil Agreement," *Yale Law Journal* 55, no. 5 (1946): 1174.

44. Lipschutz, *When Nations Clash*, 102–121.

45. Edward Mead Earle, "Another Oil War—on Paper," review of *We Fight for Oil*, by Ludwell Denny, *New Republic*, September 12, 1928, pp. 106–107. Moon, *Imperialism and World Politics*, 58–74.

46. Earle, "Oil and American Foreign Policy," 356.

47. Bert F. Hoselitz, review of *Seen from E. A.: Three International Episodes*, by Herbert Feis, *Journal of Modern History* 20, no. 4 (1948): 353.

48. Earle, "Oil and American Foreign Policy," 357.

49. Moon, *Imperialism and World Politics*, 545. In addition, see the remarkable December 1925 address by the American Economic Association president Allyn A. Young, in which he argues that the "values of the world of international rivalry are more like the irrational values of the world of consumer choice than they are like the money profits . . . for which men contend in the world of commerce." In the same address, he emphasizes the "special interests . . . served by an imperialistic policy," again, similar to Moon. Allyn A. Young, "Economics and War," *American Economic Review* 41, no. 1 (1926): 4, 3.

50. Culbertson, "Raw Materials and Foodstuffs," 129. The causes were not imaginary in all instances, he insisted, but offered no formula for determining when or how frequently these fears were "unjustified."

51. Moon, *Imperialism and World Politics*, 68.

52. Ibid., 66. Some leaders "have deliberately promoted imperialism either because they believed in it, or because they felt that it would bring prestige and votes, or campaign contributions." Ibid., 67.

53. Jack Snyder, *Myths of Empire: Domestic Politics and Political Ambition* (Ithaca, NY: Cornell University Press, 1991). See, as well, Chaim Kaufmann, "Threat Inflation and the Failure of the Marketplace of Ideas: The Selling of the Iraq War," *International Security* 29, no. 1 (2004): 5–48. The "father" of all such accounts, whether any particular descendant is aware, is Walter Lippmann, *The Stakes of Diplomacy* (New York: Henry Holt, 1915), which leads with a quotation from Admiral Alfred Thayer Mahan about the role of raw materials in "the impulse to war," and analyzes the interested parties that benefited and the ways in which such programs are sold to the public.

54. Marilyn Lake and Henry Reynolds, *Drawing the Global Colour Line: White Men's Countries and the International Challenge of Racial Equality* (Cambridge: Cambridge University Press, 2008); Linda Gordon, *The Second Coming of the KKK: The Ku Klux Klan of the 1920s and the American Political Tradition* (New York: Liveright, 2017); Vitalis, *White World Order*.

55. Earle, "Oil and American Foreign Policy," 357; Culbertson, "Raw Materials and Foodstuffs," 86.

56. Moon, *Imperialism and World Politics*, 74.

57. Anthony Anghie, "Civilization and Commerce: The Concept of Governance in Historical Perspective," *Villanova Law Review* 45, no. 5 (2000): 887–912.

58. Frederick Lugard, *The Dual Mandate in British Tropical Africa* (Edinburgh, UK: William Blackwood and Sons, 1922), 6, 61.

59. Historian Susan Pedersen calls the book "perhaps the longest job application in history," published while Lugard was being vetted for an appointment to the League of Nations Permanent Mandate Commission. See her magisterial account, *The Guardians: The League of Nations and the Crisis of Empire* (New York: Oxford, 2015), 108.

60. Elspeth Huxley, "British Aims in Africa," *Foreign Affairs* 28, no. 1 (1949): 43–55. For more on Huxley, see her obituary by Robert Cross, "A Voice from the Flame Trees," *The Guardian*, January 13, 1997, p. 16.

61. Pittman Potter, review of *America and the Race for World Dominion*, by Albert Demageon, *American Journal of International Law* 16, no. 1 (1922): 144–145. Potter criticized the French geographer for his alarmism. More generally, see Lake and Reynolds, *Drawing the Global Colour Line*, and Jeanne Morefield, *Empires Without Imperialism: Anglo-American Decline and the Politics of Deflection* (New York: Oxford University Press, 2014).

62. Nicholas Spykman, "The Social Background of Asiatic Nationalism," *American Journal of Sociology* 32, no. 3 (1926): 396. Spykman had not yet remade himself as the theorist of geopolitics described by subsequent generation of scholars.

63. Nathaniel Peffer, *The White Man's Dilemma: Climax of the Age of Imperialism* (New York: John Day, 1927), 304. Peffer was a longtime reporter residing in China, a regular contributor to the *Nation*, *New Republic*, and *Harper's Monthly*, and a Guggenheim awardee (1927). He joined the faculty of Columbia University in 1937, rising in the ranks to professor of international relations, where he continued to teach and publish on U.S.–East Asian relations.

64. Peffer, *White Man's Dilemma*, 304–305.

65. T. Lothrop Stoddard, *The New World of Islam* (New York: Scribner's, 1921), 43, 103. See also Spykman, "Social Background."

66. The first use I found for the term "have not country" in the U.S. press was by the peripatetic former Harvard professor of international relations and head of the Foreign Policy Association Raymond Leslie Buell, following his investigation of the Italian invasion. See "Buell Finds U.S. a War-Supply Base," *New York Times*, November 26, 1935, p. 12. Was it an intellectual import? For the debate and its

afterlives, see Douglas Rimmer, "Have-Not Nations: The Prototype," *Economic Development and Cultural Change* 27, no. 2 (1979): 307–325.

67. Hjalmar Schacht, "Germany's Colonial Demands," *Foreign Affairs* 15, no. 2 (1937): 223–234, quoting President Wilson's private correspondence with his adviser at Versailles, Colonel House, who identified these as legitimate grounds for German claims at the peace talks. Schacht was president of Germany's central bank and Hitler's minister of economy.

68. For example, Arnold Toynbee, "Peaceful Change or War? The Next State in the International Crisis," *International Affairs* 15, no. 1 (1936): 26–56; Norman Angell, *This Have and Have Not Business: Political Fantasy and Economic Fact* (London: Hamish Hamilton, 1936); Grover Clark, *The Balance Sheet of Imperialism: Facts and Figures on Colonies* (New York: Columbia University Press, 1936); Grover Clark, *A Place in the Sun* (New York: Macmillan, 1936); *The Colonial Problem: Report by a Study Group of Members of the Royal Institute of International Affairs* (London: Oxford University Press, 1937); Frederick Sherwood Dunn, *Peaceful Change: A Study of International Procedure* (New York: Council on Foreign Relations, 1937); Eugene Staley, *The Strategy of Raw Materials: A Study of America in Peace and War* (New York: Council on Foreign Relations, 1937); *Peaceful Change: Procedures, Population, Raw Materials, Colonies* (Paris: International Institute of Intellectual Co-operation, League of Nations, 1938); and Barbara Ward, *The International Share Out* (London: Thomas Nelson, 1938).

69. Schacht, "Germany's Colonial Demands," 230. Charles Roden Buxton, the Labor Party adviser on colonies and advocate for accommodating German demands quoted the die-hard imperialist Winston Churchill (September 29, 1935) to underscore the contradiction: "If we lost the Empire (as we may well do if this question of making concessions is pursued) we should be left starving in this little island with the population of a first-class power." Charles Roden Buxton, *The Alternative to War: A Program for Statesmen* (London: Allen and Unwin, 1936), 3. Ward repeats Buxton in *International Share Out*, 158.

70. For an account of the meeting and the question of colonial appeasement, see Pedersen, *Guardians*, chap. 11.

71. Eugene Staley (University of Chicago economist and leading post–World War II development theorist), quoted in *Peaceful Change: Procedures, Population, Raw Materials, Colonies*, 290.

72. For background, see Katharina Rietzler, "Counter-imperial Orientalism: Friedrich Berber and the Politics of International Law in Germany and India, 1920s–1960s," *Journal of Global History* 11 (2016): 113–134, and on the raw materials argument, specifically, 125.

73. *Peaceful Change: Procedures, Population, Raw Materials, Colonies*, 466–467, 485.

74. Ibid., 470.

75. John B. Parrish, "Iron and Steel in the Balance of World Power," *Journal of Political Economy* 64, no. 5 (1956): 369–388.

76. David S. Painter, *Oil and the American Century: The Political Economy of U.S. Foreign Oil Policy, 1941–1954* (Baltimore: Johns Hopkins University Press, 1986); Megan Black, *The Global Interior: Mineral Frontiers and American Power* (Cambridge, MA: Harvard University Press, 2018).

77. Stern, "Oil Scarcity Ideology"; Ian O. Lesser, *Resources and Strategy* (New York: St. Martin's Press, 1989), 105. See also Alfred E. Eckes Jr., *The United States and the Global Struggle for Minerals* (Austin: University of Texas Press, 1979).

78. Aubrey Graves, "1500 Here to Study Natural Resources," *Washington Post*, December 3, 1953, p. 20; Eckes, *United States and the Global Struggle*, 199. Ford followed up on the $180,000 or so it provided for the conference with a massive five-year grant, as reported in "Resources Group Gets $3,410,000 from Foundation," *Washington Post*, June 22, 1954, p. 12.

79. The phrase was made famous by cartoonist Walt Kelly on a poster for the first Earth Day (April 22, 1970), featuring his possum character Pogo.

80. Peter Ferdinand Drucker, "America Becomes a 'Have-Not' Nation," *Harper's Magazine*, April 1956, pp. 38–43; "Guru: Peter Drucker," *The Economist*, October 17, 2008, https://www.economist.com/node/12429448.

81. Arthur Maass, a water resources manager turned government professor at Harvard, provided a comprehensive review of the volumes. See Arthur Maass, review of *Resources for Freedom*, *American Political Science Review* 47, no. 1 (1953): 206–210. I have also relied on Alfred E. Eckes Jr., "The Paley Report," in Eckes, *United States and the Global Struggle for Minerals*, 175–198.

82. In fact, little was done during the Eisenhower administration in part because of opposition from Congress to aiding private investors and to the frank recognition that the government had little ability to influence where firms would invest. See Joanne Gowa, "Subsidizing Corporate Expansion Abroad: Pitfalls in the Analysis of Public and Private Power," *World Politics* 37, no. 2 (1985): 180–203.

83. See Herbert I. Schiller, "The Natural Resource Base: Where Do We Stand?" *World Politics* 16, no. 4 (1964): 668–676. It is a review of *Resources in America's Future* and a series of reports to the National Academy of Sciences, including one by "peak oil" theorist M. King Hubbert, who called the United States a have-not nation, a position that Schiller endorsed as well. Schiller was trained as an economist at New York University and wrote his PhD dissertation on the

U.S. Congress and its contribution to the United Nations Relief and Rehabilitation Administration. He apparently abandoned plans for his own book on natural resources and would instead emerge five years later as a radical critic of cultural imperialism. For a review of the Paley Commission's predictions, see Richard N. Cooper, "Resource Needs Revisited," *Brookings Papers on Economic Activities* 1975, no. 1 (1975): 238–245.

84. The senate maverick (R-NV) George Malone, a professional mining engineer, as quoted in Eckes, *United States and* the *Global Struggle for Minerals*, 206; I discuss Southern opposition to funding the Egyptian Aswan High Dam project in Robert Vitalis, *When Capitalists Collide: Business Conflict and the End of Empire in Egypt* (Berkeley: University of California Press, 1995).

85. Eckes, *United States and* the *Global Struggle for Minerals*, 206; Karen Merrill, "Oil, the American West, and U.S. Power," *Journal of American History* 99, no. 1 (2012): 203; Percy Bidwell, "Raw Materials and National Policy," *Foreign Affairs* 37, no. 1 (1958): 153.

86. Philip Marshall Brown, "Imperialism," *American Journal of International Law* 39, no. 1 (1945): 84–86.

87. Philip W. Bell, "Colonialism as a Problem in American Foreign Policy," *World Politics* 5, no. 1 (1952): 98, 101. Bell appeared ignorant of the so-called Prebisch-Singer thesis. For the growing influence of this thesis among development economists, see Charles P. Kindleberger, "The Terms of Trade and Economic Development," *Review of Economics and Statistics* 40, no. 1, pt. 2 (1958): 72–85; and for Singer's challenge to the costs, including opportunity costs of export development, see H. W. Singer, "The Distribution of Gains between Investing and Borrowing Countries," *American Economic Review* 40, no. 2 (1950): 473–485.

88. Bell, "Colonialism," 102.

89. The best study I know of the emergence of the norm of "resource sovereignty" is Christopher Dietrich, *Oil Revolution: Anticolonial Elites, Sovereign Rights, and the Economic Culture of Decolonization* (Cambridge: Cambridge University Press, 2017).

90. George Kennan, "Diary Notes of Trip to South America," February 28, 1950, pp. 17, 19, George F. Kennan Papers, Seeley G. Mudd Manuscript Library, Princeton, NJ. Chris Dietrich kindly shared a copy of this document with me.

91. Robert Strausz-Hupé, *The Balance of Tomorrow: Power and Foreign Policy in the United States* (New York: Putnam, 1945). It appeared virtually simultaneously with his dissertation, "The Balance of Tomorrow: A Reappraisal of Basic Trends in World Politics" (PhD diss., University of Pennsylvania, 1945). Norms may have been different back then because, in the book, Strausz-Hupé highlights the research contributed by his wartime acquaintance and, to be frank, client, Stefan Possony.

92. See Vitalis, *White World Order*, 153–155.

93. George F. Kennan, *The Kennan Diaries*, ed. Frank Costigliola (New York: Norton, 2014), entry for January 23, 1951, p. 304.

94. Ibid.

95. Ibid., 306.

96. Robert Strausz-Hupé and Stefan Possony, *International Relations in the Age of Conflict Between Democracy and Dictatorship* (New York: McGraw Hill, 1950), 621.

97. Bizarre, because there is not one iota of evidence that Nasser or the Egyptians generally thought in such terms. See Robert Vitalis, "The Midnight Ride of Kwame Nkrumah and Other Fables of Bandung," *Humanity* 4, no. 2 (2013): 261–288.

98. William Y. Elliott, "Colonialism: Freedom and Responsibility," in *The Idea of Colonialism*, ed. Robert Strausz-Hupé and Harry Hazard (New York: Praeger, 1958), 445. Thomas Meaney pointed me to the essay.

99. Kennan, *Kennan Diaries*, November 8 (p. 363) and November 27 (p. 364).

100. Stefan Possony, "Colonial Problems in Perspective," in Strausz-Hupé and Hazard, *Idea of Colonialism*, 36.

101. Peregrine Worsthorne, review of the *Idea of Colonialism*, ed. Robert Strausz-Hupé and Harry Hazard, *Encounter*, December 1958, p. 79. Worsthorne, the conservative British journalist and future editor in chief of the *Daily Telegraph*, offers a sympathetic critique. *Encounter* was a CIA-subsidized magazine.

102. Elliott, "Colonialism Reconsidered," 458.

103. To test the claim, I followed the suggestion of the California State University of Los Angeles historian Christopher Endy. I went to the website for the Office of Historian, Department of State, and searched the long-running series *Foreign Relations of the United States*, using the term *wily*. When I did, it returned descriptions of Kings Saud and Faisal of Saudi Arabia, Vietnam's Ho Chi Minh, Somalis in general, President Syngman Rhee of Korea, Iranian Prime Minister Mohammad Mosaddegh, Archbishop Makarios of Cyprus, and dozens of others.

104. The study of multinational companies and their evolving responses to nationalism was an emerging growth area. For an early account of how firms adjusted, see Theodore Moran, "New Deal of Raw Deal in Raw Materials," *Foreign Policy* 5 (Winter 1971–1972): 119–134.

105. See Noel Maurer, *The Empire Trap: The Rise and Fall of U.S. Intervention to Protect American Property Overseas, 1893–2013* (Princeton, NJ: Princeton University Press, 2013).

106. See Vitalis, review of *Money, Oil, and Empire in the Middle East*.

107. Davidson, "Visions of Political Islam."

108. Stephen J. Randall, *United States Foreign Oil Policy Since World War I: For Profits and Security*, 2nd ed. (Montreal: McGill-Queen's University Press, 2005), 251 (emphasis added).

109. Robert Vitalis, "The End of Third Worldism in Egyptian Studies," *Arab Studies Quarterly* 4, no. 1 (1996): 13–32.

110. See Greg Grandin, "Off Dead Center: William Appleman Williams," *The Nation*, July 20, 2009, https://www.thenation.com/article/dead-center-william -appleman-williams. A fiftieth anniversary edition appeared in 2009, attesting to its importance and, in the wake of the U.S. debacles in Afghanistan and Iraq, continuing relevance.

111. William Appleman Williams, *The Tragedy of American Diplomacy*, 50th anniv. ed. (New York: Norton, 2009), 206.

112. See, for example, the then-often-cited effort at refuting the revisionists by Robert W. Tucker, *The Radical Left and American Foreign Policy* (Baltimore: Johns Hopkins University Press, 1971). I cite this for convenience of the bibliographic references rather than as an endorsement of the views, although Tucker is one of those who did distinguish Williams and others from the neo-Marxists and other radicals. The phrase "private autocracy" is Noam Chomsky's, from his "Scholarship and Ideology: American Historians as 'Experts in Legitimation,'" *Social Scientist* 1, no. 7 (1973): 35, which discusses Tucker's extended essay. For another shorter, contemporaneous review of the revisionists, see Miles D. Wolpin, "American Imperialism: Leftist Illusion of Systemic Imperative," *Polity* 3, no. 3 (1971): 442–453.

113. For example, Harry Magdoff, *The Age of Imperialism: The Economics of U.S. Foreign Policy* (New York: Monthly Review Press, 1969).

114. Thomas Patterson, "Foreign Aid Under Wraps: The Point Four Program," *Wisconsin Magazine of History* 56, no. 2 (1972–1973): 119–126; Chomsky, "Scholarship and Ideology"; Michael Klare, "The New Imperialist Strategy," *Pakistan Forum* 3, no. 10–11 (1973): 46.

115. Among others, this was a pet "theory" of Harvard's Joseph Nye Jr., "Energy Nightmares," *Foreign Policy* 40 (Autumn 1980): 133.

116. Kenneth Waltz, "The Myth of National Interdependence," in *The International Corporation*, ed. Charles Kindleberger (Cambridge, MA: MIT Press, 1970), 205–223.

117. Tucker, *Radical Left*, 120. A young political theorist named William Caspary argued in much the same way. "The crucial question remains: Why must the U.S. dominate the countries that supply these materials? Why can they not simply be obtained in trade." And those who believed or acted as if a socialist revolution or a Soviet takeover would overthrow the raw materials order were also mistaken. "There is little reason to believe a priori that underdeveloped countries

after experiencing a revolution, Communist or otherwise, would not still sell their raw materials to the United States. They would still need foreign exchange for development purposes, and the Soviet Union and China cannot provide a market for every developing country in the way they have for Cuba." William Caspary, review of *The Age of Imperialism: The Economics of U.S. Foreign Policy*, by Harry Magdoff, *Midwest Journal of Political Science* 14, no. 4 (1970): 747.

118. "Interview with Robert Tucker," *SAIS Review* 1, no. 1 (1981): 84.

119. Adelman, "Is the Oil Shortage Real?" For more on the changing position of the oil firms, see Robert Keohane, "The Multinational Enterprise and World Political Economy," *International Organization* 26, no. 1 (1972): 84–120.

120. Chomsky, "Scholarship and Ideology," 21–22.

121. See Noam Chomsky, "After Pinkville," *New York Review of Books*, January 1, 1970, http://www.nybooks.com/articles/1970/01/01/after-pinkville. Chomsky's evidentiary source, in this instance, is a quotation by President Eisenhower taken from Magdoff, *Age of Imperialism*.

122. Tucker, *Radical Left*, 116.

123. Chomsky, "Scholarship and Ideology," 32 (emphasis added).

124. Noam Chomsky, "The Ethics of Intervention," reply to Stanley Hoffmann, *New York Review of Books*, March 27, 1969, http://www.nybooks.com/articles/1969/03/27/the-ethics-of-intervention.

125. Tucker would admit that "the embargo in itself was not significant in terms of its effects." Rather he was fearful that in the future the Arabs might, "if they so desired . . . deny us access." "Interview," 84.

126. Adapted from and with debt to Stephen M. Walt, *The Hell of Good Intentions: America's Foreign Policy Elite and the Decline of U.S. Primacy* (New York: Farrar, Straus and Giroux, 2018), xii.

CHAPTER 3

1. William Coughlin, "Arabs Cutting Oil Output 5% a Month to Gain War Goals," *Los Angeles Times*, October 18, 1973, p. 1. Later, the announced percentage cutback went up.

2. OAPEC had eleven members. Seven (Algeria, Iraq, Kuwait, Libya, Qatar, Saudi Arabia, and the United Arab Emirates) were OPEC members. Four (Bahrain, Egypt, Syria, and Tunisia) were not.

3. As Joel Darmstadter, the longtime economist for Resources for the Future, the organization that the Ford Foundation created in the 1950s, during the great raw-materials-are-running-out scare, argues, to prove that the embargo was followed through on "one would need to find statistical evidence of manipulated and extended export restrictions. No such evidence exists." That is, as he and

others emphasize, a few months' insignificant decline washes out when one considers annual figures for 1972–1973 and 1973–1974. See Joel Darmstadter, "Reflections on the Oil Shock of 40 Years Ago," http://www.rff.org/files/sharepoint/WorkImages/Download/RFF-Resources-186_Feature-Darmstadter.pdf. Also see Timothy Mitchell, *Carbon Democracy: Political Power in the Age of Oil* (London: Verso, 2011), 174–175.

4. The most reliable and clearly written account I know is Fiona Venn, *The Oil Crisis* (London: Longman, 2002), 8–9.

5. One can do no better here than consult the compendium *Oil Shock*, edited by Bini, Garavini, and Romero.

6. Casey Bukro, "American Oil Industry Has Only 27 Years Left Before Its Oil Runs Out," *Chicago Tribune*, March 7, 1973, p. 1. In addition, see William Hines, "Looking Forward to a Hot Summer? More Power to You," *Philadelphia Inquirer*, June 1, 1972, p. 41.

7. See Richard Vietor, *Energy Policy in America Since 1945: A Study of Business Government Relations* (Cambridge: Cambridge University Press, 1984), 144.

8. Allen L. Hammond, "Energy: Ford Foundation Study Urges Action on Conservation," *Science* 186, no. 4162 (1974): 428.

9. S. David Freeman, *Winning Our Energy Independence* (Layton, UT: Gibbs Smith, 2007); see also S. David Freeman, *The Green Cowboy: An Energetic Life* (Bloomington, IN: AuthorHouse, 2016).

10. Freeman, *Green Cowboy*, 42. The story of the Ford Foundation Energy Policy Project needs a historian to explore the archival record and provide a full account. It is indisputably true that Mobil's William Tavoulareas was Freeman's implacable foe, the author of the longest critical comment included in *Time to Choose*, which he then reprised in a stand-alone book, *Debate on a Time to Choose* (New York: Ballinger, 1977), a dialog between him and Bundy's old deputy at the National Security Council, Carl Kaysen, who had just joined the faculty at MIT. By then the foundation was distancing itself from Freeman, and Kaysen's defense of the report, for which he also served as an adviser, conceded its one-sided, populist, antibusiness, and conservationist commitments.

11. "Import Quotas Blamed for Shortages of Fuel," *Los Angeles Times*, January 26, 1973, p. 22. In his autobiography, Freeman mistakenly writes that he gave this speech during the period of the oil embargo rather than eight months earlier, while leaving out his call then for increased oil imports. Freeman, *Green Cowboy*, 43.

12. Sebastian Herbstreuth, *Oil and American Identity: A Culture of Dependency and US Foreign Policy* (London: I. B. Tauris, 2016), 91. It is by far the best study of the dramaturgy of the 1973 energy crisis.

13. Alan L. Otten, "Consumers Versus the Energy Crisis," *Wall Street Journal*, March 15, 1973, p. 16.

14. Energy Policy Project, *Time to Choose*, xi.

15. S. David Freeman, "Government's Role in Oil: A Proposal," *Washington Post*, July 7, 1974, p. B5; S. David Freeman, *Energy: The New Era* (New York: Vintage, 1974).

16. Ford Foundation, *Exploring Energy Choices: A Preliminary Report of the Ford Foundation's Energy Policy Project* (New York: Ford Foundation, 1974); Ford Foundation, *A Time to Choose: America's Energy Future* (Cambridge, MA: Ballinger, 1974). For contemporary reviews that, while sympathetic, underscore the problems, see Allen V. Kneese, "A Time to Choose: America's Energy Future," *Challenge* 18, no. 3 (1975): 57–60; Charles Stewart, "A Time to Choose: America's Energy Future," *Journal of Business* 49, no. 1 (1976): 113–114; and Richard T. Newcomb, "Review," *Journal of Economic Literature* 14, no. 1 (1976): 117–123. One that is more positive than most is Kai N. Lee, "Energy Politics vs. Energy Policies," *Public Administration Review* 36, no. 1 (1976): 110–115. Two recent histories that discuss Freeman's report are Robert L. Bradley Jr., *Capitalism at Work: Business, Government, and Energy* [dedicated to Charles Koch] (Austin, TX: Scrivener, 2009), 244–249, which recounts the controversy, and Jacobs, *Panic at the Pump*, 133–134, which does not.

17. Energy Policy Project, *Time to Choose*, 1.

18. For a contemporary account, see V. H. Oppenheim, "The Past: We Pushed Them," *Foreign Policy* 25 (Winter 1976–1977): 24–57. The works of two historians who come to some stark conclusions about these matters are Petersen, *Richard Nixon, Great Britain and the Anglo-American Alignment*, and Andrew Scott Cooper, *Oil Kings: How the U.S., Iran, and Saudi Arabia Changed the Balance of Power in the Middle East* (New York: Simon and Schuster, 2011). Guiliano Garavini rightly cautions us against the idea that the government and oil companies were behind the price increase. See his *The Rise and Fall of OPEC in the Twentieth Century* (London: Oxford University Press, 2019).

19. Kenneth E. Boulding, "Energy Policy in Black and White: Belated Reflections on a Time to Choose," in *Geography, Resources, and the Environment*, vol. 2, *Themes from the Work of Gilbert F. White*, ed. Robert W. Kates and Ian Burton (Chicago: University of Chicago Press, 1986): 311. White was the chairman of the Energy Policy Project advisory board. Contrast White with the breathless Jay Hakes, former head of the Energy Information Administration, in *A Declaration of Energy Independence: How Freedom from Foreign Oil Can Improve National Security, Our Economy, and the Environment* (New York: Wiley, 2008).

20. Douglas R. Bohi, "On the Macroeconomic Effects of Energy Price Shocks," *Resources and Energy* 13, no. 2 (1991): 145–162. The debate about precise effects continues, although this is a world removed from the popular representations. In addition, price volatility has come to matter less over time. See Kenneth Rogoff, "Oil and the Global Economy," paper presented at the International Energy Forum Secretariat Meeting of Ministers and Oil Company Presidents, Riyadh, November 19, 2005, http://citeseerx.ist.psu.edu/viewdoc/download?doi=10.1.1 .588.9031&rep=rep1&type=pdf.

21. Hendrik Houthakker, "Whatever Happened to the Energy Crisis?" *Energy Journal* 4, no. 2 (1983): 1–8. The article reprints his key address to the fourth annual meeting of the International Association of Energy Economics in 1982, which makes the point that the public debates proceed as if basic economics didn't matter. He gets the date of the Freeman report wrong, however.

22. M. A. Adelman, "U.S. Energy Policy," in *No Time to Confuse: A Critique of the Final Report of the Energy Policy Project of the Ford Foundation, "A Time to Choose: America's Energy Future"* (San Francisco: Institute for Contemporary Studies, 1975): 27. The institute was founded in 1975 by Ronald Reagan's adviser Edwin Meese III and rose to prominence with Regan's election in 1979. See Wallace Turner, "Research Institute Rises with Reagan," *New York Times*, January 26, 1981, p. 23.

23. Armen A. Alchian, "An Introduction to Confusion," in *No Time to Confuse*, 1. My description of Alchian follows Philip Mirowski and Dieter Plehwe, eds., *The Road from Mont Pelerin: The Making of the Neoliberal Thought Collective* (Cambridge, MA: Harvard University Press, 2015).

24. Kimberly Amadeo, "OPEC Oil Embargo, Its Causes, and the Effects of the Crisis," *The Balance*, March 30, 2019, https://www.thebalance.com/opec-oil -embargo-causes-and-effects-of-the-crisis-3305806. The account of causes and effects only gets worse.

25. Meghan L. O'Sullivan, "40 Years After Embargo, OPEC Is over a Barrel," *Bloomberg*, October 17, 2013, https://www.bloomberg.com/view/articles/2013 -10-17/40-years-after-embargo-opec-is-over-a-barrel. O'Sullivan was assistant to Paul Bremer in the early days of the Iraq invasion before moving to the National Security Council. She wrote a doctoral dissertation on the Sri Lankan civil war.

26. Daniel Yergin, "Why OPEC No Longer Calls the Shots," *Wall Street Journal*, October 14, 2013, https://www.wsj.com/articles/daniel-yergin-why-opec -no-longer-calls-the-shots-1381793163; Warren Stroebel, "Analysis: Awash in Oil, U.S. Reshapes Mideast Role 40 Years After OPEC Embargo," *Reuters Business News*, October 17, 2013, https://www.reuters.com/article/us-usa-energy-geopolitics -analysis/analysis-awash-in-oil-u-s-reshapes-mideast-role-40-years-after-opec

-embargo-idUSBRE99G14P20131017; Robbie Diamond (founder of Securing America's Energy Future), "OPEC Embargo: Forty Years Later," *The Hill*, October 15, 2013, http://thehill.com/blogs/congress-blog/energy-a-environment/328393 -opec-embargo-40-years-later.

27. Marc Lallanilla, "OPEC Oil Embargo: A Timeline," *Live Science*, March 21, 2014, https://www.livescience.com/44277-opec-oil-embargo-timeline.html.

28. See "The Oil Weapon: Past, Present, and Future," *Oil and Gas Journal*, May 2, 2005, https://www.ogj.com/articles/print/volume-103/issue-17/general -interest/the-oil-weapon-past-present-and-future.html.

29. "October 17, 1973 CE: OPEC Embargoes Oil to U.S.," *National Geographic*, https://www.nationalgeographic.org/thisday/oct17/opec-embargoes-oil -us (accessed October 23, 2019).

30. Andrew B. Whitford, "Estimation of Several Political Action Effects of Energy Prices," https://arxiv.org/ftp/arxiv/papers/1502/1502.07265.pdf (accessed October 23, 2019).

31. Alex Chadwick, "The Marketplace Report: OPEC Embargo Anniversary," *NPR*, October 17, 2003, https://www.npr.org/templates/story/story.php ?storyId=1469425.

32. Glenn P. Hastedt, *Encyclopedia of American Foreign Policy* (New York: Facts on File, 2004), 372–374.

33. Edward Ayers, *American Passages: A History of the United States*, 4th ed. (Boston: Wadsworth, 2009), 903.

34. National Museum of American History, "Energy Crisis," http://american history.si.edu/american-enterprise-exhibition/consumer-era/energy-crisis (accessed October 23, 2019).

35. See David S. Painter, "Letter to the Editor," *Diplomatic History* 40, no. 4 (2016): 806.

36. The ability to control production is what permits a cartel to influence price. Algeria, Iraq, and Libya were the exceptions, and Iraq opposed production cutbacks. Nationalization of the Western firms followed in the wake of 1973 as one of the outcomes of the moment. OPEC only began to assign production quotas in 1982. See Jeff Colgan, "The Emperor Has No Clothes: The Limits of OPEC in the Global Oil Market," *International Organization* 68, no. 3 (2014): 601.

37. For an exhaustive account of these ideas and their consequences at the time, see Jacobs, *Panic at the Pump*.

38. The *New York Times* published its first op-ed column on September 21, 1970. On its twentieth anniversary, in 1990, the *Times* celebrated with a twenty-page Sunday special section featuring the best op-ed pieces printed over the past two decades, the entire thing paid for (three hundred thousand dollars) by Exxon

Mobil (then Mobil), which had been buying ("advocacy advertising") space on the page routinely from the beginning.

39. Daniel Sargent, *A Superpower Transformed: The Remaking of American Foreign Relations in the 1970s* (Oxford: Oxford University Press, 2015); Mitchell, *Carbon Democracy*; Jacobs, *Panic at the Pump*; Bini, Garavini, and Romero, *Oil Shock*; Garavini, *The Rise and Fall of OPEC*.

40. See, for example, Michael Bardo and Barry Eichengreen, eds., *A Retrospective on the Bretton Woods System: Lessons for International Monetary Reform* (Chicago: University of Chicago Press, 2007).

41. Robert Mabro, the Alexandria-born development economist turned energy expert (as head of an OPEC-created Oxford think tank) offered a preliminary account in "On Oil Price Concepts," Oxford Institute for Energy Studies Working Paper 3, 1984, https://www.oxfordenergy.org/wpcms/wp-content/uploads/2010/11/WPM3-OnOilPriceConcepts-RMabro-1984.pdf. In addition, see Garavini, *Rise and Fall of OPEC*, and Mitchell, *Carbon Democracy*, 166–170, 184–185.

42. Mitchell, *Carbon Democracy*, 185.

43. Garavini, *Rise and Fall of OPEC*, 139. Venezuela's arrangements with the multinationals was different and its revenues rose and fall with the market. The newer entrants to OPEC, for example, Libya and Nigeria, insisted that the companies duplicate the arrangements that the Gulf producers enjoyed.

44. Mitchell, *Carbon Democracy*, 186.

45. Ibid., 174–175. As Adelman's later research showed, there was never any shortfall of supply. M. A. Adelman, *The Genie Out of the Bottle: World Oil Supply Since 1970* (Cambridge, MA: MIT Press, 1995), 110–111. The former Italian oil industry official Leonardo Maugeri said that the shortfall at its most severe was small enough to be covered from existing inventories. Leonardo Maugeri, *The Age of Oil: The Mythology, History, and Future of the World's Most Controversial Resource* (Guilford: Lyons Press, 2006), 113. Maugeri calls the embargo itself a myth.

46. Dietrich, *Oil Revolution*.

47. For a detailed account, see David Glasner, *Politics, Prices, and Petroleum: The Political Economy of Energy* (Cambridge, MA: Ballinger, 1985).

48. For details, see Jacobs, *Panic at the Pump*, chap. 8.

49. For an early account of the psychology of the embargo, see S. Fred Singer, "Limits to Arab Oil Power," *Foreign Policy* 30 (Spring 1978): 53–67.

50. The best account I know of the social construction of the "oil weapon" idea as an existential threat is found in Herbstreuth, *Oil and American Identity*.

51. C. Fred Bergsten, "The Threat Is Real," *Foreign Policy* 14 (Spring 1974): 84–90; Douglas R. Bohi and Joel Darmstadter, "The Energy Upheavals of the 1970s: Policy Watershed or Aberration?" in *The Energy Crisis: Unresolved Issues*

and Enduring Legacies, ed. David Lewis Feldman (Baltimore: Johns Hopkins University Press, 1996), 32–33.

52. Walter Russell Mead, testimony to the U.S. Senate Committee on Armed Services, August 5, 2015, https://www.armed-services.senate.gov/imo/media/doc/Mead_08-05-15.pdf.

53. Garavini refers to Kissinger here at the time when he was President Nixon's national security adviser: "The minutes of Kissinger's staff meeting constitute an almost inexhaustible well of caustic sarcasm and thinly veiled threat aimed at the Arab oil producers," including his nostalgia for a time when one could simply land some forces and divide up the oil fields. "I am not sure that this is so insane." Garavini, *Rise and Fall of OPEC*, 221, citing the transcript of Kissinger's October 26, 1973, staff meeting. For the "folly" of sovereignty and of tolerating "nationalization of the oil fields," see Kennan, *Diaries*, entry for January 4, 1986, p. 565. Defense Secretary James Schlesinger warned the British ambassador to the United States Lord Cromer (yes, the great-great grandson of the British banker who governed Egypt for a dozen years at the turn of the twentieth century) that the Nixon government "would not tolerate threats from "under-developed, under-populated countries." See Glenn Frankel, "U.S. Mulled Seizing Oil Fields in 1973," *Washington Post*, January 1, 2004, https://www.washingtonpost.com/archive/politics/2004/01/01/us-mulled-seizing-oil-fields-in-73/0661ef3e-027e-4758-9c41-90a40bbcfc4d/?utm_term=.9fd99f720f4e.

54. Cooper, *Oil Kings*, 156. See also David Wight, "The Petrodollar Era and Relations Between the United States and the Middle East and North Africa, 1969–1980," (PhD diss., University of California, Irvine, 2014), 114.

55. See Cooper, *Oil Kings*, 234, which confirms that Edward Luttwak ("the Machiavelli of Maryland") was a primary but not sole author, as many others have speculated over the years. Luttwak's record of routine and howlingly wrong strategic forecasts is analyzed in Posner, *Public Intellectuals*. See, as well, Thomas Meaney, "The Machiavelli of Maryland," *The Guardian*, December 9, 2015, https://www.theguardian.com/world/2015/dec/09/edward-luttwak-machiavelli-of-maryland.

56. Edward Friedland, Paul Seabury, and Aaron Wildavsky, "Oil and the Decline of Western Power," *Political Science Quarterly* 90, no. 3 (1975): 437–450. This article is the "teaser" version of their book, Edward Friedland, Paul Seabury, and Aaron Wildavsky, *The Great Détente Disaster: Oil and the Decline of American Foreign Policy* (New York: Basic Books, 1975).

57. Though not typically framed in these terms, the argument migrated leftward, as writer after writer disparaged the capacity of the oil producers to act independently of the oil companies, the "real" engineers of the price shocks. The Irish Marxist scholar of the Gulf, Fred Halliday, was among the few who refused

the caricature of the Saudis and others as puppets of the United States and of the multinationals.

58. See Peter B. Heller, review of *The Great Détente Disaster*, by Edward Friedland, Paul Seabury, and Aaron Wildavsky, *Journal of International Affairs* 30, no. 1 (1976): 125–126.

59. See Daniel Yergin, "The Economic Political Military Solution," *New York Times*, February 16, 1975, p. SM13. Yergin was a practicing journalist and fellow at Harvard's Center for International Affairs when he published his second feature in the Sunday Magazine. The first one was on Noam Chomsky's revolution in linguistics. He was also still a few years away from publishing his first book on the origins of the Cold War, based on his Cambridge University history dissertation, which he framed as a critique of the Cold War revisionists. He was said to be primarily interested in the issue of nuclear arms control until he was hired as a staffer at Harvard Business School for a project on energy. The OPEC revolution led to his making millions from the energy consulting firm he began in 1982.

60. "Oil prices continually played 'catch-up' with gold prices throughout the decade." David Hammes and Douglas Wills, "Black Gold: The End of Bretton Woods and the Oil-Price Shocks of the 1970s," *Independent Review* 9, no. 4 (2005): 507. In addition, see Mahmoud A. El-Gamal and Amy M. Jaffe, *Oil, Dollars, Debt, and Crises: The Global Curse of Black Gold* (Cambridge: Cambridge University Press, 2009), 4–5.

61. While OPEC continues to exist despite many predictions over the past half century, Colgan, "Emperor," argues that it has failed as a cartel, a position that Garavini, *Rise and Fall*, takes as well, whatever the differences between the two authors, methods, and perspectives. Leonard Maugeri, the Italian oil executive, too, sees the OPEC era as short lived. Maugeri, *Age of Oil*, 121.

62. Mabro, "Oil Price Concepts," 23. As Bohi and Darmstadter put it in "Energy Upheavals of the 1970s," "The events of the 1970s could not be repeated in the world of today. Energy markets work in fundamentally different ways than they did two decades ago. . . . Oil is now traded much like any other commodity, with active spot and futures markets, anonymous transactions at open prices, and instantaneous responses to changes in market conditions" (54).

63. Bohi and Darmstadter, "Energy Upheavals of the 1970s," 33. See also Vietor, *Energy Policy*, 263–271; and Jacobs, *Panic at the Pump*.

64. See Allan Pulsipher, "Watershed, Aberration, and Hallucination: The Last Twenty Years," in *The Energy Crisis: Unresolved Issues and Enduring Legacies*, ed. David Lewis Feldman (Baltimore: Johns Hopkins University Press, 1996), 73–80. Pulsipher trained in economics at Tulane, and between stints teaching,

served as senior staff economist for the president's Council of Economic Advisers (1973–1975), program officer for the Ford Foundation's division of resources for the environment (1977–1980), and chief economist for the Tennessee Valley Authority (1980–1988). At the time of his death, he was associate executive director and Marathon Oil Company Professor of Energy Policy for the Center for Energy Studies and a professor of environmental policy at Louisiana State University. See LSU Center for Energy Studies, Allan G. Pulsipher obituary, November 16, 2017, https://lsu.edu/ces/about/facultystaff/pulsipher.php.

65. Andrew Bacevich, *America's War for the Middle East: A Military History* (New York: Random House, 2016).

66. Kai Bird's riveting *A Good Spy: The Life and Death of Robert Ames* (New York: Broadway Books, 2014), tells the story of the Lebanon intervention and the behind-the-scenes intelligence operations better than any other.

67. On the Iran-Iraq War, see the luminous Toby Craig Jones, "After the Pipelines: Energy and the Flow of War in the Persian Gulf," *South Atlantic Quarterly* 116, no. 2 (2017): 417–425.

68. F. Gregory Gause III, "The Illogic of Dual Containment," *Foreign Affairs*, March–April 1994, pp. 56–66.

69. Pulsipher, "Watershed," 74.

70. Olav Njølstad, "Shifting Priorities: The Persian Gulf in U.S. Strategic Planning in the Carter Years," *Cold War History* 4, no. 3 (2004): 21. Tellingly, when the U.S. embassy in Tehran, in April 1977, enumerated the country's principal interest in Iran, oil was not even mentioned. Rather, it was to maintain "a stable, independent, non-communist and cooperative Iran [that was able] . . . to resist potential Soviet aggressiveness . . . and to continue its role for stability in the Persian Gulf, Middle East, and South Asia" (25).

71. Soviet energy exports increased by 270 percent between 1970 and 1988, making the country almost totally dependent on the oil and gas sector for foreign exchange. See Jeronim Perovic, "The Soviet Union's Rise as an International Energy Power: A Short History," in *Cold War Energy: A Transnational History of Soviet Oil and Gas,* ed. Jeronim Perovic (Cham, Switzerland: Palgrave Macmillan, 2017), 26; and Jeronim Perovic and Dunja Krempin, "'The Key Is in Our Hands': Soviet Energy Strategy During Détente and the Global Oil Crises of the 1970s," in "The Energy Crises of the 1970s: Anticipations and Reactions in the Industrialized World," ed. Frank Bösch and Rüdiger Graf, special issue, *Historical Social Research/ Historiche Sozialforschung* 39, no. 4 (2014): 138. For a contemporary account of then highly contested claims about the Soviets running out of oil, see Richard Burt, "U.S. Aides Say Soviet May Look to Persian Gulf for Oil in the 1980's," *New York Times,*

April 15, 1980, p. A1. For a historian's account of the pervasiveness of these highly problematic beliefs, see Davidson, "Visions of Political Islam."

72. John Gosliko, "World Speculates on Nature of a Reagan Foreign Policy," *Washington Post*, July 12, 1980, p. A8.

73. Ibid.; Francis Fukuyama, "The Soviet Threat to the Persian Gulf," Paper P-6596, presented at the Security Conference on Asia and the Pacific, Tokyo, January 1980, Afghanistan Collection, Digital National Security Archive. For Kemp and Ross, see James Mann, *The Rise of the Vulcans: The History of Bush's War Cabinet* (New York: Viking, 2004), 79–81, and Geoffrey Kemp, "Scarcity and Strategy," *Foreign Affairs* 56, no. 2 (1978): 396–414.

74. See Dennis Ross, "Considering Soviet Threats to the Persian Gulf," *International Security* 6, no. 2 (1981): 159–180. Biographies of Ross note that he completed a PhD dissertation at UCLA, but I have not been able to find it either in the University of California library catalog or in the ProQuest database of dissertations. In addition, see W. Scott Thompson, "The Persian Gulf and the Correlation of Forces," *International Security* 7, no. 1 (1982): 157–180. Thompson, who taught at the Fletcher School and joined the Reagan administration, believed that international relations scholars failed to judge the Soviet threat seriously enough!

75. Dennis Ross, "The Soviet Union and the Persian Gulf," *Political Science Quarterly* 99, no. 4 (1984–1985): 615–636.

76. See Brian Auten, *Carter's Conversion: The Hardening of American Defense Policy* (Columbia: University of Missouri Press, 2008), 156–165.

77. Robert Kaiser, "Memo Sets Stage in Assessing U.S., Soviet Strength," *Washington Post*, July 6, 1977, https://www.washingtonpost.com/archive/politics/1977/07/06/memo-sets-stage-in-assessing-us-soviet-strength/079e53ff-0d84-48ba-81c1-b890f0412a5d/?utm_term=.65112f51846c.

78. Odom, "Cold War Origins"; Njølstad, "Shifting Priorities." See, as well, David S. Painter, "From Linkage to Economic Warfare: Soviet-American Relations and the End of the Cold War," in Perovic, *Cold War Energy*, 282–318.

79. Andrew Bacevich has a nice account of the increased number of expert (and not so expert) views of Soviet expansion in *America's War for the Middle East*, 31–32, ranging from Richard Pipes to George Ball.

80. "Ritual Reagan," *Wall Street Journal*, November 15, 1979, p. 26.

81. "Reagan Says Soviets Intend to Use Russian-Armed Cuban Troops in Mideast," *Los Angeles Times*, February 8, 1980, p. 23.

82. Amos Perlmutter, "The Conflagration Now Threatening the Persian Gulf," *Wall Street Journal*, November 20, 1980, p. 10. For the larger list of military men, intellectuals associated with conservative think tanks such as the Hoover Institution, the Center for Strategic and International Studies, the American Enter-

prise Institute, and assorted Beltway insiders assembled to advise Reagan, see Don Oberdorfer, "Reagan Names 67 Foreign, Defense Policy Advisers," *Washington Post*, April 22, 1980, p. A4.

83. Hoagland, "How Strong Are the Saudis?"

84. It is no coincidence that the first challenges to the strategic rationales for securing oil access by professors of international relations in a generation appeared at this time. Robert Johnson, "The Persian Gulf in U.S. Strategy: A Skeptical View," *International Security* 14, no. 1 (1989): 122–160, would become a touchstone for later skeptics writing after the 2003 invasion of Iraq. Lipschutz, *When Nations Clash*.

85. David Painter, "From Linkage to Economic Warfare," in Perovic, *Cold War Energy*, 304.

86. Zbigniew Brzezinski, "We Need More Muscle in the Gulf, Less in NATO," *Washington Post*, June 7, 1987, p. B1. My old colleague at Penn, Alvin Rubenstein, was another true believer who warned that the Soviets were poised to undertake a new wave of expansion into the Third World in the 1990s. See his *Moscow's Third World Strategy* (Princeton, NJ: Princeton University Press, 1988).

87. Alexei Vasiliev, *Russia's Middle East Policy: From Lenin to Putin* (London: Routledge, 2018), 241–242.

88. Fred Halliday, *Soviet Policy in the Arc of Crisis* (Washington, DC: Institute of Policy Studies, 1981). Halliday was a pioneering researcher and journalist who covered the revolutionary movements in the Arabian Peninsula. He was a fellow at the Amsterdam-based Transnational Institute in the 1970s and early 1980s, before completing his doctorate on the foreign policy of the People's Democratic Republic of Yemen at the School of Oriental and African Studies, and starting to teach international relations at the London School of Economics in 1983.

89. Ibid., 2. The point still holds. The main takeaway of Council on Foreign Relations senior fellow Steven Cook's study *False Dawn: Protest, Democracy, and Violence in the New Middle East* (New York: Oxford University Press, 2017) is that the United States has virtually no capacity to shape the politics of the region going forward.

90. Halliday, *Soviet Policy*, 10–17.

91. Ibid., 49.

92. Halliday drives home his point about this geo-ignorance in *Soviet Policy*: "By compressing geography [like the Risk game board does, by the way], Soviet advances in Afghanistan or Ethiopia are seen as threatening the Gulf itself: such interpretations ignore the fact that the easiest way for Russia to hit at Western assets and communications lines in the Gulf is by rocket and air strikes from bases within Soviet territory" (17). Others were equally skeptical of the strategic wherewithal of the Beltway's militarists. Fred Kaplan exposed the flaws in the reigning assessment of Soviet nuclear capacities while still a PhD student at MIT. See Fred Kaplan,

Dubious Specter: A Skeptical Look at the Soviet Nuclear Threat (Washington, DC: Institute for Policy Studies, 1980). Back then, the IPS mattered.

93. See Brandon Wolfe-Hunnicutt, "The Paranoid Style in American Diplomacy: Oil and the Limits of Power in Iraq, 1958–1972" (unpublished manuscript, 2019).

94. Vasiliev, *Russia's Middle East Policy*, 281.

95. See Davidson, "Visions of Political Islam," 151–180. He was a PhD student of Marilyn Young's who I pressed to look for evidence of any self-consciousness on the part of men like Brzezinski about the problems in their ideas regarding access to oil and so forth.

96. Ragaei El Mallakh, book reviews, *Journal of Economic Literature* 18, no. 2 (1980): 642–647.

97. Vitalis, *America's Kingdom*, 274–275.

98. For a far less rosy view of the future of the "fracking boom," see Bethany McLean, *Saudi America: The Truth About Fracking and How It's Changing the World* (New York: Columbia Global Reports, 2018).

99. Lawrence Wright, "The Dark Bounty of Texas Oil," *New Yorker*, January 1, 2018, https://www.newyorker.com/magazine/2018/01/01/the-dark-bounty-of-texas-oil (emphasis added).

100. I am grateful to Michael Lynch for this last point.

CHAPTER 4

1. Vitalis, *America's Kingdom*.

2. On this and other clichés in the Aramco arsenal that its executives began to worry about as Saudi nationalists began to challenge the company's privileges, see Robert Vitalis, "Wallace Stegner's Arabian Discovery: The Imperial Blind Spots in a Continental Vision," *Pacific Historical Review* 76, no. 3 (2007): 405–438.

3. Robert Vitalis, "Black Gold, White Crude: An Essay on American Exceptionalism, Hierarchy, and Hegemony in the Gulf," *Diplomatic History* 26, no. 2 (2002): 185–213.

4. Will Dana, "Recipe for Disaster," interview with Thomas Friedman, *Rolling Stone*, October 17, 2002, pp. 62–64.

5. "Trump: Saudi King Wouldn't Last 'Two Weeks' without U.S. Support," *Al Jazeera*, October 3, 2018, https://www.aljazeera.com/news/2018/10/trump-saudi-king-wouldn-weeks-support-181003053438418.html.

6. David Ottaway, "U.S.-Saudi Relations Are at Their Lowest Point Since 9/11," *Axios*, October 16, 2018, https://www.axios.com/ussaudi-relations-are-at-their-lowest-point-since-911-d107b2a2-171e-4c6a-bf47-91f95b3fbac3.html.

7. For a reminder of those dark days, see Vitalis, *America's Kingdom*, xxvi–xxvii.

8. On Sanger and his study, *Arabian Peninsula* (Ithaca: Cornell University Press, 1954), drafted in 1948–1949, see Vitalis, *America's Kingdom*, 32–33.

9. Fern Racine Gold and Melvin Conant, *Access to Oil—the United States Relationship with Saudi Arabia and Iran* (Washington, DC: U.S. Government Printing Office, 1977).

10. Douglas Little, *American Orientalism: The United States and the Middle East Since 1945* (Chapel Hill: University of North Carolina Press, 2002).

11. Robert Kaiser and David Ottaway, "Saudi Leader's Anger Revealed Shaky Ties," *Washington Post*, February 10, 2001, p. A1.

12. Ibid.

13. Rudy Abramson, "1945 Meeting of FDR and Saudi King Was Pivotal for Relations," *Los Angeles Times*, August 9, 1990, http://articles.latimes.com/1990-08-09/news/mn-388_1_king-saud.

14. Kaiser and Ottaway, "Saudi Leader's Anger Revealed Shaky Ties," A1, A10. Prince Bandar was a main source for the account, and Ottaway would go on to write his biography, *The King's Messenger: Prince Bandar bin Sultan and America's Tangled Relationship with Saudi Arabia* (New York: Walker, 2008).

15. See Robert Vitalis, "Sons and Heirs," review of *The Bin Ladens: The Story of a Family and Its Fortune*, by Steve Coll, *London Review of Books*, December 4, 2008, pp. 15–16.

16. Robert Kaiser and David Ottaway, "Oil for Security Fueled Close Ties," *Washington Post*, February 11, 2001, pp. A1, A7, A16–A17.

17. Ibid., A1, A17. A graduate school friend of mine wrote a dissertation and first book on the question back in the 1990s. See David Spiro, *The Hidden Hand of American Hegemony: Petrodollar Recycling and International Markets* (Ithaca, NY: Cornell University Press, 1999). But twelve years after the *Post* story, a Bloomberg reporter purports to finally unlock the secret; see Andrea Wong, "The Untold Story Behind Saudi Arabia's 41-Year U.S. Debt Secret," *Bloomberg*, May 30, 1916, https://www.bloomberg.com/news/features/2016-05-30/the-untold-story-behind-saudi-arabia-s-41-year-u-s-debt-secret, and scroll down to find an off-hand reference to Spiro's book!

18. See Comptroller General of the United States, "The U.S.-Saudi Arabian Joint Commission on Economic Cooperation," ID-79-7, March 22, 1979, https://www.gao.gov/assets/130/126054.pdf. The best scholarly account we have to date is found toward the end of Victor McFarland, "Living in Never-Never Land: The United States, Saudi Arabia, and Oil in the 1970s" (PhD diss., Yale University, 2014).

19. J. B. Kelly, *Arabia, the Gulf and the West* (New York: Basic Books, 1980), 263–264. J. B. Kelly argues that the West suffered numerous illusions about the oilcrats. The book was his entrée to Washington and for a while the Reagan administration, before the latter opted to sell Airborne Warning and Control System (AWACS) aircraft to the Saudis, which Kelly tried to stop. See "Professor JB Kelly," *The Telegraph*, September 24, 2009, https://www.telegraph.co.uk/news/obituaries/politics-obituaries/6227955/Professor-JB-Kelly.html.

20. Kelly was "wrong in thinking that any such agreement was ever reached or even seriously contemplated." William Quandt, *Saudi Arabia in the 1980s: Foreign Policy, Security, and Oil* (Washington, DC: Brookings Institution, 1980), 130.

21. Kaiser and Ottaway, "Oil for Security Fueled Close Ties," A7.

22. Rachel Bronson, *Thicker than Oil: America's Uneasy Partnership with Saudi Arabia* (New York: Oxford University Press, 2006), 3, 42; see also Robert Vitalis, "Thinner than Air," review of *Thicker than Oil*, by Rachel Bronson, *Middle East Report* 242 (March 2007): 44–45.

23. See Daniel Yergin, "Protecting Oil Means Protecting Balance of Power," *Los Angeles Times*, March 10, 1991, p. M2, which argues that, in stopping Saddam Hussein, who was allegedly seeking domination over Gulf oil reserves, President Bush was following a policy laid down by FDR. Yergin, then head of Cambridge Energy Resources, would publish his tome *The Prize* that year, although it would take another ten years for the idea to catch on.

24. Vitalis, *America's Kingdom*, xxv.

25. Quoted in Ben Norton, "'Oil for Security': Ex–CIA Director Michael Hayden Describes Cozy U.S. Relationship with Saudi Dictatorship in New Book," *Salon*, February 26, 2016, https://www.salon.com/2016/02/26/oil_for_security _ex_cia_director_michael_hayden_describes_cozy_u_s_relationship_with_saudi _dictatorship_in_new_book (emphasis added).

26. "Saudi Arabia Fast Facts," *CNN*, October 2, 2019, https://www.cnn.com/2015/04/01/middleeast/saudi-arabia-fast-facts/index.html.

27. Bruce Riedel, *Kings and Presidents: Saudi Arabia and the United States Since 1945* (Washington, DC: Brookings Institution Press, 2018), 4.

28. "A Chronology: The House of Saud," *Frontline*, August 1, 2005, https://www.pbs.org/wgbh/pages/frontline/shows/saud/cron (emphasis added).

29. Jeanne Leroux, "The Secret to Our Nation's Security," Counterpunch, March 10, 2017, https://www.counterpunch.org/2017/03/10/the-secret-to-our -nations-security.

30. See the trailer for the film *Blood and Oil*, at https://mediaed.wistia .com/medias/pf59bp467a?goal=0_8555fd0625-a0189497e7-393387605&mc_cid= a0189497e7&mc_eid=888abf784e.

31. Gawdat Baghat, "Saudi Arabia and the War on Terrorism," *Arab Studies Quarterly* 26, no. 1 (2004): 51–63.

32. Huber, *Lifeblood*, 104.

33. Sarah, "Account for the Importance of the United States during the Twentieth Century," *Tutor Hunt*, September 29, 2013, https://www.tutorhunt.com/resource/7614.

34. Phyllis Bennis, introductory remarks to a panel on U.S.-Saudi relations, 2016 Summit on Saudi Arabia, Washington, DC, March 5, 2016. Video of the event is available at https://www.salon.com/2016/03/10/inside_the_first_ever_summit_calling_for_an_end_to_the_suicidal_death_pact_between_the_u_s_and_saudi_arabia. In the video—I was on the panel, where I previewed the argument of this book—you can see my bewilderment, and not just at her garbling many basic facts.

35. "Kingdom of the Unjust," *C-SPAN*, November 14, 2016, https://www.c-span.org/video/?418395-1/medea-benjamin-discusses-kingdom-unjust.

36. William A. Eddy, *F.D.R. Meets Ibn Saud* (New York: American Friends of the Middle East, 1954); "Memorandum of Conversation between the King of Saudi Arabia (Abdul Aziz Al Saud) and President Roosevelt, February 14, 1945, Aboard the U.S.S. 'Quincy,'" February 14, 1945, https://history.state.gov/historicaldocuments/frus1945v08/d2. Even Yergin says the record is silent about oil: "Whatever was or was not said, both men knew that it was central to the emerging relationship between their two countries." Yergin, *Prize*, 404. Bennis and Benjamin go quite a bit further, not only intuiting what both leaders thought but also imagining what was said, based on false beliefs and factitious evidence. I am indebted to Rosie Bsheer for providing me a copy of Ibn Saud's record of the meeting, which confirms the above.

37. Eddy, *FDR*, 32–33.

38. Ibid., 34. See the retrospective account of career diplomat Parker T. Hart, *Saudi Arabia and the United States: Birth of a Security Partnership* (Bloomington: Indiana University Press, 1998), 38–50. FDR's meeting was the focus of one newspaper account on the eve of President Nixon's visit to the kingdom. Needless to say, the myth of the oil for security pact had not yet been invented. See William Coughlin, "U.S. Navy Bent Its Protocol for Saudi Monarch," *Los Angeles Times*, June 11, 1974, p. A1.

39. Vitalis, *America's Kingdom*, 80–81.

40. Nadav Safran, *Saudi Arabia: The Ceaseless Quest for Security* (Cambridge, MA: Harvard University Press, 1985), 172. As I put it in *America's Kingdom*, Saudi Arabia "was not that different from Panama and El Salvador in the same era, and, like these two latter American dependencies, lacked the capacity or will of other nearby states to challenge the prevailing order" (6).

41. Black, *Crude Reality*, 143. He is the rare historian comfortable with making sweeping claims while admitting no documentary evidence exists for them.

42. Nick Thimmesch, "Saudis Are Our Best Arab Friends," *Chicago Tribune*, August 7, 1974, p. 22.

43. The cliché "camels to Cadillacs" is still in use today to describe the United Arab Emirates. Meanwhile, the *New York Times* mixed it up a little when it reported during the 1990 Gulf War that Saudis had gone "from camels to Mercedeses." James LeMoyne, "Fuel for Saudi Debate: Opening Society without Causing Strife," *New York Times*, October 31, 1990, p. A1.

44. "Exit King Saud," *Washington Post*, November 6, 1964, p. A20; Paul L. Montgomery, "Faisal, Rich and Powerful, Led Saudis into 20th Century and to Arab Forefront," *New York Times*, March 26, 1975, p. 10.

45. Abdullah Al-Arian, "Seventy Years of the New York Times Describing Saudi Royals as Reformers," *Jadaliyya*, November 27, 2017, http://www.jadaliyya.com/Details/34727.

46. Associated Press, "Explained: Behind the Saudi Crown Prince's Carefully Managed Image Lurks a Dark Side," *Haaretz*, October 15, 2018, https://www.haaretz.com/middle-east-news/saudi-crown-prince-s-carefully-managed-rise-hides-dark-side-1.6555677; Karen De Young and Kareem Fahim, "After Journalist Vanishes, Focus Shifts to Young Prince's 'Dark' and Bullying Side," *Washington Post*, October 13, 2018, https://www.washingtonpost.com/world/national-security/the-dashing-prince-with-a-dark-and-bullying-side/2018/10/13/61f64ea0-ce41-11e8-a360-85875bacob1f_story.html; "Rumors Swirl About MBS's 'Dark Side' After 2nd Saudi Crisis This Year," *Geostrategy-Direct*, October 30, 2018, http://geostrategy-direct-subscribers.com/rumors-swirl-about-mbss-dark-side-after-2nd-saudi-crisis-this-year.

47. Vitalis, *America's Kingdom*, chaps. 6, 8. Gregory Gause concludes that my careful look at the documents effectively debunks the idea of the United States pressuring Saudi Arabia, for instance, to end slavery. Gregory Gause, *International Relations of the Persian Gulf* (Cambridge: Cambridge University Press, 2010), 147. Riedel repeats the myth without citing any U.S. records and instead relies on a court hagiographer and a misquotation of the Russian historian Alexei Vasiliev. Riedel, *Kings and Presidents*, 40. The London-based Anti-Slavery Society continued to report on the persistence of slavery and slave markets in Saudi Arabia long after 1963, when slaves were said to have been freed. No scholarly study I know has pursued this matter. For details, see Paul Kennedy, "Group Urging U.N. to Halt Slavery," *New York Times*, December 4, 1966, p. 16; Thomas Hamilton, "U.N. Commission to Consider Report on World Slave Trade," *New York Times*, March 20, 1967, p. 11; Andrew Jaffee and Marvin Kypfer, "Two Million Still Toiling in Slavery,"

Washington Post, May 14, 1970, p. 1; "Children Still Sold into Slavery in Several Reactionary Countries," *Philadelphia Tribune*, December 29, 1973, p. 5; "Slavery Is Still Widespread," *Afro-American*, September 4, 1976, p. 16; and Leonard Colvin, "Slavery Still Exists in Saudi Arabia According to Human Rights Magazine," *Norfolk Journal and Guide*, November 14, 1990, p. 1.

48. "King Faisal," *Washington Post*, March 26, 1975, p. A14.

49. "Fahd Has Guided the Saudis Since 1975," *Los Angeles Times*, June 14, 1982, p. B12; "New Saudi King Fahd: Key Backer of U.S. Was Top Policy Maker Even Before Taking Throne," *Washington Post*, June 14, 1982, p. A12; "King Fahd's Delicate Job," *Chicago Tribune*, June 15, 1982, p. 14; Peter Kihss, "Saudis' King: Ally of West; Fahd," *New York Times*, June 16, 1982, p. A6; Oswald Johnson, "Saudi Power Has Limits, U.S. Policy-Makers Find," *Los Angeles Times*, July 5, 1983, p. B1. Fahd's brother, prince Abdullah, the new crown prince, was by contrast "not a deep thinker." Johnson, "Saudi Power, B1.

50. "New Leader Termed Kingdom's 'Nicest Man,'" *Los Angeles Times*, March 25, 1975, p. 2; "Steady Course: Saudi Arabian Regime Is Expected to Hew to Late King's Policy," *Wall Street Journal*, March 26, 1975, p. 1. Meanwhile, Khaled would go on to spend millions on real estate, yachts, private jets, and the like. Stories of his corrupt dealings date back to 1972.

51. Ray Vicker, "The Saudis Look to the Future," *Wall Street Journal*, March 28, 1975, p. 4; Walter Pincus, "U.S.-Saudi Involvement Grows," *Los Angeles Times*, March 30, 1975, p. A3.

52. Stanley Reed, "Saudis' Ties Loosen; Little U.S. Can Do," *New York Times*, September 27, 1984, p. A23. See, as well, David Ottaway, "Saudi Leaders Turn Inward as Nation Faces Uncertain Era," *Washington Post*, November 25, 1984, p. 1.

53. David Ottaway, "Saudi King Seeks Islamic Law Review," *Washington Post*, June 16, 1983, p. A1; Nicholas Moore, "Saudi Main Goal: The Cause of Islam," *Los Angeles Times*, December 10, 1984, p. C5.

54. Justin Coe, "To Saudi, King Fahd Falls Short of Ideals," *Christian Science Monitor*, February 13, 1985, p. 9; Peter Kilborn, "In a Land of Palaces, Saudi King Is Special," *New York Times*, February 13, 1987, p. A11.

55. Elaine Sciolino, "In Saudi Oasis of Calm, Some See Seeds of Unrest," *New York Times*, May 15, 1985, p. A2. For the rising activism of those years, see the superb account by Stéphane Lacroix, *Awakening Islam: The Politics of Religious Dissent in Contemporary Saudi Arabia* (Cambridge, MA: Harvard University Press, 2011).

56. Norman Kempster, "Saudis Struggle to Face Reality—Hard Times," *Los Angeles Times*, August 18, 1985, p. A1, quoting the ex-NSC staffer William Quandt, from his new perch at Brookings. Quandt guessed that the regime would "weather the storm," but "since we missed the Iranian situation so bad I think we

should admit that we don't know what the situation will be." See, as well, Patrick Tyler, "King Fahd Tries to Meet Challenge to Stability," *Washington Post*, February 22, 1987, p. A26.

57. David Ottaway, "Saudis Use Bush Visit to Signal Displeasure," *Washington Post*, April 21, 1986, p. A4. Also see Norman Kempster, "U.S.-Arab Relations Plummet," *Los Angeles Times*, May 19, 1986, p. 5.

58. Ottaway, "Saudis Use Bush," A4. In addition, see Robert Hershey Jr., "U.S., in Shift, Seems to View Fall in Oil Prices as a Risk, Not a Boon," *New York Times*, April 3, 1986, p. A1, which links Bush's push to his planned 1988 presidential run; Peter Behr and Cass Peterson, "White House Won't Interfere in Oil Pricing," *Washington Post*, April 3, 1986, p. A14; and Timothy McNulty, "Bush Sees Oil Glut Undermining U.S.," *Chicago Tribune*, April 7, 1986, p. 1.

59. Ottaway, *King's Messenger*, 66–75.

60. Malcolm Byrne, *Iran-Contra: Reagan's Scandal and the Unchecked Abuse of Presidential Power* (Lawrence: University of Kansas Press, 2014).

61. Terry Atlas and James O'Shea, "Saudis, CIA Partners in Afghan Aid," *Chicago Tribune*, December 7, 1986, p. 1; Jeff Gerth, "'81 Saudi Deal: Help for Rebels for U.S. Arms," *New York Times*, February 4, 1987, p. A1; Bob Woodward, "The Secret Wars of the CIA, 1981–1987: Casey's 'Active' Counterterrorism," *Washington Post*, September 27, 1987, p. A1; Ottaway, *King's Messenger*, 60–65. Fahd helped bankroll First Lady Nancy Reagan's "Just Say No" antidrug campaign in those years as well. "Saudi Rulers 'Just Said Yes' to Nancy," *Los Angeles Times*, March 7, 1990, p. 2.

62. Caryle Murphy, "Fahd: Cautious King in Saudi Arabia Hot Seat," *Washington Post*, December 5, 1990, p. A27; Riedel, *Kings and Presidents*, 105.

63. Douglas Jehl and James Gerstenzang, "Saudis to Buy $20 Billion in U.S. Weapons," *Los Angeles Times*, September 15, 1990, p. OCA1; William Hartung, "U.S. Military Support for Saudi Arabia and the War in Yemen," *Lobe Log*, November 23, 2018, https://lobelog.com/u-s-military-support-for-saudi-arabia-and-the-war-in-yemen.

64. Tom Hundley, "Royalty's Fears Keep Saudi Military Weak," *Chicago Tribune*, November 11, 1990, p. C1.

65. Paul Wolfowitz, "Remarks on the Conclusion of the Gulf War," *American-Arab Affairs*, December 30, 1990, p. 1.

66. Kim Murphy, "Saudis Cite U.S. for Growing Social Gulf," *Los Angeles Times*, November 23, 1990, p. OCA10; Caryle Murphy, "Saudi Religious Police Turn More Aggressive: Foreigners, Private Homes Become Targets," *Washington Post*, December 13, 1990, p. A43. For the war's costs, I have relied on Clay Chan-

dler, "Bentsen Urges Saudis to Make Spending Cuts," *Washington Post*, October 6, 1994, p. D11.

67. Michael Wines, "Saudis Plan to Supply U.S. with Fuel for Military Use," *New York Times*, August 23, 1990, p. A1.

68. See Judith Miller, "The Struggle Within: Saudi Arabia," *New York Times*, March 10, 1991, p. SM26. Use of the term "the blob" to stand in for "the interconnected system of think tanks in Washington that churns out dozens of reports and op-eds every week" originates with President Barack Obama's deputy national security adviser, Ben Rhodes. See Daniel DePetris, "Rhodes Is Right About 'The Blob,'" *National Interest*, May 11, 2016, https://nationalinterest.org/blog/the-skeptics/rhodes-right-about-the-blob-16147.

69. Lacroix, *Awakening Islam*, 181. The movement's militarization would come a year or two later.

70. Stephen Engelberg, "U.S.-Saudi Deals in 90's Shifting from Cash Toward Credit," *New York Times*, August 23, 1993, p. A1.

71. Patrick Tyler, "U.S. Strategy Plan Calls for Insuring No Rivals Develop: A One Superpower World," *New York Times*, March 8, 1992, p. 1; Micah Zenko, "U.S. Military Policy in the Middle East: An Appraisal," October 2018, https://reader.chathamhouse.org/us-military-policy-middle-east-appraisal#domestic-academic-and-political-debates.

72. See Osama bin Laden, "A Declaration of Jihad against the Americans Occupying the Land of the Two Holy Sanctuaries," in *Messages to the World: The Statements of Osama Bin Laden*, ed. Bruce Lawrence (London: Verso, 2005), 23–26.

73. "Crossroads in Riyadh," *Wall Street Journal*, January 9, 1996, p. A14.

74. See, for example, Geraldine Brooks, "Saudi Arabia Is Facing Debts and Defections That Test U.S. Ties," *Wall Street Journal*, October 25, 1994, p. A1.

75. Engelberg, "U.S.-Saudi Deals."

76. "We don't know and may never know exactly what Clinton and Fahd said to each other. It could be that it's in the American national interest to defend the Saudi monarchy. But the American people ought to know the terms of the barter, if any." Hobart Rowen, "Clinton's Deal with King Fahd," *Washington Post*, August 26, 1993, p. A27. Also see James Peltz and John Broder, "Clinton Helps Sell Saudis on Jet Deal Worth $6 Billion," *Los Angeles Times*, August 20, 1993, p. A1.

77. See Tim Weiner, "Clinton and His Ties to the Influential Saudis," *New York Times*, August 23, 1993, p. A6. Bruce Riedel, the CIA officer then serving as director of Gulf and South Asia Affairs on the National Security Council, claims it was his idea to have the Saudis buy the commercial aircraft and so keep the U.S. firms from competing for Iran's business. See Riedel, *Kings and Presidents*, 122. The

costs of this adventure go undiscussed, and while he says the Iran connection was "not mentioned" in the publicity, it was nonetheless discussed in the U.S. press at the time. See Peltz and Broder, "Clinton Helps Sell Saudis on Jet Deal."

78. Jeff Gerth, "Saudi Stability Hit by Heavy Spending over Last Decade," *New York Times*, August 22, 1993, p. 2; Engelberg, "U.S.-Saudi Deals." My original account of the council meeting can be found in Robert Vitalis, "Gun Belt in the Beltway," *Middle East Report* 197 (November 1995): 14.

79. See, for example, Geraldine Brooks, "Saudi Arabia Is Facing Debts and Defections," A1.

80. Thomas Hegghammer, *Jihad in Saudi Arabia: Violence and Pan-Islamism Since 1979* (Cambridge: Cambridge University Press, 2010), 70–71.

81. "The clash between the Administration's goals—preaching fiscal restraint and economic reform while at the same time pitching billions of dollars in sales—has sent mixed signals to the Saudi kingdom." Elaine Sciolino with Eric Schmitt, "Saudi Arabia, Its Purse Thinner, Learns How to Say No," *New York Times*, November 4, 1994, p. A1.

82. Hegghammer, *Jihad*, 72–73.

83. Terry Atlas, "Terrorist Blast Point to Saudis' Vulnerability," *Chicago Tribune*, November 14, 1995, p. D1.

84. Elaine Sciolino, "Blast Wrecks U.S. Military Aid Installation—35 to 50 Are Wounded," *New York Times*, November 14, 1995, p. A1. Bin Laden himself took explicit note of the tensions underlying these competing accounts of the bombing. See the interview titled "The New Powder Keg in the Middle East" reproduced in Lawrence, ed., *Messages to the World*, 31–43.

85. One of the smartest Saudis I knew, the businessman and chamber of commerce member Abd al-Muhsin Akkas, challenged the overheated talk of "crisis." See Kim Murphy, "Tremors of Unrest Rock Long-Stable Saudi Arabia," *Los Angeles Times*, January 3, 1995, p. A1.

86. Marie Colvin, "An Ailing Fahd Fuels Fear in the West over Threat to Oil Kingdom," *Times of India*, December 13, 1995, p. 15; Thomas Lippman and R. Jeffrey Smith, "In Smooth Transfer of Power, Saudis Allay Short-Term Fears," *Washington Post*, January 7, 1996, p. A23; David Hirst, "Fall of the House of Fahd," *The Guardian*, August 10, 1999, https://www.theguardian.com/world/1999/aug/11/saudiarabia.

87. To those who questioned Abdallah's worldliness (for example, he didn't speak English), his top aide and adviser could testify to finding him once absorbed in the Arabic translation of Dale Carnegie's *How to Win Friends and Influence People*. John Lancaster, "Fahd Holds Throne but Not Reins," *Washington Post*, May 22, 1996, p. A23.

88. In January 2001, the U.S. indicted thirteen Saudis and one Lebanese member of Saudi Hezbollah for the killings. Riedel says the Clinton administration retaliated against Iranian intelligence operations in 1997 under the assumption that Saudi Hezbollah had some kind of backing from Tehran. Riedel, *Kings and Presidents*, 122–125. Hegghammer disputes the idea that al-Qaeda was behind the bombing. Hegghammer, *Jihad*, 73. Gareth Porter continues to insist that U.S. investigators were prevented by their superiors from exploring the bin Laden connection. See Gareth Porter, "Who Bombed Khobar Towers? Anatomy of a Crooked Terrorism Investigation," *Truthout*, September 1, 2015, https://truthout.org/articles/who-bombed-khobar-towers-anatomy-of-a-crooked-terrorism-investigation. The indictment is available at https://nsarchive2.gwu.edu/NSAEBB/NSAEBB318/doc05.pdf.

89. Bruce Riedel, *The Prince of Counterterrorism* (Washington, DC: Brookings Institution, 2015), Kindle ed., loc.93.

90. David Ottaway and Robert G. Kaiser, "After Sept. 11, Severe Tests Loom for Relationship: The U.S.-Saudi Alliance," *Washington Post*, February 12, 2002, p. A1.

91. Hence the ambivalence of Abdullah's response and need for deniability at home while permitting U.S. forces to operate, which Gregory Gause details in *International Relations of the Persian Gulf*, 146–147.

92. Hegghammer, *Jihad*, 143–144.

93. Ibid., 153–155.

94. Faye Bowers, "Bombs' Intent: To Fray U.S.-Saudi Ties," *Christian Science Monitor*, May 14, 2003, p. 1; Neil MacFarquhar, "A Bombing Shatters the Saudi Art of Denial," *New York Times*, May 18, 2003, p. WK5; Alfred Prados, "Saudi Arabia: Current Issues and U.S. Relations," April 28, 2005, pp. 4–6, https://fas.org/asmp/resources/govern/109th/CRSIB93113.pdf; Hegghammer, *Jihad*, 182–185, 202–217.

95. Hegghammer, *Jihad*, 189.

96. Ibid., 193. If leaders' views differed and if the long-term strategy of someone like bin Laden was the overthrow of the Al Saud, these were kept secret from recruits.

97. Elaine Sciolino, "U.S. Rethinks Its Role in Saudi Arabia," *New York Times*, March 10, 2002, p. 24; Michael Gordon and Eric Schmitt, "U.S. Will Move Air Operations to Qatar Base," *New York Times*, April 30, 2003, p. A1. A dilemma for the United States was how to make it seem that it was not responding to bin Laden's demand. Militants, meanwhile, continued to portray the kingdom as occupied. Hegghammer, *Jihad*, 226.

98. Kenneth Pollock, "Saudi Arabia's Big Leap," *New York Times*, October 16, 2003, p. A29.

99. Patrick Tyler, "The Saudi Exit: No Sure Cure for Royals' Trouble," *New York Times*, April 30, 2003, p. A14.

100. Nicholas Blanford, "Reformist Impulse in Saudi Arabia Suffers Setback," *Christian Science Monitor*, June 5, 2003, p. 7.

101. "Nation-Building in Saudi Arabia," *Christian Science Monitor*, June 3, 2004, p. 8; Faiza Salah Ambah, "Moves Toward Reform Wane," *Christian Science Monitor*, October 4, 2004, p. 6.

102. On the rise and fall of the Bush administration's democratization agenda in the Middle East, see Jason Brownlee, *Democracy Prevention: The Politics of the U.S.-Egyptian Alliance* (Cambridge: Cambridge University Press, 2012).

103. Roger Owen, *The Rise and Fall of Arab Presidents for Life* (Cambridge, MA: Harvard University Press, 2014).

104. "A Promise of Reform in Saudi Arabia," *New York Times*, February 26, 2009, p. A30.

105. Toby Craig Jones, quoted in Dan Murphy, "Saudi Arabia Has New King, Same Agenda," *Christian Science Monitor*, August 2, 2005, p. 1.

106. Hegghammer, *Jihad*, 217–226.

107. Riedel, who dined there with Vice President Al Gore in 1998, calls it something "right out of the first James Bond novel, *Dr. No*." Riedel, *Kings and Presidents*, 113.

108. David Ottaway, "Saudi Court Case Raises Questions of Corruption by Leadership," *Washington Post*, January 2, 1996, p. A1.

109. Kevin Sullivan et al., "Crown Prince Mohammed bin Salman Is 'Chief of the Tribe' in a Cowed House of Saud," *Washington Post*, October 30, 2018, https://www.washingtonpost.com/world/national-security/crown-prince-mohammed-bin-salman-is-chief-of-the-tribe-in-a-cowed-house-of-saud/2018/10/30/f6fa4b68-d946-11e8-aeb7-ddcad4a0a54e_story.html.

110. Dexter Filkins, "A Saudi Prince's Quest to Remake the Middle East," *New Yorker*, April 9, 2018, https://www.newyorker.com/magazine/2018/04/09/a-saudi-princes-quest-to-remake-the-middle-east?reload=true.

111. "Saudi Prince Miteb bin Abdullah Pays $1bn in Corruption Settlement," *The Guardian*, November 29, 2017, https://www.theguardian.com/world/2017/nov/29/saudi-prince-miteb-bin-abdullah-pays-1bn-in-corruption-settlement.

112. Rania El Gamal and Katie Paul, "Two Saudi Princes Released from Detention in Anti-Corruption Probe," *Reuters*, December 28, 2017, https://www.reuters.com/article/us-saudi-corruption/two-saudi-princes-released-from-detention-in-anti-corruption-probe-source-idUSKBN1EM1L4.

113. Kevin Sullivan and Kareem Fahim, "A Year After the Ritz-Carlton Roundup, Saudi Elites Remain Jailed by the Crown Prince," *Washington Post*,

November 5, 2018, https://www.washingtonpost.com/world/a-year-after-the
-ritz-carlton-roundup-saudi-elites-remain-jailed-by-the-crown-prince/2018/11/
05/32077a5c-e066-11e8-b759-3d88a5ce9e19_story.html?utm_term=.12e4f1a34fe2.

114. Thomas L. Friedman, "Saudis to Cover U.S. Troop Costs and Help Middle East Countries," *New York Times*, September 7, 1990, p. A1. Friedman was reporting from Jidda for this story.

115. Thomas L. Friedman, "The Oil Factor," *New York Times*, July 3, 1996, p. A23 (emphasis added).

116. Thomas L. Friedman, "Smoking or Non-smoking," *New York Times*, September 14, 2001, p. A27.

117. Thomas L. Friedman, "Drilling for Tolerance," *New York Times*, October 30, 2001, p. A17.

118. Thomas L. Friedman, "Fighting bin Ladenism," *New York Times*, November 6, 2001, p. A21.

119. "And so the circle is complete. President Bush won't tell Americans the truth, so we won't tell Saudis the truth, so they won't tell their extremists the truth." Thomas L. Friedman, "Hummers Here, Hummers There," *New York Times*, May 25, 2003, p. WK9.

120. Lacroix, *Awakening*; David Commins, *The Wahhabi Mission and Saudi Arabia* (London: I. B. Tauris, 2009).

121. Thomas L. Friedman, "Reaping What It Sowed," *New York Times*, May 4, 2005, p. A23. Stock completed a long-delayed PhD on Egyptian writer Naguib Mahfouz's fiction in 2008 after his expulsion from Cairo. He promotes himself as an expert in Middle East politics, as well as Mahfouz's biographer, and now writes mainly for institutions of the Islamophobic right—for example, the Foreign Policy Research Institute and Middle East Forum.

122. Thomas L. Friedman, "1977 vs. 1979," *New York Times*, February 14, 2010, p. WK8. Fandy is an Egyptian-born political scientist who, after failing to gain tenure in the United States, moved to London and began a consulting business. His PhD dissertation, "State Islam and State Violence: The Case of Saudi Arabia" (Southern Illinois University at Carbondale, 1993), ignores the actual construction of state institutions from the 1940s to the 1970s, the oversized role of the two migrant waves of Egyptian Muslim Brothers (who, quoting a Saudi intellectual, Riedel says, "literally built the Saudi states and most Saudi institutions," especially in education, "thanks to Faisal"), and much else germane to the subject. So does his book, *Saudi Arabia and the Politics of Dissent* (New York: St. Martins Press, 1999). Fandy simply doesn't know the history of the country in any depth, which I demonstrated at a 2004 workshop, for which he wrote a commissioned paper condemning Saudi Arabia's alleged recent transformation into a rogue state. After

I challenged both the claim and his account of the origins of the state's repressive apparatus, he abruptly quit the workshop.

123. Even Faisal's recent champion, the ex-CIA analyst Bruce Riedel, reports that as crown prince and then king he had begun "the large-scale export of Saudi Islamic values and teaching to the *umma* across the world to counter secularists" in the 1960s. Riedel, *Kings and Presidents*, 45. Also see Mitchell, *Carbon Democracy*, chap. 8.

124. Friedman, "Hummers Here, Hummers There."

125. Thomas L. Friedman, "Our Radical Islamic BFF," *New York Times*, September 2, 2015, p. A25.

126. Thomas L. Friedman, "Letter from Arabia," *New York Times*, November 25, 2015, p. A31.

127. Thomas L. Friedman, "Saudi Arabia's Arab Spring, at Last," *New York Times*, November 23, 2017, p. A27. The sad state of knowledge about the kingdom is illustrated by the *Intercept* repeating this queer idea based on a story in *Vice News!* See Sarah Aziza, "Muhammad bin Salman Is Running Saudi Arabia Like a Man Who Got Away with Murder," *Intercept*, February 1, 2019, https://theintercept .com/2019/02/01/mohammed-bin-salman-saudi-arabia-entertainment.

128. Truth in advertising. I was one of seven professors of Middle East politics who signed an open letter to the *Times* complaining that Friedman had passed over in silence the crown prince's use of torture at home and mass murder abroad in Yemen. See Sheila Carapico et al., "Open Letter by Senior Middle East Scholars to the *New York Times* Regarding 'Saudi Arabia's Arab Spring, at Last,'" Global Research, December 5, 2017, https://www.globalresearch.ca/an-open-letter-by-senior -middle-east-scholars-to-the-new-york-times-regarding-saudi-arabias-arab-spring -at-last/5621673.

129. Thomas Friedman, comments at Brookings Institution Center for Middle East Policy, Saban Forum 2017: "America First" and the Middle East; The Future of Saudi Arabia and Its Regional Role, Washington, DC, December 3, 2017, https://www.brookings.edu/wp-content/uploads/2017/11/fp_20171205_future _saudi_arabia.pdf.

130. Robert Lacey, *The Kingdom* (New York: Harcourt, Brace and Jovanovich, 1982); David Holden and Richard Johns, *The House of Saud* (New York: Holt, Rinehart and Winston, 1982). For a discussion of these sources, see Robert Vitalis, "Into the Saudi Enigma," *The National* (Dubai), March 11, 2010, http:// www.thenational.ae/apps/pbcs.dll/article?AID=/20100311/REVIEW/703119988& SearchID=7338446533192. A longer version appeared as Robert Vitalis, "Pitching the Princes," review of *Inside the Kingdom*, by Robert Lacey, *Middle East Report* 254 (Spring 2010): 45–46.

131. Neil Ulman, "Fitting In: Americans Who Work in Saudi Arabia Find It Strange but Nice," *Wall Street Journal*, January 20, 1975, p. 1. The firms also held clandestine church services and, famously, women inside Aramco compounds have always been permitted to drive, but, surely, Friedman doesn't consider it evidence of a liberalizing and pluralist era among the "Wahhabis." For the history of these matters, see Vitalis, *America's Kingdom*.

132. Phyllis Kepler, "A Family Ventures into Off-Limits Saudi Arabia," *Los Angeles Times*, June 1, 1975, p. J1. For their careers as specialists, see Emily Achenbaum, "John Kepler: 1928–2008," *Chicago Tribune*, September 16, 2008, https://www.chicagotribune.com/news/ct-xpm-2008-09-16-0809150716-story.html.

133. Randal, who back then spelled his name with a second *L*, couldn't resist. "Hard core porn classics such as 'Deep Throat' and 'Behind the Green Door' are said to be readily available." Jonathan Randall, "Sly Sin in Stern Kingdom," *Washington Post*, March 11, 1976, p. A37.

134. Judith Miller, "Growing Pains in Arabia: A Rush to Industrialize While the Oil Lasts," *Washington Post*, February 13, 1977, p. 30.

135. Joe Alex Morris Jr., "New Passion on Arabian Peninsula: Revival of Islamic Puritanism Endangers Gambling Casino," *Los Angeles Times*, May 15, 1977, p. A8.

136. Thomas Ferris, "Riding the Saudi Boom," *New York Times*, March 25, 1979, p. SM6.

137. Pascal Menoret, *Joyriding in Riyadh: Oil, Urbanism, and Road Revolt* (Cambridge: Cambridge University Press, 2014). Prince Turki al-Faisal commanded one of his scholars for hire, Joseph Kéchichian, to produce a pamphlet intended to discredit Menoret's research. See Joseph Kéchichian, "Pascal Menoret and Saudi Arabia," King Faisal Center for Research and Islamic Studies, August 2016, in Menoret's possession.

138. Gregory Gause, discussion with the author, Austin, TX, October 26, 2018. Some critics treated the so-called "Reagan Corollary" to the Carter Doctrine as a promise to guarantee the "internal stability," along with the territorial integrity, of Saudi Arabia. See William Safire, "Essay: The Reagan Corollary," *New York Times*, October 4, 1981, p. 19.

139. That is, this was back when Aramco paid for and aided Saudi Arabia's representatives at the new United Nations and was conspiring to block the UN partition resolution that would lead to the creation of Israel. For details and documentation, see Vitalis, "Black Gold, White Crude," 206.

140. Thomas Friedman, "Saudi Royals and Reality," *New York Times*, October 16, 2001, p. A23.

141. Vitalis, *America's Kingdom*; "Saudi King Gives French Newsmen Anti-Jewish Writings," *Jewish Advocate*, January 31, 1974, p. 1; Quandt, *Saudi Arabia in the 1980s*, 31.

142. From the controversial PowerPoint presentation by Laurent Murawiec to the Pentagon's civilian advisory board, headed at the time by Richard Perle. The presentation was leaked to the *Washington Post*, and Murawiec had to resign his post in the uproar, before joining the Hudson Institute. His arguments and follow-up book, *Princes of Darkness: The Saudi Assault on the West* (Lanham, MD: Rowman and Littlefield, 2005), received strong endorsement by like-minded thinkers such as Daniel Pipes and fraternal organizations that, today, are champions of MBS. See Patricia Sullivan, "Laurent Murawiec, 58; Strategist Said Saudis Backed Terror," *Washington Post*, October 14, 2009, http://www.washingtonpost.com/wp-dyn/content/article/2009/10/13/AR2009101303329.html.

143. Adam Taylor, "Did Saudi Arabia Have a Reputation to Ruin?" *Washington Post*, October 19, 2018, https://www.washingtonpost.com/world/2018/10/19/did-saudi-arabia-have-reputation-ruin/?noredirect=on&utm_term=.6b158d0b53e3.

144. Gause, *International Relations*, 144–145.

145. "This desire to solve difficult foreign policy issues by trying to manage the domestic politics of foreign countries is the kind of thinking that got us into the Iraq war." F. Gregory Gause III, "After the Killing of Jamal Khashoggi: Muhammad bin Salman and the Future of Saudi-U.S. Relations," Center for Strategic and International Studies, December 12, 2018, https://www.csis.org/analysis/after-killing-jamal-khashoggi-muhammad-bin-salman-and-future-saudi-us-relations. The comparison with Saud is mine, not Gause's. For the bungled assassination, see Vitalis, *America's Kingdom*, 190–193.

146. Matt Schiavenza, "Why the U.S. Is Stuck with Saudi Arabia," *The Atlantic*, January 24, 2015, http://www.theatlantic.com/international/archive/2015/01/why-the-us-is-stuck-with-saudi-arabia/384805.

147. "What's Going on in Iraq and Syria? Understanding ISIS/ISIL: A Political Science Roundtable Discussion," September 24, 2014, https://www.sas.upenn.edu/slice/whats-going-on-iraq-and-syria-understanding-isisisil-political-science-roundtable-discussion. The United States may have been the biggest oil producer in 2018, but it was at the same time the second largest importer of crude after China, and in 2017 Saudi Arabia was the second largest supplier after Canada. Daniel Workman, "Crude Oil Imports by Country," World's Top Exports, September 16, 2019, http://www.worldstopexports.com/crude-oil-imports-by-country.

148. Elisabeth Bumiller and Adam Nagourney, "Bush: America Is Addicted to Oil," *New York Times*, February 1, 2006, https://www.nytimes.com/2006/02/01/

NOTES TO CHAPTER 5

world/americas/01iht-state.html. Search "addicted to oil" for the spike in discussion following the State of the Union from Brookings, NPR, CNN, the Army War College, and others, although the idea continues to circulate. For a critique, see Michael Lynch, "The Myth of America's Addiction to Oil," *Forbes*, October 25, 2015, https://www.forbes.com/sites/michaellynch/2015/10/25/the-myth-of-americas -addiction-to-oil/#11386ca624f9.

149. "Transcript/Film Clip of Thomas Friedman's *Addicted to Oil* Documentary," CalCars, June 30, 2006, http://www.calcars.org/calcars-news/462.html.

150. Thomas Friedman, "Let's Roll," *New York Times*, January 2, 2002, p. A15. This piece is his call on the Bush administration to launch a "national project" of "energy independence."

151. "Transcript/Film Clip."

CHAPTER 5

1. "Race" as a naturally occurring difference is illusion. "Racism," the practice of applying a double standard in law and custom "based on ancestry," together with "the ideology surrounding such a double standard," is a real social practice. Racism takes the objective reality of race for granted. Fields and Fields, *Racecraft*, 17.

2. Ibid., 19, 24.

3. Mitchell, *Carbon Democracy*; Huber, *Lifeblood*, 150, citing Mazen Labban, *Space, Oil and Capital* (London: Routledge, 2008); Shimshon Bichler and Jonathan Nitzan, "Arms and Oil in the Middle East: A Biography of Research," *Rethinking Marxism* 30, no. 3 (2018): 418–440.

4. Securing America's Future Energy, "Military Cost of Defending the Global Oil Supply."

5. See McFarland, "Living in Never-Never Land," 118. This is the conventional interpretation, taking the demands for Israeli withdrawal from the territories occupied in 1967 and restitution for the Palestinians at face value. Some might argue that, regardless, a political consequence of the boycott is the U.S. engagement in the "peace process," the return of Sinai to Egypt, and so on. On how the United States worked to prevent a Palestinian state from emerging subsequently, see Salim Yaqub, *Imperfect Strangers: Americans, Arabs, and U.S.-Middle East Relations in the 1970s* (Ithaca, NY: Cornell University Press, 2016), and Seth Anziska, *Preventing Palestine: A Political History from Camp David to Oslo* (Princeton, NJ: Princeton University Press, 2018).

6. Securing America's Future Energy, "Military Cost of Defending the Global Oil Supply," 6. Roger Stern's older estimate was much higher, and these authors criticize his calculations. Meanwhile, my old friend Neta Crawford's continuing

Costs of War project at Brown University puts the price through fiscal year 2019 for all post–September 11 wars at $5.9 trillion. See the project's home page at https://watson.brown.edu/costsofwar.

7. Pulsipher, "Watershed, Aberration, and Hallucination."

8. Posen, *Restraint*.

9. "Allocating costs between protecting global oil and other military missions is extremely contentious, and any resources freed by reducing or dropping this mission would be reallocated immediately to other existing military priorities." Securing America's Future Energy, "Military Cost of Defending the Global Oil Supply," 2.

10. Fields and Fields, *Racecraft*, 18.

11. For a recent attempt to rehabilitate the idea in the context of so-called state failure, see Stephen Krasner, "Sharing Sovereignty: New Institutions for Collapsed and Failing States," *International Security* 29, no. 2 (2004): 113–115.

12. Vitalis, *White World Order*, 123–128.

13. Otherwise "oil" came to stand for "raw materials" as a whole. See the late resort to belief that "radical Third World governments" such as Iran could not be counted on to "maintain the large-scale constant supply of vital resources to the industrialized world." Bruce Russett, "Security and the Resources Scramble: Will 1984 Be Like 1914?" *International Affairs* 58, no. 1 (1981–1982): 42.

14. Chittaranjan Alva, "Ideology and the Vietnam War," *Social Scientist* 1, no. 3 (1972): 74. But see the work of Vijay Prashad, who imagines that the U.S. Army in Iraq and Afghanistan is there to secure "raw materials" for global corporations. Vijay Prashad, "Orientalism," in *Keywords for American Cultural Studies*, 2nd ed., ed. Bruce Burgett (New York: New York University Press, 2014): 190.

15. Lipschutz, *When Nations Clash*, xxix. His book is the exception to my argument about the discipline's failure to correct for its errors, and it went unreviewed in all professional journals—for example, the *American Political Science Review*, *Diplomatic History*, *International Organization*, and *International Studies Quarterly*. *Foreign Affairs*, not a peer-reviewed journal, published a signature two-liner about it.

16. Karen Merrill's history, with documents for undergraduates, ignores Adelman's dismissal of the "oil weapon" and the entire field of energy economics, which she calls a "byzantine subject." Karen Merrill, *The Oil Crisis of 1973–1974* (Boston: Bedford, 2007), 165. Tyler Priest shows in his review of *Panic at the Pump* that Meg Jacobs, ostensibly a historian of regulatory policies, never actually explains "the causes, effects, and resolution" of the energy crisis." Tyler Priest, "Priest on Jacobs, 'Panic at the Pump: The Energy Crisis and the Transformation of American Politics in the 1970s,'" *H-Energy*, November 2016, https://networks.h-net.org/node/

19200/reviews/153504/priest-jacobs-panic-pump-energy-crisis-and-transformation
-american. Priest is one of a handful of historians who recognize that Adelman and
other economists needed to be taken seriously and the histories of the era rethought
in light of the empirical evidence they marshal.

17. Lipschutz, *When Nations Clash*, 147.

18. Posen, *Restraint*, 112.

19. Lipschutz, *When Nations Clash*, 111.

20. Holdren, foreword to Lipschutz, *When Nations Clash*, xxii–xxiii. For a
biography of Holdren, see "John P. Holdren," Belfer Center for Science and International Affairs, September 30, 2019, https://www.belfercenter.org/person/john
-p-holdren. For a recent account of the U.S. decision to go to war in Iraq in 2003
on these grounds, see Butt, "Why Did the United States Invade Iraq in 2003?"

21. Lipschutz, *When Nations Clash*, xix.

22. James A. Paul, "Oil Companies in Iraq," *Global Policy Forum*, November
2003, https://www.globalpolicy.org/component/content/article/185/40586.html. I
served on the editorial committee of MERIP's successor publication, *Middle East
Report*, between 1993 and 1998, when I resigned because others were up in arms
about my claim that the United States had no way to "control" Saudi Aramco's
oil price and production policies. See Simon Bromley, "Oil and the Middle East:
The End of U.S. Hegemony," *Middle East Report*, 208 (Fall 1998), for the piece the
Report commissioned that it imagined told the truth about U.S. imperial power.

23. Fields and Fields, *Racecraft*, 6.

24. Yergin, "Protecting Oil."

25. Quoted in Vitalis, "Black Gold, White Crude," 208.

26. Madawi al-Rasheed, "Introduction," in *Kingdom without Borders: Saudi
Arabia's Political, Religious, and Media Frontiers*, ed. Madawi al-Rasheed (London:
Hurst, 2008), 3.

27. David Ottaway, "The King and Us: U.S.-Saudi Relations in the Wake of
9/11," *Foreign Affairs*, May–June 2009, pp. 121–131.

28. Freedom House, "Freedom in the World, 2019: Saudi Arabia," 2019,
https://freedomhouse.org/report/freedom-world/2019/saudi-arabia.

29. See Jamal Khashoggi, "By Blaming 1979 for Saudi Arabia's Problems,
the Crown Prince is Peddling Revisionist History," *Washington Post*, April 3,
2018, https://www.washingtonpost.com/news/global-opinions/wp/2018/04/03/
by-blaming-1979-for-saudi-arabias-problems-the-crown-prince-is-peddling
-revisionist-history; and H. A. Hellyer, "Saudi Arabia's Crown Prince Is Not Interested in Islamic Reform," *Newsweek*, October 24, 2018, https://www.newsweek
.com/saudi-arabias-crown-prince-not-interested-islamic-reform-opinion-1184821.
Madawi al-Rasheed argues that the Saudi crown prince's escalating the rivalry

with Iran was largely as a means to cow his own population into submission. "What Fuels the Saudi Rivalry with Iran?" *New York Times*, April 23, 2018, https://www.nytimes.com/2018/04/23/opinion/international-world/saudi-iran-prince-mohammed.html.

30. Jeanne Morefield cautions, correctly, against the tendency of the commentariat to treat the Trump administration as having "departed from everything that came before and demanding a return to more familiar times." See Jeanne Morefield, "Intellectuals against Noticing," in "Evil Empire," ed. Deborah Chasman and Joshua Cohen, special issue, *Boston Review* 8 (2018): 90.

31. Sharon LaFraniere et al., "Federal Inquiry of Trump Friend Focused on Foreign Lobbying," *New York Times*, July 28, 2019, p. 1. During my own visit to Riyadh, I spied both ex-Senator George McGovern and James Zogby, head of the Arab-American Institute, hunting for donations. Abd al-Muhsin Akkas of the Riyadh Chamber of Commerce told me this was hardly unusual.

32. The best account of Saudi Arabia's support for Salafism in many Muslim societies is al-Rasheed, *Kingdom without Borders*. You will look in vain, however, for a critical word on Saudi money in U.S. politics in Bronson's *Thicker than Oil*, Reidel's *Kings and Presidents*, and other exemplars of the genre.

33. For discussion of elite management of the relationship, see Steven Emerson, *The American House of Saud: The Secret Petrodollar Connection* (New York: Franklin Watts, 1985); Craig Unger, *House of Bush, House of Saud: The Secret Relationship between the Two Most Powerful Dynasties* (New York: Scribner, 2004); Philip Bump and Justin Wm. Moyer, "This Is What Saudi Arabia's Influence Network Looks Like," *Washington Post*, October 19, 2018, https://www.washingtonpost.com/politics/2018/10/19/this-is-what-saudi-arabias-influence-network-washington-looks-like; Fred Halliday, "A Curious and Close Liaison: Saudi Arabia's Relations with the United States," in *State, Society, and Economy in Saudi Arabia*, ed. Tim Niblock (London: Croom Helm, 1992): 125–147; and Gause, *International Relations*, 144.

34. Andrew T. Price-Smith, *Oil, Illiberalism, and War: An Analysis of Energy and U.S. Foreign Policy* (Cambridge: MIT Press, 2015), 73, 137.

35. Jon Alterman, director of CSIS's Middle East program, quoted in Karen De Young, "Trump's Decision to Withdraw U.S. Troops from Syria Startles Aides and Allies," *Washington Post*, December 19, 2018, https://www.washingtonpost.com/world/national-security/trumps-decision-to-withdraw-us-troops-from-syria-startles-aides-and-allies/2018/12/19/8odd8ab2-o3b2-11e9-b5df-5d3874f1ac36_story.html?utm_term=.314ccda266e2.

36. "Transcript of Interview between Noam Chomsky and Andrew Marr," February 14, 1996, *Scratchindog Pisses on a Tree* (blog), July 2, 2015, http://

scratchindog.blogspot.com/2015/07/transcript-of-interview-between-noam.html. The 2017 firing of a Google critic by the think tank that employed him is telling. See John B. Judis, "The Credible Think Tank Is Dead," *New Republic*, September 15, 2017, https://newrepublic.com/article/144818/credible-think-tank-dead.

37. David Long, "Review of *America's Kingdom* by Robert Vitalis," *Middle East Journal* 61, no. 2 (2007): 361.

38. Porter, "Why America's Grand Strategy Has Not Changed."

39. Quoted in Nicholas Kristof, "She Wanted to Drive, So Saudi Arabia's Ruler Imprisoned and Tortured Her," *New York Times*, January 26, 2019, https://www.nytimes.com/2019/01/26/opinion/sunday/loujain-al-hathloul-saudi.html.

40. See Madawi al-Rasheed, "Can Saudi Arabia Survive without the House of Saud?" *Middle East Eye*, October 22, 1978, https://www.middleeasteye.net/opinion/can-saudi-arabia-survive-without-house-saud, in which she evoked Fred Halliday's classic *Arabia without Sultans* (New York: Random House, 1975).

41. See Stephen Wertheim, "Paeans to the 'Postwar Order' Won't Save Us," *War on the Rocks*, August 6, 2018, https://warontherocks.com/2018/08/paeans-to-the-postwar-order-wont-save-us. The article discusses the ossification of national security experts, on the one hand, and a rising generation of millennials "maturing in the war on terror and the crash" who need to be engaged, on the other. Stephen Wertheim calls for "the emergence of new thinkers, leaders, and institutions" to meet "the legitimate aspirations of the American people."

BIBLIOGRAPHY

Abramson, Rudy. "1945 Meeting of FDR and Saudi King Was Pivotal for Relations." *Los Angeles Times*, August 9, 1990. http://articles.latimes.com/1990-08 -09/news/mn-388_1_king-saud.

Achenbaum, Emily. "John Kepler: 1928–2008." *Chicago Tribune*, September 16, 2008. https://www.chicagotribune.com/news/ct-xpm-2008-09-16-0809150716 -story.html.

Adelman, M. A. "The Clumsy Cartel." *Energy Journal* 1, no. 1 (1980): 43–53.

———. *The Economics of Petroleum Supply: Papers by M. A. Adelman, 1962–1993.* Cambridge, MA: MIT Press, 1993.

———. *The Genie Out of the Bottle: World Oil Supply Since 1970.* Cambridge, MA: MIT Press, 1995.

———. "Is the Oil Shortage Real? Oil Companies as OPEC Tax Collectors." *Foreign Policy* 9 (Winter 1972–1973): 69–107.

———. "The Real Oil Problem." *Regulation* 27, no. 1 (2004): 16–21.

———. "U.S. Energy Policy." In *No Time to Confuse: A Critique of the Final Report of the Energy Policy Project of the Ford Foundation, "A Time to Choose America's Energy Future,"* 27–42. San Francisco: Institute for Contemporary Studies, 1975.

Alchian, Armen A. "An Introduction to Confusion." In *No Time to Confuse: A Critique of the Final Report of the Energy Policy Project of the Ford Foundation, "A Time to Choose America's Energy Future,"* 1–25. San Francisco: Institute for Contemporary Studies, 1975.

Alva, Chittaranjan. "Ideology and the Vietnam War." *Social Scientist* 1, no. 3 (1972): 68–75.

Amadeo, Kimberly. "OPEC Oil Embargo, Its Causes, and the Effects of the Crisis." *The Balance*, March 30, 2019. https://www.thebalance.com/opec-oil-embargo -causes-and-effects-of-the-crisis-3305806.

American Empire Project. "Blood and Oil." http://americanempireproject.com/
blood-and-oil (accessed October 19, 2019).

"American Position in Oil Industry Supreme." *Wall Street Journal*, June 5,
1920, p. 8.

Angell, Norman. *This Have and Have Not Business: Political Fantasy and Economic
Fact.* London: Hamish Hamilton, 1936.

Anghie, Anthony. "Civilization and Commerce: The Concept of Governance in
Historical Perspective." *Villanova Law Review* 45, no. 5 (2000): 887–912.

Anziska, Seth. *Preventing Palestine: A Political History from Camp David to Oslo.*
Princeton, NJ: Princeton University Press, 2018.

Al-Arian, Abdullah. "Seventy Years of the New York Times Describing Saudi
Royals as Reformers." *Jadaliyya*, November 27, 2017. http://www.jadaliyya
.com/Details/34727.

Associated Press. "Explained: Behind the Saudi Crown Prince's Carefully Managed
Image Lurks a Dark Side." *Haaretz*, October 15, 2018. https://www.haaretz
.com/middle-east-news/saudi-crown-prince-s-carefully-managed-rise-hides
-dark-side-1.6555677.

Atlas, Terry. "Terrorist Blast Point to Saudis' Vulnerability." *Chicago Tribune*,
November 14, 1995, p. D1.

Atlas, Terry, and James O'Shea. "Saudis, CIA Partners in Afghan Aid." *Chicago
Tribune*, December 7, 1986, p. 1.

Auten, Brian. *Carter's Conversion: The Hardening of American Defense Policy.* Columbia: University of Missouri Press, 2008.

Axelrod, Alan. *Adversaries and Allies: Mastering Strategic Relationships.* New York:
Sterling, 2009.

Ayers, Edward. *American Passages: A History of the United States.* 4th ed. Boston:
Wadsworth, 2009.

Aziza, Sarah. "Muhammad bin Salman Is Running Saudi Arabia Like a Man Who
Got Away with Murder." *Intercept*, February 1, 2019. https://theintercept.com/
2019/02/01/mohammed-bin-salman-saudi-arabia-entertainment.

Bacevich, Andrew. *America's War for the Middle East: A Military History.* New York:
Random House, 2016.

Baghat, Gawdat. "Saudi Arabia and the War on Terrorism." *Arab Studies Quarterly*
26, no. 1 (2004): 51–63.

Bardo, Michael, and Barry Eichengreen, eds. *A Retrospective on the Bretton Woods
System: Lessons for International Monetary Reform.* Chicago: University of Chicago Press, 2007.

Barnhart, Michael. *Japan Prepares for Total War: The Search for Economic Security,
1919–1941.* Ithaca, NY: Cornell University Press, 2013.

Baumeister, Christiane, and Lutz Kilian. "Lower Oil Prices and the U.S. Economy: Is This Time Different?" *Brookings Papers on Economic Activity*, Fall 2016, pp. 287–357.

Behr, Peter, and Cass Peterson. "White House Won't Interfere in Oil Pricing." *Washington Post*, April 3, 1986, p. A14.

Bell, Philip W. "Colonialism as a Problem in American Foreign Policy." *World Politics* 5, no. 1 (1952): 86–109.

Bergsten, C. Fred. "The Threat Is Real." *Foreign Policy* 14 (Spring 1974): 84–90.

Bichler, Shimshon, and Jonathan Nitzan. "Arms and Oil in the Middle East: A Biography of Research." *Rethinking Marxism* 30, no. 3 (2018): 418–440.

Bidwell, Percy. "Raw Materials and National Policy." *Foreign Affairs* 37, no. 1 (1958): 144–155.

———. *Raw Materials: A Study of American Policy*. New York: Harper Brothers, 1959.

Bini, Elisabetta, Giuliano Garavini, and Federico Romero, eds. *Oil Shock: The 1973 Crisis and its Economic Legacy*. London: I. B. Tauris, 2016.

Bin Laden, Osama. "A Declaration of Jihad against the Americans Occupying the Land of the Two Holy Sanctuaries." In *Messages to the World: The Statements of Osama Bin Laden*, edited by Bruce Lawrence, 23–26. London: Verso, 2005.

Bird, Kai. *A Good Spy: The Life and Death of Robert Ames*. New York: Broadway Books, 2014.

Black, Brian. *Crude Reality: Petroleum in World History*. Lanham, MD: Rowman and Littlefield, 2012.

Black, Megan. *The Global Interior: Mineral Frontiers and American Power*. Cambridge, MA: Harvard University Press, 2018.

Blanford, Nicholas. "Reformist Impulse in Saudi Arabia Suffers Setback." *Christian Science Monitor*, June 5, 2003, p. 7.

Blankmeyer, Eric. "Do Commodity Prices Still Show Excess Co-movement?" *Southwestern Economic Review* 33, no. 1 (2006): 149–160.

Bohi, Douglas R. "On the Macroeconomic Effects of Energy Price Shocks." *Resources and Energy* 13, no. 2 (1991): 145–162.

Bohi, Douglas R., and Joel Darmstadter. "The Energy Upheavals of the 1970s: Policy Watershed or Aberration?" In *The Energy Crisis: Unresolved Issues and Enduring Legacies*, edited by David Lewis Feldman, 25–61. Baltimore: Johns Hopkins University Press, 1996.

Boulding, Kenneth E. "Energy Policy in Black and White: Belated Reflections on a Time to Choose." In *Geography, Resources, and the Environment*, vol. 2, *Themes from the Work of Gilbert F. White*, edited by Robert W. Kates and Ian Burton, 310–325. Chicago: University of Chicago Press, 1986.

Bowers, Faye. "Bombs' Intent: To Fray US-Saudi Ties." *Christian Science Monitor*, May 14, 2003, p. 1.

Bradley, Robert L., Jr. *Capitalism at Work: Business, Government and Energy*. Austin, TX: Scrivener, 2009.

Brodie, Bernard. "Foreign Oil and American Security." Yale Institute of International Studies Memorandum no. 23, September 15, 1947. http://www.fdrlibrary .marist.edu/_resources/images/ergen/ergen1937.pdf.

Bromley, Simon. "Oil and the Middle East: The End of U.S. Hegemony." *Middle East Report* 208 (Fall 1998): 19–22.

———. "The United States and the Control of World Oil." *Government and Opposition* 40, no. 2 (2005): 225–255.

Bronson, Rachel. *Thicker than Oil: America's Uneasy Partnership with Saudi Arabia*. New York: Oxford University Press, 2006.

Brooks, Geraldine. "Saudi Arabia Is Facing Debts and Defections That Test U.S. Ties." *Wall Street Journal*, October 25, 1994, p. A1.

Brooks, Stephen, and William Wohlforth. *America Abroad: The United States' Global Role in the 21st Century*. New York: Oxford University Press, 2017.

Brown, Philip Marshall. "Imperialism." *American Journal of International Law* 39, no. 1 (1945): 84–86.

Brownlee, Jason. *Democracy Prevention: The Politics of the U.S.-Egyptian Alliance*. Cambridge: Cambridge University Press, 2012.

Brzezinski, Zbigniew. "We Need More Muscle in the Gulf, Less in NATO." *Washington Post*, June 7, 1987, p. B1.

"Buell Finds U.S. a War-Supply Base." *New York Times*, November 26, 1935, p. 12.

Bukharin, Nikolai. "Imperialism and Communism." *Foreign Affairs* 14 (1936): 563–577.

Bukro, Casey. "American Oil Industry Has Only 27 Years Left Before Its Oil Runs Out." *Chicago Tribune*, March 7, 1973, p. 1.

Bumiller, Elisabeth, and Adam Nagourney. "Bush: America Is Addicted to Oil." *New York Times*, February 1, 2006. https://www.nytimes.com/2006/02/01/world/ americas/01iht-state.html.

Bump, Philip, and Justin Wm. Moyer. "This Is What Saudi Arabia's Influence Network Looks Like." *Washington Post*, October 19, 2018. https://www .washingtonpost.com/politics/2018/10/19/this-is-what-saudi-arabias-influence -network-washington-looks-like.

Burt, Richard. "U.S. Aides Say Soviet May Look to Persian Gulf for Oil in the 1980's." *New York Times*, April 15, 1980, p. A1.

Butt, Ahsan I. "Why Did the United States Invade Iraq in 2003?" *Security Studies* 28, no. 2 (2019): 250–285.

Buxton, Charles Roden. *The Alternative to War: A Program for Statesmen*. London: Allen and Unwin, 1936.

Byrne, Malcolm. *Iran-Contra: Reagan's Scandal and the Unchecked Abuse of Presidential Power*. Lawrence: University of Kansas Press, 2014.

Carapico, Sheila, Lisa Hajjar, Toby C. Jones, Mark LeVine, Joshua Stacher, Bob Vitalis, and Jessica Winegar. "Open Letter by Senior Middle East Scholars to the *New York Times* Regarding 'Saudi Arabia's Arab Spring, at Last.'" Global Research, December 5, 2017. https://www.globalresearch.ca/an-open-letter-by -senior-middle-east-scholars-to-the-new-york-times-regarding-saudi-arabias -arab-spring-at-last/5621673.

Caspary, William. Review of *The Age of Imperialism: The Economics of U.S. Foreign Policy*, by Harry Magdoff. *Midwest Journal of Political Science* 14, no. 4 (1970): 745–749.

"Caucasian Solidarity Urged to Insure Safety of World." *Christian Science Monitor*, August 27, 1923, p. 3.

Chadwick, Alex. "The Marketplace Report: OPEC Embargo Anniversary." *NPR*, October 17. 2003, https://www.npr.org/templates/story/story.php?storyId= 1469425.

Chandler, Clay. "Bentsen Urges Saudis to Make Spending Cuts." *Washington Post*, October 6, 1994, p. D11.

"Children Still Sold into Slavery in Several Reactionary Countries." *Philadelphia Tribune*, December 29, 1973, p. 5.

Chomsky, Noam. "After Pinkville." *New York Review of Books*, January 1, 1970. http://www.nybooks.com/articles/1970/01/01/after-pinkville.

———. "The Ethics of Intervention." Reply to Stanley Hoffmann. *New York Review of Books*, March 27, 1969. http://www.nybooks.com/articles/1969/03/ 27/the-ethics-of-intervention.

———. Letter to the editor. *London Review of Books*, August 17, 2017, p. 4.

———. "Scholarship and Ideology: American Historians as 'Experts in Legitimation.'" *Social Scientist* 1, no. 7 (1973): 20–37.

"A Chronology: The House of Saud." *Frontline*, August 1, 2005. https://www.pbs .org/wgbh/pages/frontline/shows/saud/cron.

Clark, Grover. *The Balance Sheet of Imperialism: Facts and Figures on Colonies*. New York: Columbia University Press, 1936.

———. *A Place in the Sun*. New York: Macmillan, 1936.

Clayton, Blake. "The Case for Allowing U.S. Crude Oil Exports." Council on Foreign Relations *Policy Memorandum* 34 (July 2013).

Coe, Justin. "To Saudi, King Fahd Falls Short of Ideals." *Christian Science Monitor*, February 13, 1985, p. 9.

Colgan, Jeff. "The Emperor Has No Clothes: The Limits of OPEC in the Global Oil Market." *International Organization* 68, no. 3 (2014): 599–632.

———. *Petro-Aggression: When Oil Causes War*. Cambridge: Cambridge University Press, 2013.

Coll, Steve. *Private Empire: ExxonMobil and American Power*. New York: Penguin, 2012.

The Colonial Problem: Report by a Study Group of Members of the Royal Institute of International Affairs. London: Oxford University Press, 1937.

Colvin, Leonard. "Slavery Still Exists in Saudi Arabia According to Human Rights Magazine." *Norfolk Journal and Guide*, November 14, 1990, p. 1.

Colvin, Marie. "An Ailing Fahd Fuels Fear in the West over Threat to Oil Kingdom." *Times of India*, December 13, 1995, p. 15.

Commins, David. *The Wahhabi Mission and Saudi Arabia*. London: I. B. Tauris, 2009.

Comptroller General of the United States. "The U.S.-Saudi Arabian Joint Commission on Economic Cooperation." ID-79-7. March 22, 1979. https://www.gao.gov/assets/130/126054.pdf.

Cook, Steven. *False Dawn: Protest, Democracy, and Violence in the New Middle East*. New York: Oxford University Press, 2017.

Cooper, Andrew Scott. *Oil Kings: How the U.S., Iran, and Saudi Arabia Changed the Balance of Power in the Middle East*. New York: Simon and Schuster, 2011.

Cooper, Richard N. "Resource Needs Revisited." *Brookings Papers on Economic Activities* 1975, no. 1 (1975): 238–245.

Coughlin, William. "Arabs Cutting Oil Output 5% a Month to Gain War Goals." *Los Angeles Times*, October 18, 1973, p. 1.

———. "U.S. Navy Bent Its Protocol for Saudi Monarch." *Los Angeles Times*, June 11, 1974, p. A1.

Cross, Robert. "A Voice from the Flame Trees." *The Guardian*, January 13, 1997, p. 16.

"Crossroads in Riyadh." *Wall Street Journal*, January 9, 1996, p. A14.

Culbertson, William S. "Economic Control Urged to End War." *New York Times*, July 31, 1923, p. 4.

———. *International Economic Policies: A Survey of the Economics of Diplomacy*. New York: Appleton, 1925.

———. "Problems of Raw Materials and Foodstuffs in the Commercial Policies of Nations." Special issue, *Annals of the American Academy of Political and Social Science* 12 (March 1924).

———. "Raw Materials Breed Animosities." *New York Times*, December 17, 1924, p. X17.

Dana, Will. "Recipe for Disaster." Interview with Thomas Friedman. *Rolling Stone*, October 17, 2002, pp. 62–64.

Darmstadter, Joel. "Reflections on the Oil Shock of 40 Years Ago." http://www.rff.org/files/sharepoint/WorkImages/Download/RFF-Resources-186_Feature-Darmstadter.pdf.

Davenport, E. H., and Sidney Russell Cooke. *Oil Trusts and Anglo American Relations*. London: Macmillan, 1923.

Davidson, Ezra. "Visions of Political Islam and the American Military Presence in the Middle East—from Carter to Reagan." PhD diss., New York University, 2011.

"Declares Oil Industry Can't Fulfill Contracts." *Los Angeles Times*, November 14, 1920, p. V6.

DePetris, Daniel. "Rhodes Is Right About 'The Blob.'" *National Interest*, May 11, 2016. https://nationalinterest.org/blog/the-skeptics/rhodes-right-about-the-blob-16147.

Desjardins, Jeff. "The Oil Market Is Bigger than All Metal Markets Combined." *Visual Capitalist*, October 14, 2016. https://www.visualcapitalist.com/size-oil-market/.

De Young, Karen. "Trump's Decision to Withdraw U.S. Troops from Syria Startles Aides and Allies." *Washington Post*, December 19, 2018. https://www.washingtonpost.com/world/national-security/trumps-decision-to-withdraw-us-troops-from-syria-startles-aides-and-allies/2018/12/19/80dd8ab2-03b2-11e9-b5df-5d3874f1ac36_story.html?utm_term=.314ccda266e2.

De Young, Karen, and Kareem Fahim. "After Journalist Vanishes, Focus Shifts to Young Prince's 'Dark' and Bullying Side." *Washington Post*, October 13, 2018. https://www.washingtonpost.com/world/national-security/the-dashing-prince-with-a-dark-and-bullying-side/2018/10/13/61f64ea0-ce41-11e8-a360-85875bacob1f_story.html.

Diamond, Robbie. "OPEC Embargo: Forty Years Later." *The Hill*, October 15, 2013. http://thehill.com/blogs/congress-blog/energy-a-environment/328393-opec-embargo-40-years-later.

Dietrich, Christopher. *Oil Revolution: Anticolonial Elites, Sovereign Rights, and the Economic Culture of Decolonization*. Cambridge: Cambridge University Press, 2017.

Di Tommaso, Gaetano. "America's Energy Transition, the Evolution of the National Interest, and the Middle Eastern Connection at the Dawn of the Twentieth Century." PhD diss., University of Bologna, 2017.

Drucker, Peter Ferdinand. "America Becomes a 'Have-Not' Nation." *Harper's Magazine*, April 1956, pp. 38–43.

Dunn, Frederick Sherwood. *Peaceful Change: A Study of International Procedure.* New York: Council on Foreign Relations, 1937.

Earle, Edward Mead. "Another Oil War—on Paper." Review of *We Fight For Oil,* by Ludwell Denny. *New Republic,* September 12, 1928, pp. 106–107.

———. "The New Mercantilism." *Political Science Quarterly* 40, no. 4 (1925): 594–600.

———. "Oil and American Foreign Policy." *New Republic,* August 20, 1924, pp. 355–357.

———. *Turkey, the Great Powers, and the Baghdad Railway.* New York: Macmillan, 1923.

Eckes, Alfred E., Jr. "The Paley Report." In *United States and the Global Struggle for Minerals,* 175–198. Austin: University of Texas Press, 1979.

———. *The United States and the Global Struggle for Minerals.* Austin: University of Texas Press, 1979.

Eddy, William A. *F.D.R. Meets Ibn Saud.* New York: American Friends of the Middle East, 1954.

Elliott, William Y. "Colonialism: Freedom and Responsibility." In *The Idea of Colonialism,* edited by Robert Strausz-Hupé and Harry Hazard, 430–458. New York: Praeger, 1958.

Emeny, Brooks. *The Strategy of Raw Materials: A Study of America in Peace and War.* New York: Macmillan, 1938.

Emerson, Steven. *The American House of Saud: The Secret Petrodollar Connection.* New York: Franklin Watts, 1985.

Engelberg, Stephen. "U.S.-Saudi Deals in 90's Shifting from Cash Toward Credit." *New York Times,* August 23, 1993, p. A1.

Esterbrook, John. "Rumsfeld: It Would Be a Short War." *CBS News,* November 15, 2002. http://www.cbsnews.com/news/rumsfeld-it-would-be-a-short-war.

"Exit King Saud." *Washington Post,* November 6, 1964, p. A20.

"Fahd Has Guided the Saudis Since 1975." *Los Angeles Times,* June 14, 1982, p. B12.

Fandy, Mamoun. *Saudi Arabia and the Politics of Dissent.* New York: St. Martins Press, 1999.

———. "State Islam and State Violence: The Case of Saudi Arabia." PhD diss., Southern Illinois University at Carbondale, 1993.

Feis, Herbert. "The Anglo-American Oil Agreement." *Yale Law Journal* 55, no. 5 (1946): 1174–1190.

———. *Seen from E. A.* New York: Knopf, 1947.

Feith, Douglas. "Love and Oil." *New Republic,* November 22, 1980, pp. 20–23.

———. "Radical Sheiks." *American Spectator,* April 1980, pp. 11–15.

Feldman, David Lewis. ed. *The Energy Crisis: Unresolved Issues and Enduring Legacies*. Baltimore: Johns Hopkins University Press, 1996.

Ferris, Thomas. "Riding the Saudi Boom." *New York Times*, March 25, 1979, p. SM6.

Fields, Karen E., and Barbara J. Fields. *Racecraft: The Soul of Inequality in American Life*. London: Verso, 2012.

Filkins, Dexter. "A Saudi Prince's Quest to Remake the Middle East." *New Yorker*, April 9, 2018. https://www.newyorker.com/magazine/2018/04/09/a-saudi-princes-quest-to-remake-the-middle-east?reload=true.

Ford Foundation. *Exploring Energy Choices: A Preliminary Report of the Ford Foundation's Energy Policy Project*. New York: Ford Foundation, 1974.

———. *A Time to Choose: America's Energy Future*. Cambridge, MA: Ballinger, 1974.

Fox, Jon Gilbert. "Powerful Ideas about Oil." *JHU Engineering*, Summer 2007. https://engineering.jhu.edu/magazine/2007/07/powerful-ideas-oil/#.We9f3oZrz-Z.

Frankel, Glenn. "U.S. Mulled Seizing Oil Fields in 1973." *Washington Post*, January 1, 2004. https://www.washingtonpost.com/archive/politics/2004/01/01/us-mulled-seizing-oil-fields-in-73/0661ef3e-027e-4758-9c41-90a40bbcfc4d/?utm_term=.9fd99f720f4e.

Freedom House. "Freedom in the World, 2019: Saudi Arabia." 2019. https://freedomhouse.org/report/freedom-world/2019/saudi-arabia.

Freeman, S. David. *Energy: The New Era*. New York: Vintage, 1974.

———. "Government's Role in Oil: A Proposal." *Washington Post*, July 7, 1974, p. B5.

———. *The Green Cowboy: An Energetic Life*. Bloomington, IN: AuthorHouse, 2016.

———. *Winning Our Energy Independence*. Layton, UT: Gibbs Smith, 2007.

Friedberg, Aaron. *Beyond Air-Sea Battle: The Debate over US Military Strategy in Asia*. London: Routledge, 2014.

Friedland, Edward, Paul Seabury, and Aaron Wildavsky. "Oil and the Decline of Western Power." *Political Science Quarterly* 90, no. 3 (1975): 437–450.

———. *The Great Détente Disaster: Oil and the Decline of American Foreign Policy*. New York: Basic Books, 1975.

Friedman, Thomas L. "Drilling for Tolerance." *New York Times*, October 30, 2001, p. A17.

———. "Fighting bin Ladenism." *New York Times*, November 6, 2001, p. A21.

———. "Hummers Here, Hummers There." *New York Times*, May 25, 2003, p. WK9.

———. "Let's Roll." *New York Times*, January 2, 2002, p. A15.

———. "Letter from Arabia." *New York Times*, November 25, 2015, p. A31.

———. "1977 vs. 1979." *New York Times*, February 14, 2010, p. WK8.

———. "The Oil Factor," *New York Times*, July 3, 1996, p. A23.

———. "Our Radical Islamic BFF." *New York Times*, September 2, 2015, p. A25.

———. "Reaping What It Sowed." *New York Times*, May 4, 2005, p. A23.

———. "Saudi Arabia's Arab Spring, at Last." *New York Times*, November 23, 2017, p. A27.

———. "Saudi Royals and Reality." *New York Times*, October 16, 2001, p. A23.

———. "Saudis to Cover U.S. Troop Costs and Help Middle East Countries." *New York Times*, September 7, 1990, p. A1.

———. "Smoking or Non-smoking." *New York Times*, September 14, 2001, p. A27.

Fukuyama, Francis. "The Soviet Threat to the Persian Gulf." Paper P-6596, presented at the Security Conference on Asia and the Pacific, Tokyo, January 1980. Afghanistan Collection, Digital National Security Archive.

Galpern, Steven. *Money, Oil, and Empire in the Middle East: Sterling and Postwar Imperialism, 1944–1971.* New York: Cambridge University Press, 2009.

El-Gamal, Mahmoud A., and Amy M. Jaffe. *Oil, Dollars, Debt, and Crises: The Global Curse of Black Gold.* Cambridge: Cambridge University Press, 2009.

El Gamal, Rania, and Katie Paul. "Two Saudi Princes Released from Detention in Anti-Corruption Probe." *Reuters*, December 28, 2017. https://www.reuters.com/article/us-saudi-corruption/two-saudi-princes-released-from-detention-in-anti-corruption-probe-source-idUSKBN1EM1L4.

Garavini, Guiliano. *The Rise and Fall of OPEC in the Twentieth Century.* London: Oxford University Press, 2019.

Gause, F. Gregory, III. "After the Killing of Jamal Khashoggi: Muhammad bin Salman and the Future of Saudi-U.S. Relations." Center for Strategic and International Studies, December 12, 2018. https://www.csis.org/analysis/after-killing-jamal-khashoggi-muhammad-bin-salman-and-future-saudi-us-relations.

———. "British and American Policies in the Persian Gulf, 1968–1973." *Review of International Studies* 11, no. 4 (1985): 247–273.

———. "The Illogic of Dual Containment." *Foreign Affairs*, March–April 1994, pp. 56–66.

———. *International Relations of the Persian Gulf.* Cambridge: Cambridge University Press, 2010.

Gerth, Jeff. "'81 Saudi Deal: Help for Rebels for U.S. Arms." *New York Times*, February 4, 1987, p. A1.

———. "Saudi Stability Hit by Heavy Spending over Last Decade." *New York Times*, August 22, 1993, p. 2.

Glaser, Charles, and Rosemary Kelanic, eds. *Crude Strategy: Rethinking the US Military Commitment to Defend Persian Gulf Oil*. Washington, DC: Georgetown University Press, 2016.

Glasner, David. *Politics, Prices, and Petroleum: The Political Economy of Energy*. Cambridge, MA: Ballinger, 1985.

Gold, Fern Racine, and Melvin Conant. *Access to Oil—the United States Relationship with Saudi Arabia and Iran*. Washington, DC: U.S. Government Printing Office, 1977.

Goldstein, Joshua S., and Steven Pinker. "Inconvenient Truths for the Environmental Movement." *Boston Globe*, November 23, 2015. https://www.bostonglobe.com/opinion/2015/11/23/inconvenient-truths-for-environmental-movement/esDloe97894keW16Ywa9MP/story.html.

Gordon, Linda. *The Second Coming of the KKK: The Ku Klux Klan of the 1920s and the American Political Tradition*. New York: Liveright, 2017.

Gordon, Michael, and Eric Schmitt. "U.S. Will Move Air Operations to Qatar Base." *New York Times*, April 30, 2003, p. A1.

Gowa, Joanne. "Subsidizing Corporate Expansion Abroad: Pitfalls in the Analysis of Public and Private Power." *World Politics* 37, no. 2 (1985): 180–203.

Grandin, Greg. "Off Dead Center: William Appleman Williams." *The Nation*, July 20, 2009. https://www.thenation.com/article/dead-center-william-appleman-williams.

Grann, David. *Killers of the Flower Moon: The Osage Murders and the Birth of the FBI*. New York: Random House, 2017.

Graves, Aubrey. "1500 Here to Study Natural Resources." *Washington Post*, December 3, 1953, p. 20.

Greenspan, Alan. *The Age of Turbulence: Adventures in a New World*. New York: Penguin, 2007.

"Guru: Peter Drucker." *The Economist*, October 17, 2008. https://www.economist.com/node/12429448.

Hakes, Jay. *A Declaration of Energy Independence: How Freedom from Foreign Oil Can Improve National Security, Our Economy, and the Environment*. New York: Wiley, 2008.

Halliday, Fred. *Arabia without Sultans*. New York: Random House, 1975.

———. "A Curious and Close Liaison: Saudi Arabia's Relations with the United States." In *State, Society, and Economy in Saudi Arabia*, edited by Tim Niblock, 125–147. London: Croom Helm, 1992.

———. *Soviet Policy in the Arc of Crisis.* Washington, DC: Institute of Policy Studies, 1981.

Hamilton, Thomas. "U.N. Commission to Consider Report on World Slave Trade." *New York Times*, March 20, 1967, p. 11.

Hammes, David, and Douglas Wills. "Black Gold: The End of Bretton Woods and the Oil-Price Shocks of the 1970s." *Independent Review* 9, no. 4 (2005): 501–511.

Hammond, Allen L. "Energy: Ford Foundation Study Urges Action on Conservation." *Science* 186, no. 4162 (1974): 426–428.

Handelshøyskole, Norges. "Price Comovement in Energy and Commodity Markets." Master's thesis, Norwegian School of Economics, Bergen, Norway, 2011.

"Harding Sees Oil in British Control." *New York Times*, October 10, 1920, p. 2.

Hart, Parker T. *Saudi Arabia and the United States: Birth of a Security Partnership.* Bloomington: Indiana University Press, 1998.

Hartung, William. "U.S. Military Support for Saudi Arabia and the War in Yemen." *Lobe Log*, November 23, 2018. https://lobelog.com/u-s-military -support-for-saudi-arabia-and-the-war-in-yemen.

Harvey, David. *The New Imperialism.* Oxford: Oxford University Press, 2003.

Hastedt, Glenn P. *Encyclopedia of American Foreign Policy.* New York: Facts on File, 2004.

Hayes, Carlton, and Parker Thomas Moon. *Modern History.* New York: Macmillan, 1928.

Hegghammer, Thomas. *Jihad in Saudi Arabia: Violence and Pan-Islamism Since 1979.* Cambridge: Cambridge University Press, 2010.

Heilbrunn, Jacob. *They Knew They Were Right: The Rise of the Neocons.* New York: Doubleday, 2008.

Heller, Peter B. Review of *The Great Détente Disaster*, by Edward Friedland, Paul Seabury, and Aaron Wildavsky. *Journal of International Affairs* 30, no. 1 (1976): 125–126.

Hellyer, H. A. "Saudi Arabia's Crown Prince Is Not Interested in Islamic Reform." *Newsweek*, October 24, 2018. https://www.newsweek.com/saudi-arabias-crown -prince-not-interested-islamic-reform-opinion-1184821.

Herbstreuth, Sebastian. *Oil and American Identity: A Culture of Dependency and US Foreign Policy.* London: I. B. Tauris, 2016.

Hershey, Robert, Jr. "U.S., in Shift, Seems to View Fall in Oil Prices as a Risk, Not a Boon." *New York Times*, April 3, 1986, p. A1.

Hines, William. "Looking Forward to a Hot Summer? More Power to You." *Philadelphia Inquirer*, June 1, 1972, p. 41.

Hirst, David. "Fall of the House of Fahd." *The Guardian*, August 10, 1999. https:// www.theguardian.com/world/1999/aug/11/saudiarabia.

Hoagland, Jim. "How Strong Are the Saudis?" *New York Review of Books*, April 1, 1982, https://www.nybooks.com/articles/1982/04/01/how-strong-are-the-saudis.

Hobson, John A. *Imperialism: A Study*. London: James Nisbet, 1902.

Hochschild, Adam. Review of *Empire of Cotton*, by Sven Beckert. *New York Times*, December 31, 2014. https://www.nytimes.com/2015/01/04/books/review/empire -of-cotton-by-sven-beckert.html.

Holden, David, and Richard Johns, *The House of Saud*. New York: Holt, Rinehart and Winston, 1982.

Hoselitz, Bert F. Review of *Seen from E. A.: Three International Episodes*, by Herbert Feis. *Journal of Modern History* 20, no. 4 (1948): 352–354.

Houthakker, Hendrik. "Whatever Happened to the Energy Crisis?" *Energy Journal* 4, no. 2 (1983): 1–8.

Huber, Matthew. *Lifeblood: Oil, Freedom, and the Forces of Capital*. Minneapolis: University of Minnesota Press, 2013.

Hundley, Tom. "Royalty's Fears Keep Saudi Military Weak." *Chicago Tribune*, November 11, 1990, p. C1.

Huxley, Elspeth. "British Aims in Africa." *Foreign Affairs* 28, no. 1 (1949): 43–55.

Ikenberry, G. John. *Liberal Leviathan: The Origins, Crisis, and Transformation of the American World Order*. Princeton, NJ: Princeton University Press, 2011.

"Import Quotas Blamed for Shortages of Fuel." *Los Angeles Times*, January 26, 1973, p. 22.

"Interview with Robert Tucker." *SAIS Review* 1, no. 1 (1981): 83–91.

Jacks, David S. "From Boom to Bust: A Typology of Real Commodity Prices in the Long Run." NBER Working Paper no. 18874, March 2013. https://www .nber.org/papers/w18874.pdf.

Jacobs, Meg. *Panic at the Pump: The Energy Crisis and the Transformation of American Politics in the 1970s*. New York: Hill and Wang, 2016.

Jaffee, Andrew, and Marvin Kypfer. "Two Million Still Toiling in Slavery." *Washington Post*, May 14, 1970, p. 1.

Jehl, Douglas, and James Gerstenzang. "Saudis to Buy $20 Billion in U.S. Weapons." *Los Angeles Times*, September 15, 1990, p. OCA1.

Jenks, Leland. *Migration of British Capital to 1875*. New York: Knopf, 1927.

———. *Our Cuban Colony: Sugar*. New York: Vanguard, 1928.

———. Review of *Oil Trusts and Anglo-American Relations*, by E. H. Davenport and Sidney Russell Cooke. *Social Forces* 2, no. 5 (1924): 761–763.

"John P. Holdren." Belfer Center for Science and International Affairs, September 30, 2019. https://www.belfercenter.org/person/john-p-holdren.

Johnson, Oswald. "Saudi Power Has Limits, U.S. Policy-Makers Find." *Los Angeles Times*, July 5, 1983, p. B1.

Johnson, Robert. "The Persian Gulf in U.S. Strategy: A Skeptical View." *International Security* 14, no. 1 (1989): 122–160.

Jones, Chester Lloyd, Henry Kittredge Norton, Parker Thomas Moon. *The United States and the Caribbean*. Chicago: University of Chicago Press, 1929.

Jones, Toby Craig. "After the Pipelines: Energy and the Flow of War in the Persian Gulf." *South Atlantic Quarterly* 116, no. 2 (2017): 417–425.

Judis, John B. "The Credible Think Tank Is Dead." *New Republic*, September 15, 2017. https://newrepublic.com/article/144818/credible-think-tank-dead.

Kaiser, Robert. "Memo Sets Stage in Assessing U.S., Soviet Strength." *Washington Post*, July 6, 1977. https://www.washingtonpost.com/archive/politics/1977/07/06/memo-sets-stage-in-assessing-us-soviet-strength/079e53ff-0d84-48ba-81c1-b890f0412a5d/?utm_term=.65112f51846c.

Kaiser, Robert, and David Ottaway. "Oil for Security Fueled Close Ties." *Washington Post*, February 11, 2001, pp. A1, A7, A16–A17.

———. "Saudi Leader's Anger Revealed Shaky Ties." *Washington Post*, February 10, 2001, pp. A1, A10.

Kaplan, Fred. *Daydream Believers: How a Few Grand Ideas Wrecked American Power*. New York: Wiley, 2008.

———. *Dubious Specter: A Skeptical Look at the Soviet Nuclear Threat*. Washington, DC: Institute for Policy Studies, 1980.

———. *Wizards of Armageddon*. New York: Simon and Schuster, 1983.

Kaufmann, Chaim. "Threat Inflation and the Failure of the Marketplace of Ideas: The Selling of the Iraq War." *International Security* 29, no. 1 (2004): 5–48.

Kéchichian, Joseph. "Pascal Menoret and Saudi Arabia." King Faisal Center for Research and Islamic Studies, August 2016. In Menoret's possession.

Kelly, J. B. *Arabia, the Gulf, and the West*. New York: Basic Books, 1980.

Kemp, Geoffrey. "Scarcity and Strategy." *Foreign Affairs* 56, no. 2 (1978): 396–414.

Kempster, Norman. "Saudis Struggle to Face Reality—Hard Times." *Los Angeles Times*, August 18, 1985, p. A1.

———. "U.S.-Arab Relations Plummet." *Los Angeles Times*, May 19, 1986, p. 5.

Kennan, George. "Diary Notes of Trip to South America." February 28, 1950. George F. Kennan Papers, Seeley G. Mudd Manuscript Library, Princeton, NJ.

———. *The Kennan Diaries*. Edited by Frank Costigliola. New York: Norton, 2014.

Kennedy, Paul. "Group Urging U.N. to Halt Slavery." *New York Times*, December 4, 1966, p. 16.

Keohane, Robert. "The Multinational Enterprise and World Political Economy." *International Organization* 26, no. 1 (1972): 84–120.

Kepler, Phyllis. "A Family Ventures into Off-Limits Saudi Arabia." *Los Angeles Times*, June 1, 1975, p. J1.

Khalidi, Rashid. *Sowing Crisis: The Cold War and American Dominance in the Middle East*. Boston: Beacon Press, 2009.

Khashoggi, Jamal. "By Blaming 1979 for Saudi Arabia's Problems, the Crown Prince Is Peddling Revisionist History." *Washington Post*, April 3, 2018. https://www.washingtonpost.com/news/global-opinions/wp/2018/04/03/by-blaming-1979-for-saudi-arabias-problems-the-crown-prince-is-peddling-revisionist-history.

Kihss, Peter. "Saudis' King: Ally of West; Fahd." *New York Times*, June 16, 1982, p. A6.

Kilborn, Peter. "In a Land of Palaces, Saudi King Is Special." *New York Times*, February 13, 1987, p. A11.

Kindleberger, Charles P. "The Terms of Trade and Economic Development." *Review of Economics and Statistics* 40, no. 1, pt. 2 (1958): 72–85.

"King Fahd's Delicate Job." *Chicago Tribune*, June 15, 1982, p. 14.

"King Faisal." *Washington Post*, March 26, 1975, p. A14.

"Kingdom of the Unjust." *C-SPAN*, November 14, 2016. https://www.c-span.org/video/?418395-1/medea-benjamin-discusses-kingdom-unjust.

Klare, Michael. *Blood and Oil: The Dangers and Consequences of America's Growing Dependency on Imported Petroleum*. New York: Henry Holt, 2004.

———. "The New Imperialist Strategy." *Pakistan Forum* 3, no. 10–11 (1973): 7–16, 46.

Kneese, Allen V. "A Time to Choose: America's Energy Future." *Challenge* 18, no. 3 (1975): 57–60.

Koebner, Richard. "The Concept of Economic Imperialism." *Economic History Review* 2, no. 1 (1949): 1–29.

Koeppel, Dan. *Banana: The Fate of a Fruit That Changed the World*. New York: Hudson Street Press, 2008.

Krasner, Stephen. "Sharing Sovereignty: New Institutions for Collapsed and Failing States." *International Security* 29, no. 2 (2004): 85–120.

Kristof, Nicholas. "She Wanted to Drive, So Saudi Arabia's Ruler Imprisoned and Tortured Her." *New York Times*, January 26, 2019. https://www.nytimes.com/2019/01/26/opinion/sunday/loujain-al-hathloul-saudi.html.

Labban, Mazen. *Space, Oil, and Capital*. London: Routledge, 2008.

Lacey, Robert. *The Kingdom*. New York: Harcourt, Brace and Jovanovich, 1982.

Lacroix, Stéphane. *Awakening Islam: The Politics of Religious Dissent in Contemporary Saudi Arabia*. Cambridge, MA: Harvard University Press, 2011.

LaFraniere, Sharon, Maggie Haberman, William K. Rashbaum, Ben Protess, and David D. Kirkpatrick. "Federal Inquiry of Trump Friend Focused on Foreign Lobbying." *New York Times*, July 28, 2019, p. 1.

Lake, Marilyn, and Henry Reynolds. *Drawing the Global Colour Line: White Men's Countries and the International Challenge of Racial Equality.* Cambridge: Cambridge University Press, 2008.

Lallanilla, Marc. "OPEC Oil Embargo: A Timeline." *Live Science*, March 21, 2014. https://www.livescience.com/44277-opec-oil-embargo-timeline.html.

Lancaster, John. "Fahd Holds Throne but Not Reins." *Washington Post*, May 22, 1996, p. A23.

Lawrence, Bruce, ed. *Messages to the World: The Statements of Osama Bin Laden.* London: Verso, 2005.

Lee, Kai N. "Energy Politics vs. Energy Policies." *Public Administration Review* 36, no. 1 (1976): 110–115.

Leigh, Devin. Review of *Capitalism and Slavery*, by Eric Williams. *Lakefront Historian*, July 8, 2014. https://lakefronthistorian.com/2014/07/08/review-of-capitalism-and-slavery-by-eric-williams.

LeMoyne, James. "Fuel for Saudi Debate: Opening Society without Causing Strife." *New York Times*, October 31, 1990, p. A1.

Leroux, Jeanne. "The Secret to Our Nation's Security." *Counterpunch*, March 10, 2017. https://www.counterpunch.org/2017/03/10/the-secret-to-our-nations-security.

L'Espagnol de la Tramerye, Pierre. *The World Struggle for Oil.* New York: Knopf, 1924.

Lesser, Ian O. *Resources and Strategy.* New York: St. Martin's Press, 1989.

Lippman, Thomas, and R. Jeffrey Smith. "In Smooth Transfer of Power, Saudis Allay Short-Term Fears." *Washington Post*, January 7, 1996, p. A23.

Lipschutz, Ronnie. *When Nations Clash: Raw Materials, Ideology and Foreign Policy.* New York: Harper and Row, 1989.

Little, Douglas. *American Orientalism: The United States and the Middle East Since 1945.* Chapel Hill: University of North Carolina Press, 2002.

Long, David. Review of *America's Kingdom*, by Robert Vitalis. *Middle East Journal* 61, no. 2 (2007): 361.

LSU Center for Energy Studies. Allan G. Pulsipher obituary. November 16, 2017. https://lsu.edu/ces/about/facultystaff/pulsipher.php.

Lugard, Frederick. *The Dual Mandate in British Tropical Africa.* Edinburgh, UK: William Blackwood and Sons, 1922.

Lynch, Michael. "The Myth of America's Addiction to Oil." *Forbes*, October 25, 2015. https://www.forbes.com/sites/michaellynch/2015/10/25/the-myth-of-americas-addiction-to-oil/#11386ca624f9.

———. *The "Peak Oil" Scare and the Coming Oil Flood*. Santa Barbara, CA: Praeger, 2016.

Maass, Arthur. Review of *Resources for Freedom*. *American Political Science Review* 47, no. 1 (1953): 206–210.

Mabro, Robert. "On Oil Price Concepts." Oxford Institute for Energy Studies Working Paper 3, 1984. https://www.oxfordenergy.org/wpcms/wp-content/uploads/2010/11/WPM3-OnOilPriceConcepts-RMabro-1984.pdf.

MacFarquhar, Neil. "A Bombing Shatters the Saudi Art of Denial." *New York Times*, May 18, 2003, p. WK5.

Magdoff, Harry. *The Age of Imperialism: The Economics of U.S. Foreign Policy*. New York: Monthly Review Press, 1969.

El Mallakh, Ragaei. Book reviews. *Journal of Economic Literature* 18, no. 2 (1980): 642–647.

Mann, James. *The Rise of the Vulcans: The History of Bush's War Cabinet*. New York: Viking, 2004.

Martin, Douglas. "Morris A. Adelman Dies at 96; Saw Oil as Inexhaustible." *New York Times*, June 9, 2014, p. B8.

Maugeri, Leonardo. *The Age of Oil: The Mythology, History, and Future of the World's Most Controversial Resource*. Guilford, CT: Lyons Press, 2006.

Maurer, Noel. *The Empire Trap: The Rise and Fall of U.S. Intervention to Protect American Property Overseas, 1893–2013*. Princeton, NJ: Princeton University Press, 2013.

McFarland, Victor. "Living in Never-Never Land: The United States, Saudi Arabia, and Oil in the 1970s." PhD diss., Yale University, 2014.

McLean, Bethany. *Saudi America: The Truth About Fracking and How It's Changing the World*. New York: Columbia Global Reports, 2018.

McNulty, Timothy. "Bush Sees Oil Glut Undermining U.S." *Chicago Tribune*, April 7, 1986, p. 1.

Mead, Walter Russell. Testimony to the United States Senate Committee on Armed Services. August 5, 2015. https://www.armed-services.senate.gov/imo/media/doc/Mead_08-05-15.pdf.

Meaney, Thomas. "The Machiavelli of Maryland." *The Guardian*, December 9, 2015. https://www.theguardian.com/world/2015/dec/09/edward-luttwak-machiavelli-of-maryland.

"Memorandum of Conversation between the King of Saudi Arabia (Abdul Aziz Al Saud) and President Roosevelt, February 14, 1945, Aboard the U.S.S. 'Quincy.'" February 14, 1945. https://history.state.gov/historicaldocuments/frus1945v08/d2.

Menoret, Pascal. *Joyriding in Riyadh: Oil, Urbanism, and Road Revolt*. Cambridge: Cambridge University Press, 2014.

Merleaux, April. *Sugar and Civilization: American Empire and the Cultural Politics of Sweetness*. Chapel Hill: University of North Carolina Press, 2015.

Merriam, Gordon. "Draft Memorandum to President Truman." Enclosed with "Memorandum by the Under Secretary of State (Acheson) to the Secretary of State," October 9, 1945. https://history.state.gov/historicaldocuments/frus1945v08/d20.

Merrill, Karen. *The Oil Crisis of 1973–1974*. Boston: Bedford, 2007.

———. "Oil, the American West, and U.S. Power." *Journal of American History* 99, no. 1 (2012): 197–207.

Miller, Judith. "Growing Pains in Arabia: A Rush to Industrialize While the Oil Lasts." *Washington Post*, February 13, 1977, p. 30.

———. "The Struggle Within: Saudi Arabia." *New York Times*, March 10, 1991, p. SM26.

Miller, Keith. "How Important Was Oil in World War II?" *History News Network*, October 11, 2001. http://hnn.us/articles/339.html.

Mirowski, Philip, and Dieter Plehwe, eds. *The Road from Mont Pelerin: The Making of the Neoliberal Thought Collective*. Cambridge, MA: Harvard University Press, 2015.

Mitchell, Timothy. *Carbon Democracy: Political Power in the Age of Oil*. London: Verso, 2011.

Mommer, Bernard. "The Shocking History of Oil." In *Oil Shock: The 1973 Crisis and Its Economic Legacy*, edited by Elisabetta Bini, Giuliano Garavini, and Federico Romero, Kindle ed., loc. 310–672. London: I. B. Tauris, 2016.

Montgomery, Paul L. "Faisal, Rich and Powerful, Led Saudis into 20th Century and to Arab Forefront." *New York Times*, March 26, 1975, p. 10.

Moon, Parker Thomas. *Imperialism and World Politics*. New York: Macmillan, 1927.

———. "Raw Materials and Imperialism." *Proceedings of the Academy of Political Science in the City of New York* 1 (July 1926): 180–187.

———. *The United States and the Caribbean*. Chicago: University of Chicago Press, 1929.

Moore, Nicholas. "Saudi Main Goal: The Cause of Islam." *Los Angeles Times*, December 10, 1984, p. C5.

Moran, Theodore. "New Deal of Raw Deal in Raw Materials." *Foreign Policy* 5 (Winter 1971–1972): 119–134.

Morefield, Jeanne. *Empires without Imperialism: Anglo-American Decline and the Politics of Deflection*. New York: Oxford University Press, 2014.

———. "Intellectuals against Noticing." In "Evil Empire," edited by Deborah Chasman and Joshua Cohen. Special issue, *Boston Review* 8 (2018): 89–97.

Morris, Joe Alex, Jr. "New Passion on Arabian Peninsula: Revival of Islamic Puritanism Endangers Gambling Casino." *Los Angeles Times*, May 15, 1977, p. A8.

Mowlana, Hamid. "Roots of War: The Long Road of Intervention." In *Triumph of the Image: The Media's War in the Persian Gulf—a Global Perspective*, edited by Hamid Mowlana, George Gerbner, and Herbert Schiller, 30–50. Boulder, CO: Westview Press, 1992.

Mueller, John. *Overblown: How Politicians and the Terrorism Industry Inflate National Security Threats, and Why We Believe Them*. New York: Free Press, 2006.

Murawiec, Laurent. *Princes of Darkness: The Saudi Assault on the West*. Lanham, MD: Rowman and Littlefield, 2005.

Murphy, Caryle. "Fahd: Cautious King in Saudi Arabia Hot Seat." *Washington Post*, December 5, 1990, p. A27.

———. "Saudi Religious Police Turn More Aggressive: Foreigners, Private Homes Become Targets." *Washington Post*, December 13, 1990, p. A43.

Murphy, Dan. "Saudi Arabia Has New King, Same Agenda." *Christian Science Monitor*, August 2, 2005, p. 1.

Murphy, Kim. "Saudis Cite U.S. for Growing Social Gulf." *Los Angeles Times*, November 23, 1990, p. OCA10.

———. "Tremors of Unrest Rock Long-Stable Saudi Arabia." *Los Angeles Times*, January 3, 1995, p. A1.

Muttitt, Greg. *Fuel on the Fire: Oil and Politics in Occupied Iraq*. New York: New Press, 2012.

"Nation-Building in Saudi Arabia." *Christian Science Monitor*, June 3, 2004, p. 8.

National Museum of American History. "Energy Crisis." http://americanhistory.si.edu/american-enterprise-exhibition/consumer-era/energy-crisis (accessed October 23, 2019).

"New Leader Termed Kingdom's 'Nicest Man.'" *Los Angeles Times*, March 25, 1975, p. 2.

"New Saudi King Fahd: Key Backer of U.S. Was Top Policy Maker Even Before Taking Throne." *Washington Post*, June 14, 1982, p. A12.

Newcomb, Richard T. "Review." *Journal of Economic Literature* 14, no. 1 (1976): 117–123.

Njølstad, Olav. "Shifting Priorities: The Persian Gulf in U.S. Strategic Planning in the Carter Years." *Cold War History* 4, no. 3 (2004): 21–55.

Norton, Ben. "'Oil for Security': Ex–CIA Director Michael Hayden Describes Cozy U.S. Relationship with Saudi Dictatorship in New Book." *Salon*, February 26, 2016. https://www.salon.com/2016/02/26/oil_for_security_ex_cia_director

_michael_hayden_describes_cozy_u_s_relationship_with_saudi_dictatorship_in_new_book.

Nye, Joseph, Jr. "Energy Nightmares." *Foreign Policy* 40 (Autumn 1980): 132–154.

Oberdorfer, Don. "Reagan Names 67 Foreign, Defense Policy Advisers." *Washington Post*, April 22, 1980, p. A4.

"October 17, 1973 CE: OPEC Embargoes Oil to U.S." *National Geographic*. https://www.nationalgeographic.org/thisday/oct17/opec-embargoes-oil-us (accessed October 23, 2019).

Odom, William E. "The Cold War Origins of the U.S. Central Command." *Cold War Studies* 8, no. 2 (2006): 52–82.

"The Oil Weapon: Past, Present, and Future." *Oil and Gas Journal*, May 2, 2005. https://www.ogj.com/articles/print/volume-103/issue-17/general-interest/the-oil-weapon-past-present-and-future.html.

Oppenheim, V. H. "The Past: We Pushed Them." *Foreign Policy* 25 (Winter 1976–1977): 24–57.

Ortiz-Ospina, Esteban, Diana Beltekian, and Max Roser. "Trade and Globalization." *Our World and Data*, 2014. https://ourworldindata.org/international-trade.

O'Sullivan, Meghan L. "40 Years After Embargo, OPEC Is over a Barrel." *Bloomberg*, October 17, 2013. https://www.bloomberg.com/view/articles/2013-10-17/40-years-after-embargo-opec-is-over-a-barrel.

Ottaway, David. "The King and Us: U.S.-Saudi Relations in the Wake of 9/11." *Foreign Affairs*, May–June 2009, pp. 121–131.

———. *The King's Messenger: Prince Bandar bin Sultan and America's Tangled Relationship with Saudi Arabia.* New York: Walker, 2008.

———. "Saudi Court Case Raises Questions of Corruption by Leadership." *Washington Post*, January 2, 1996, p. A1.

———. "Saudi King Seeks Islamic Law Review." *Washington Post*, June 16, 1983, p. A1.

———. "Saudi Leaders Turn Inward as Nation Faces Uncertain Era." *Washington Post*, November 25, 1984, p. 1.

———. "Saudis Use Bush Visit to Signal Displeasure." *Washington Post*, April 21, 1986, p. A4.

———. "U.S.-Saudi Relations Are at Their Lowest Point Since 9/11." *Axios*, October 16, 2018. https://www.axios.com/ussaudi-relations-are-at-their-lowest-point-since-911-d107b2a2-171e-4c6a-bf47-91f95b3fbac3.html.

Ottaway, David, and Robert G. Kaiser. "After Sept. 11, Severe Tests Loom for Relationship: The U.S.-Saudi Alliance." *Washington Post*, February 12, 2002, p. A1.

Otten, Alan L. "Consumers Versus the Energy Crisis." *Wall Street Journal*, March 15, 1973, p. 16.

Owen, Roger. *The Rise and Fall of Arab Presidents for Life*. Cambridge, MA: Harvard University Press, 2014.

Painter, David S. "From Linkage to Economic Warfare: Soviet-American Relations and the End of the Cold War." In *Cold War Energy: A Transnational History of Soviet Oil and Gas*, edited by Jeromin Perovic, 282–318. Cham, Switzerland: Palgrave Macmillan, 2017.

———. "Letter to the Editor." *Diplomatic History* 40, no. 4 (2016): 806.

———. *Oil and the American Century: The Political Economy of U.S. Foreign Oil Policy, 1941–1954*. Baltimore: Johns Hopkins University Press, 1986.

———. "Oil and U.S. Foreign Policy." *Oxford Energy Forum* 53 (May 2003): 9.

Palast, Greg. *Armed Madhouse*. New York: Penguin, 2006.

Parrish, John B. "Iron and Steel in the Balance of World Power." *Journal of Political Economy* 64, no. 5 (1956): 369–388.

Patterson, Thomas. "Foreign Aid under Wraps: The Point Four Program." *Wisconsin Magazine of History* 56, no. 2 (1972–1973): 119–126.

Paul, James A. "Oil Companies in Iraq." *Global Policy Forum*, November 2003. https://www.globalpolicy.org/component/content/article/185/40586.html.

Peaceful Change: Procedures, Population, Raw Materials, Colonies. Paris: International Institute of Intellectual Co-operation, League of Nations, 1938.

Pedersen, Susan. *The Guardians: The League of Nations and the Crisis of Empire*. New York: Oxford, 2015.

Peffer, Nathaniel. *The White Man's Dilemma: Climax of the Age of Imperialism*. New York: John Day, 1927.

Peltz, James, and John Broder. "Clinton Helps Sell Saudis on Jet Deal Worth $6 Billion." *Los Angeles Times*, August 20, 1993, p. A1.

Percival, A. "Giant Struggle for Control of World's Oil Supply; Standard and Royal Dutch Shell Engaged in Battle of Billions for Mastery of Fuel Vital to Merchant Marine—Vest Stakes Awaiting the Victor." *New York Times*, June 27, 1920. https://www.nytimes.com/1920/06/27/archives/giant-struggle-for-control -of-worlds-oil-supply-standard-and-royal.html.

Perlmutter, Amos. "The Conflagration Now Threatening the Persian Gulf." *Wall Street Journal*, November 20, 1980, p. 10.

Perovic, Jeronim. "The Soviet Union's Rise as an International Energy Power: A Short History." In *Cold War Energy: A Transnational History of Soviet Oil and Gas*, edited by Jeromin Perovic, 1–43. Cham, Switzerland: Palgrave Macmillan, 2017.

Perovic, Jeronim, and Dunja Krempin. "'The Key Is in Our Hands': Soviet Energy Strategy during Détente and the Global Oil Crises of the 1970s." In "The Energy Crises of the 1970s: Anticipations and Reactions in the Industrialized

World," edited by Frank Bösch and Rüdiger Graf. Special issue, *Historical Social Research/Historiche Sozialforschung* 39, no. 4 (2014): 113–144.

Petersen, Tore T. *Richard Nixon, Great Britain and the Anglo-American Alignment in the Persian Gulf and Arabian Peninsula: Making Allies Out of Clients*. Brighton, UK: Sussex Academic Press, 2009.

Pincus, Walter. "U.S.-Saudi Involvement Grows." *Los Angeles Times*, March 30, 1975, p. A3.

Pinkyck, Robert S., and Julio Rotemberg. "The Excess Co-movement of Commodity Prices." *Economic Journal* 100, no. 403 (1990): 1173–1189.

Pollock, Kenneth. "Saudi Arabia's Big Leap." *New York Times*, October 16, 2003, p. A29.

Popper, David. "Arms and the World." Review of *The Strategy of Raw Materials: A Study of America in Peace and War*, by Eugene Staley. *Saturday Review*, August 28, 1937, p. 16.

Porter, Gareth. "Who Bombed Khobar Towers? Anatomy of a Crooked Terrorism Investigation." *Truthout*, September 1, 2015. https://truthout.org/articles/who-bombed-khobar-towers-anatomy-of-a-crooked-terrorism-investigation.

Porter, Patrick. *Blunder: Britain's War in Iraq*. Oxford: Oxford University Press, 2018.

———. "Why America's Grand Strategy Has Not Changed: Power, Habit, and the U.S. Foreign Policy Establishment." *International Security* 42, no. 4 (2018): 9–46.

Posen, Barry. *Restraint: A New Foundation for U.S. Grand Strategy*. Ithaca, NY: Cornell University Press, 2014.

Posner, Richard. *Public Intellectuals*. Cambridge, MA: Harvard University Press, 2003.

Potter, Pittman. Review of *America and the Race for World Dominion*, by Albert Demageon. *American Journal of International Law* 16, no. 1 (1922): 144–145.

Prados, Alfred. "Saudi Arabia: Current Issues and U.S. Relations." April 28, 2005. https://fas.org/asmp/resources/govern/109th/CRSIB93113.pdf.

Prashad, Vijay. "Orientalism." In *Keywords for American Cultural Studies*, 2nd ed., edited by Bruce Burgett, 187–190. New York: New York University Press, 2014.

———. "Saudi Arabia's Oversupply of Oil Has Little to Do with Economics and Everything to Do with Politics." *AlterNet*, March 3, 2016. https://www.alternet.org/world/saudi-arabias-oversupply-oil-has-little-do-economics-and-everything-do-politics.

Price-Smith, Andrew T. *Oil, Illiberalism, and War: An Analysis of Energy and U.S. Foreign Policy*. Cambridge, MA: MIT Press, 2015.

Priest, Tyler. "Priest on Jacobs, 'Panic at the Pump: The Energy Crisis and the Transformation of American Politics in the 1970s.'" *H-Energy*, November 2016. https://networks.h-net.org/node/19200/reviews/153504/priest-jacobs-panic -pump-energy-crisis-and-transformation-american.

"Professor JB Kelly." *The Telegraph*, September 24, 2009. https://www.telegraph .co.uk/news/obituaries/politics-obituaries/6227955/Professor-JB-Kelly.html.

"A Promise of Reform in Saudi Arabia." *New York Times*, February 26, 2009, p. A30.

Pulsipher, Allan. "Watershed, Aberration, and Hallucination: The Last Twenty Years." In *Energy Crisis*, edited by David Lewis Feldman, 73–80. Baltimore: Johns Hopkins University Press, 1996.

Quandt, William. *Saudi Arabia in the 1980s: Foreign Policy, Security, and Oil.* Washington, DC: Brookings Institution, 1981.

Randall, Jonathan. "Sly Sin in Stern Kingdom." *Washington Post*, March 11, 1976, p. A37.

Randall, Stephen J. *United States Foreign Oil Policy Since World War I: For Profits and Security.* 2nd ed. Montreal: McGill-Queen's University Press, 2005.

al-Rasheed, Madawi. "Can Saudi Arabia Survive without the House of Saud?" *Middle East Eye*, October 22, 1978. https://www.middleeasteye.net/opinion/can -saudi-arabia-survive-without-house-saud.

———. "Introduction." In *Kingdom without Borders: Saudi Arabia's Political, Religious, and Media Frontiers*, edited by Madawi al-Rasheed, 1–38. London: Hurst, 2008.

———, ed. *Kingdom without Borders: Saudi Arabia's Political, Religious, and Media Frontiers.* London: Hurst, 2008.

———. "What Fuels the Saudi Rivalry with Iran?" *New York Times*, April 23, 2018. https://www.nytimes.com/2018/04/23/opinion/international-world/saudi -iran-prince-mohammed.html.

Reagan, Ronald. "The President's News Conference." October 1, 1981. https:// www.reaganlibrary.gov/research/speeches/100181b.

"Reagan Says Soviets Intend to Use Russian-Armed Cuban Troops in Mideast." *Los Angeles Times*, February 8, 1980, p. 23.

Reed, Stanley. "Saudis' Ties Loosen; Little U.S. Can Do." *New York Times*, September 27, 1984, p. A23.

"Resources Group Gets $3,410,000 from Foundation." *Washington Post*, June 22, 1954, p. 12.

Review of *The Age of Imperialism: The Economics of U.S. Foreign Policy*, by Harry Magdoff. *Midwest Journal of Political Science* 14, no. 4 (1970): 745–749.

Riedel, Bruce. *Kings and Presidents: Saudi Arabia and the United States Since 1945.* Washington, DC: Brookings Institution Press, 2018.

―――. *The Prince of Counterterrorism.* Washington, DC: Brookings Institution Press, 2015.

Rietzler, Katharina. "Counter-imperial Orientalism: Friedrich Berber and the Politics of International Law in Germany and India, 1920s–1960s." *Journal of Global History* 11 (2016): 113–134.

Rimmer, Douglas. "Have-Not Nations: The Prototype." *Economic Development and Cultural Change* 27, no. 2 (1979): 307–325.

"Ritual Reagan." *Wall Street Journal*, November 15, 1979, p. 26.

Rogoff, Kenneth. "Oil and the Global Economy." Paper presented at the International Energy Forum Secretariat Meeting of Ministers and Oil Company Presidents, Riyadh, November 19, 2005.

Ross, Dennis. "Considering Soviet Threats to the Persian Gulf." *International Security* 6, no. 2 (1981): 159–180.

―――. "The Soviet Union and the Persian Gulf." *Political Science Quarterly* 99, no. 4 (1984–1985): 615–636.

Rowen, Hobart. "Clinton's Deal with King Fahd." *Washington Post*, August 26, 1993, p. A27.

Rubenstein, Alvin. *Moscow's Third World Strategy.* Princeton, NJ: Princeton University Press, 1988.

"Rumors Swirl About MBS's 'Dark Side' After 2nd Saudi Crisis This Year." *Geostrategy-Direct*, October 30, 2018. http://geostrategy-direct-subscribers.com/rumors-swirl-about-mbss-dark-side-after-2nd-saudi-crisis-this-year.

Russett, Bruce. "Security and the Resources Scramble: Will 1984 Be Like 1914?" *International Affairs* 58, no. 1 (1981–1982): 42–58.

Safire, William. "Essay: The Reagan Corollary." *New York Times*, October 4, 1981, p. 19.

―――. "Glut to the Gluttons." *New York Times*, June 3, 1981, p. A23.

Safran, Nadav. *Saudi Arabia: The Ceaseless Quest for Security.* Cambridge, MA: Harvard University Press, 1985.

Said, Edward. "Thoughts on a War: Ignorant Armies Clash by Night." In *Beyond the Storm: A Gulf Crisis Reader*, edited by Phyllis Bennis and Michel Moushabeck, 1–6. New York: Olive Branch Press, 1991.

Salah Ambah, Faiza. "Moves Toward Reform Wane." *Christian Science Monitor*, October 4, 2004, p. 6.

Sanger, Richard H. *The Arabian Peninsula.* Ithaca, NY: Cornell University Press, 1954.

Sarah. "Account for the Importance of the United States during the Twentieth Century." *Tutor Hunt*, September 29, 2013. https://www.tutorhunt.com/resource/7614.

Sargent, Daniel. *A Superpower Transformed: The Remaking of American Foreign Relations in the 1970s.* Oxford: Oxford University Press, 2015.

"Saudi Arabia Fast Facts." *CNN*, October 2, 2019. https://www.cnn.com/2015/04/01/middleeast/saudi-arabia-fast-facts/index.html.

"Saudi King Gives French Newsmen Anti-Jewish Writings." *Jewish Advocate*, January 31, 1974, p. 1.

"Saudi Prince Miteb bin Abdullah Pays $1bn in Corruption Settlement." *The Guardian*, November 29, 2017. https://www.theguardian.com/world/2017/nov/29/saudi-prince-miteb-bin-abdullah-pays-1bn-in-corruption-settlement.

"Saudi Rulers 'Just Said Yes' to Nancy." *Los Angeles Times*, March 7, 1990, p. 2.

Schacht, Hjalmar. "Germany's Colonial Demands." *Foreign Affairs* 15, no. 2 (1937): 223–234.

Schiavenza, Matt. "Why the U.S. Is Stuck with Saudi Arabia." *The Atlantic*, January 24, 2015. http://www.theatlantic.com/international/archive/2015/01/why-the-us-is-stuck-with-saudi-arabia/384805.

Schiller, Herbert I. "The Natural Resource Base: Where Do We Stand?" *World Politics* 16, no. 4 (1964): 668–676.

Sciolino, Elaine. "Blast Wrecks U.S. Military Aid Installation—35 to 50 Are Wounded." *New York Times*, November 14, 1995, p. A1.

———. "In Saudi Oasis of Calm, Some See Seeds of Unrest." *New York Times*, May 15, 1985, p. A2.

———. "U.S. Rethinks Its Role in Saudi Arabia." *New York Times*, March 10, 2002, p. 24.

Sciolino, Elaine, with Eric Schmitt. "Saudi Arabia, Its Purse Thinner, Learns How to Say No." *New York Times*, November 4, 1994, p. A1.

Securing America's Future Energy. "The Military Cost of Defending the Global Oil Supply." *Issue Brief*, September 21, 2018. http://secureenergy.org/wp-content/uploads/2018/09/Military-Cost-of-Defending-the-Global-Oil-Supply.-Sep.-18.-2018.pdf.

Sheller, Mimi. *Aluminum Dreams: The Making of Light Mobility.* Cambridge, MA: MIT Press, 2014.

Silverstein, Ken. *The Secret World of Oil.* London: Verso, 2014.

Singer, H. W. "The Distribution of Gains between Investing and Borrowing Countries." *American Economic Review* 40, no. 2 (1950): 473–485.

Singer, S. Fred. "Limits to Arab Oil Power." *Foreign Policy* 30 (Spring 1978): 53–67.

"Slavery Is Still Widespread." *Afro-American*, September 4, 1976, p. 16.

Snyder, Jack. *Myths of Empire: Domestic Politics and Political Ambition*. Ithaca, NY: Cornell University Press, 1991.

Spiro, David. *The Hidden Hand of American Hegemony: Petrodollar Recycling and International Markets*. Ithaca, NY: Cornell University Press, 1999.

Spykman, Nicholas. "The Social Background of Asiatic Nationalism." *American Journal of Sociology* 32, no. 3 (1926): 396–411.

Staley, Eugene. *The Strategy of Raw Materials: A Study of America in Peace and War*. New York: Council on Foreign Relations, 1937.

"Steady Course: Saudi Arabian Regime Is Expected to Hew to Late King's Policy." *Wall Street Journal*, March 26, 1975, p. 1.

Stern, Roger. "The Lie That Changed History: Peak Oil, Science, and America's Path to the Middle East." Unpublished manuscript, 2017. In author's possession.

———. "Oil Scarcity Ideology in U.S. Foreign Policy, 1908–97." *Security Studies* 25, no. 2 (2016): 214–257.

———. "United States Cost of Military Force Projection, 1976–2007." *Energy Policy* 38, no. 6 (2010): 2816–2825.

Stevenson, Tom. "What Are We There For." *London Review of Books*, May 9, 2019, pp. 11–12.

Stewart, Charles. "A Time to Choose: America's Energy Future." *Journal of Business* 49, no. 1 (1976): 113–114.

Stoddard, T. Lothrop. *The New World of Islam*. New York: Scribner's, 1921.

Stokes, Doug, and Sam Raphael. *Global Energy Security and American Hegemony*. Baltimore: Johns Hopkins University Press, 2010.

Strausz-Hupé, Robert. "The Balance of Tomorrow: A Reappraisal of Basic Trends in World Politics." PhD diss., University of Pennsylvania, 1945.

———. *The Balance of Tomorrow: Power and Foreign Policy in the United States*. New York: Putnam, 1945.

Strausz-Hupé, Robert, and Harry Hazard, eds. *The Idea of Colonialism*. New York: Praeger, 1958.

Strausz-Hupé, Robert, and Stefan Possony. *International Relations in the Age of Conflict between Democracy and Dictatorship*. New York: McGraw Hill, 1950.

Stroebel, Warren. "Analysis: Awash in Oil, U.S. Reshapes Mideast Role 40 Years After OPEC Embargo." *Reuters Business News*, October 17, 2013. https://www.reuters.com/article/us-usa-energy-geopolitics-analysis/analysis-awash-in-oil-u-s-reshapes-mideast-role-40-years-after-opec-embargo-idUSBRE99G14P20131017.

Sullivan, Kevin, and Kareem Fahim. "A Year After the Ritz-Carlton Roundup, Saudi Elites Remain Jailed by the Crown Prince." *Washington Post*, Novem-

ber 5, 2018. https://www.washingtonpost.com/world/a-year-after-the-ritz
-carlton-roundup-saudi-elites-remain-jailed-by-the-crown-prince/2018/11/05/
32077a5c-e066-11e8-b759-3d88a5ce9e19_story.html?utm_term=.12e4f1a34fe2.

Sullivan, Kevin, Karen De Young, Souad Mekhennet, and Kareem Fahim. "Crown Prince Mohammed bin Salman Is 'Chief of the Tribe' in a Cowed House of Saud." *Washington Post*, October 30, 2018. https://www.washingtonpost.com/world/national-security/crown-prince-mohammed-bin-salman-is-chief-of-the-tribe-in-a-cowed-house-of-saud/2018/10/30/f6fa4b68-d946-11e8-aeb7-ddcad4a0a54e_story.html.

Sullivan, Patricia. "Laurent Murawiec, 58; Strategist Said Saudis Backed Terror." *Washington Post*, October 14, 2009. http://www.washingtonpost.com/wp-dyn/content/article/2009/10/13/AR2009101303329.html.

Tavoulareas, William. *Debate on a Time to Choose*. New York: Ballinger, 1977.

Taylor, Adam. "Did Saudi Arabia Have a Reputation to Ruin?" *Washington Post*, October 19, 2018. https://www.washingtonpost.com/world/2018/10/19/did-saudi-arabia-have-reputation-ruin/?noredirect=on&utm_term=.6b158d0b53e3.

Telhami, Shibley, and Fiona Hill. "America's Vital Stakes in Saudi Arabia." *Foreign Affairs* 81, no. 6 (2002): 167–173.

Thimmesch, Nick. "Saudis Are Our Best Arab Friends." *Chicago Tribune*, August 7, 1974, p. 22.

Thompson, W Scott. "The Persian Gulf and the Correlation of Forces." *International Security* 7, no. 1 (1982): 157–180.

Toynbee, Arnold. "Peaceful Change or War? The Next State in the International Crisis." *International Affairs* 15, no. 1 (1936): 26–56.

"Transcript/Film Clip of Thomas Friedman's *Addicted to Oil* Documentary." CalCars, June 30, 2006. http://www.calcars.org/calcars-news/462.html.

"Transcript of Interview between Noam Chomsky and Andrew Marr." February 14, 1996. *Scratchindog Pisses on a Tree* (blog), July 2, 2015. http://scratchindog.blogspot.com/2015/07/transcript-of-interview-between-noam.html.

Trubowitz, Peter. *Politics and Strategy: Partisan Ambition and American Statecraft*. Princeton, NJ: Princeton University Press, 2011.

"Trump: Saudi King Wouldn't Last 'Two Weeks' without U.S. Support." *Al Jazeera*, October 3, 2018. https://www.aljazeera.com/news/2018/10/trump-saudi-king-wouldn-weeks-support-181003053438418.html.

Tucker, Robert W. "The Middle East: Carterism without Carter." *Commentary* 72, no. 3 (1981): 27–36.

———. *The Radical Left and American Foreign Policy*. Baltimore: Johns Hopkins Press, 1971.

Turner, Wallace. "Research Institute Rises with Reagan." *New York Times*, January 26, 1981, p. 23.

Tyler, Patrick. "King Fahd Tries to Meet Challenge to Stability." *Washington Post*, February 22, 1987, p. A26.

———. "The Saudi Exit: No Sure Cure for Royals' Trouble." *New York Times*, April 30, 2003, p. A14.

———. "U.S. Strategy Plan Calls for Insuring No Rivals Develop: A One Superpower World." *New York Times*, March 8, 1992, p. 1.

Ulman, Neil. "Fitting In: Americans Who Work in Saudi Arabia Find It Strange but Nice." *Wall Street Journal*, January 20, 1975, p. 1.

Unger, Craig. *House of Bush, House of Saud: The Secret Relationship between the Two Most Powerful Dynasties*. New York: Scribner, 2004.

Vasiliev, Alexei. *Russia's Middle East Policy: From Lenin to Putin*. London: Routledge, 2018.

Venn, Fiona. *The Oil Crisis*. London: Longman, 2002.

Vicker, Ray. "The Saudis Look to the Future." *Wall Street Journal*, March 28, 1975, p. 4.

Victor, David G. "What Resource Wars?" *National Interest* 92 (November–December 2007): 48–55.

Vietor, Richard. *Energy Policy in America Since 1945: A Study of Business Government Relations*. Cambridge: Cambridge University Press, 1984.

Vitalis, Robert. *America's Kingdom: Mythmaking on the Saudi Oil Frontier*. Stanford, CA: Stanford University Press, 2005.

———. "Black Gold, White Crude: An Essay on American Exceptionalism, Hierarchy, and Hegemony in the Gulf." *Diplomatic History* 26, no. 2 (2002): 185–213.

———. "The Closing of the Arabian Oil Frontier and the Future of Saudi-American Relations." *Middle East Report* 204 (July–September 1997): 15–21, 25

———. "The End of Third Worldism in Egyptian Studies." *Arab Studies Quarterly* 4, no. 1 (1996): 13–32.

———. "Gun Belt in the Beltway." *Middle East Report* 197 (November 1995): 14.

———. "Into the Saudi Enigma." *The National* (Dubai), March 11, 2010. http://www.thenational.ae/apps/pbcs.dll/article?AID=/20100311/REVIEW/703119988&SearchID=7338446533192.

———. "The Midnight Ride of Kwame Nkrumah and Other Fables of Bandung." *Humanity* 4, no. 2 (2013): 261–288.

———. "Pitching the Princes." Review of *Inside the Kingdom*, by Robert Lacey. *Middle East Report* 254 (Spring 2010): 45–46.

———. Review of *Money, Oil, and Empire in the Middle East: Sterling and Postwar Imperialism, 1944–1971*, by Steven Galpern. *Business History Review* 84, no. 2 (2010): 371–373.

———. "Sons and Heirs." Review of *The Bin Ladens: The Story of a Family and Its Fortune*, by Steve Coll. *London Review of Books*, December 4, 2008, pp. 15–16.

———. "Thinner than Air." Review of *Thicker than Oil*, by Rachel Bronson. *Middle East Report* 242 (March 2007): 44–45.

———. "Wallace Stegner's Arabian Discovery: The Imperial Blind Spots in a Continental Vision." *Pacific Historical Review* 76, no. 3 (2007): 405–438.

———. *When Capitalists Collide: Business Conflict and the End of Empire in Egypt*. Berkeley: University of California Press, 1995.

———. *White World Order, Black Power Politics: The Birth of American International Relations*. Ithaca, NY: Cornell University Press, 2015.

Vogler, Gary. *Iraq and the Politics of Oil: An Insider's Perspective*. Lawrence: University Press of Kansas, 2017.

Volcker, Paul A., Richard J. Goldstone, and Mark Pieth. "Manipulation of the Oil-For-Food Programme by the Iraqi Regime." October 27, 2005. https://www.foxnews.com/projects/pdf/final_off_report.pdf.

Walt, Stephen M. *The Hell of Good Intentions: America's Foreign Policy Elite and the Decline of U.S. Primacy*. New York: Farrar, Straus and Giroux, 2018.

Waltz, Kenneth. "The Myth of National Interdependence." In *The International Corporation*, edited by Charles Kindelberger, 205–223. Cambridge, MA: MIT Press, 1970.

"War with Iraq Is *Not* in America's National Interest." *New York Times*, September 26, 2002. http://www.bear-left.com/archive/2002/0926oped.html.

Ward, Barbara. *The International Share Out*. London: Thomas Nelson, 1938.

Weiner, Tim. "Clinton and His Ties to the Influential Saudis." *New York Times*, August 23, 1993, p. A6.

Wertheim, Stephen. "Paeans to the 'Postwar Order' Won't Save Us." *War on the Rocks*, August 6, 2018. https://warontherocks.com/2018/08/paeans-to-the-postwar-order-wont-save-us.

White, David. "Petroleum Resources of the World." *Annals of the American Academy of Political and Social Science* 89 (May 1920): 111–134.

Whitford, Andrew B. "Estimation of Several Political Action Effects of Energy Prices." https://arxiv.org/ftp/arxiv/papers/1502/1502.07265.pdf (accessed October 23, 2019).

Wight, David. "The Petrodollar Era and Relations Between the United States and the Middle East and North Africa, 1969–1980." PhD diss., University of California, Irvine, 2014.

Williams, William Appleman. *The Tragedy of American Diplomacy*. 50th anniv. ed. New York: Norton, 2009.

Wines, Michael. "Saudis Plan to Supply U.S. with Fuel for Military Use." *New York Times*, August 23, 1990, p. A1.

Winslow, E. M. "Marxian, Liberal, and Sociological Theories of Imperialism." *Journal of Political Economy* 39, no. 6 (1931): 713–758.

Wolfe-Hunnicutt, Brandon. "The Paranoid Style in American Diplomacy: Oil and the Limits of Power in Iraq, 1958–1972." Unpublished manuscript, 2019.

Wolfowitz, Paul. "Remarks on the Conclusion of the Gulf War." *American-Arab Affairs*, December 30, 1990, pp. 1–10.

Wolpin, Miles D. "American Imperialism: Leftist Illusion of Systemic Imperative." *Polity* 3, no. 3 (1971): 442–453.

Wong, Andrea. "The Untold Story Behind Saudi Arabia's 41-Year U.S. Debt Secret." *Bloomberg*, May 30, 1916. https://www.bloomberg.com/news/features/2016-05-30/the-untold-story-behind-saudi-arabia-s-41-year-u-s-debt-secret.

Woodward, Bob. "Ouster of Hussein Crucial for Oil Security." *Washington Post*, September 17, 2007. http://www.washingtonpost.com/wp-dyn/content/article/2007/09/16/AR2007091601287.html.

———. "The Secret Wars of the CIA, 1981–1987: Casey's 'Active' Counterterrorism." *Washington Post*, September 27, 1987, p. A1.

Workman, Daniel. "Crude Oil Imports by Country." World's Top Exports, September 16, 2019. http://www.worldstopexports.com/crude-oil-imports-by-country.

"World's Oil Resources Practically Unlimited." *Wall Street Journal*, July 27, 1920, p. 7.

Worsthorne, Peregrine. Review of the *Idea of Colonialism*, edited by Robert Strausz-Hupé and Harry Hazard. *Encounter* (December 1958): 79–85.

Wright, Lawrence. "The Dark Bounty of Texas Oil." *New Yorker*, January 1, 2018. https://www.newyorker.com/magazine/2018/01/01/the-dark-bounty-of-texas-oil.

Wright, Robin. "Donald Trump, Pirate-in-Chief." *New Yorker*, January 30, 2017. http://www.newyorker.com/news/news-desk/donald-trump-pirate-in-chief.

Wueschner, Silvano. "Herbert Hoover, Great Britain, and the Rubber Crisis, 1923–1926." *Essays in Economic and Business History* 18 (2000): 211–221.

Yaqub, Salim. *Imperfect Strangers: Americans, Arabs, and U.S.-Middle East Relations in the 1970s*. Ithaca, NY: Cornell University Press, 2016.

Yergin, Daniel "The Economic Political Military Solution." *New York Times*, February 16, 1975, p. SM13.

———. *The Prize: The Epic Quest for Oil, Money, and Power*. New York: Simon and Schuster, 1991.

———."Protecting Oil Means Protecting Balance of Power." *Los Angeles Times*, March 10, 1991, p. M2.

———. "Why OPEC No Longer Calls the Shots." *Wall Street Journal*, October 14, 2013. https://www.wsj.com/articles/daniel-yergin-why-opec-no-longer-calls -the-shots-1381793163.

Young, Allyn A. "Economics and War." *American Economic Review* 41, no. 1 (1926): 1–13.

Zenko, Micah. "U.S. Military Policy in the Middle East: An Appraisal." October 2018. https://reader.chathamhouse.org/us-military-policy-middle-east-appraisal #domestic-academic-and-political-debates.

INDEX

Lightning Source UK Ltd.
Milton Keynes UK
UKHW010827260620
365611UK00002B/138/J

9 781503 600904